# He Was a Midwestern Boy
# On His Own

# He Was a Midwestern Boy On His Own

## BOB GREENE

**ATHENEUM**
NEW YORK 1991
COLLIER MACMILLAN CANADA TORONTO
MAXWELL MACMILLAN INTERNATIONAL
NEW YORK OXFORD SINGAPORE SYDNEY

Atheneum
Macmillan Publishing Company
866 Third Avenue, New York, NY 10022

Collier Macmillan Canada, Inc.
1200 Eglinton Avenue East, Suite 200
Don Mills, Ontario M3C 3N1

Library of Congress Cataloging-in-Publication Data
Greene, Bob.
   He was a midwestern boy on his own / Bob Greene.
     p.   cm.
   ISBN 0-689-12117-2
     1. Journalism—United States—History—20th century—
Sources.   2. American newspapers—Sections, columns, etc.
I. Title
PN4867.G68   1991
814'.54—dc20        90-19322        CIP

Macmillan books are available at special discounts for bulk
purchases for sales promotions, premiums, fund-raising,
or educational use. For detail, contact:
Special Sales Director
Macmillan Publishing Company
866 Third Avenue
New York, NY 10022

10  9  8  7  6  5  4  3  2  1

Printed in the United States of America

For Lisa Bain

# Contents

# Introduction

When people talk about the business of covering the news today, it is often in terms of technology: satellite uplinks and computerized word processors and laser printing techniques. All of this is important; our world is smaller because we are able to reach each other instantaneously, and it is the technology that enables us to do this.

Long ago, though, it was said that all you needed to cover a story was a man, a pencil, and a train ticket. When, as a boy, I first heard that phrase, I was mesmerized by the possibilities it conjured up. By the time I heard the phrase, it was already outmoded, in the literal sense—trains were already being replaced by airplanes. But that idea—the idea of a person making his living by traveling from place to place, looking for stories—was wondrous. To live such a life seemed like a great and distant dream.

I have been lucky; I have been able to live that life. I have never considered myself to be a detached and deep-thinking commentator on the news—never considered myself to be a learned pundit. I avoid attempting to decipher the geopolitical and economic meanings of momentous global events. Instead, I like to go out and see things and talk with people and then sit down and write the stories of what I have found. A man, a pencil, and a train ticket—in essence, the dream still holds.

Back in those days when I first thought about spending my life this way, my assumption was that to be truly successful in reporting stories that reached people, a person had to live in New York or Washington or California, the famous centers of power and glamour. Growing up in the middle of the country, it seemed to me that no one would ever pay attention to the work of a person who lived so far away from where the demonstrably important events of the world were taking place. In my mind's eye, the people in those great and glittering cities were always rushing in excited groups from a Broadway opening to a gala party at a nightclub to a reception given by a distinguished senator. I thought about those things as I stood on Main Street in central Ohio, where the geographic limits of my horizons seemed destined to be forever bound by the Eskimo Queen ice cream stand on the east and the Bexley Public Library on the west.

In many ways, I am still that kid on Main Street, dreaming about what's out there. The stories in this book range in locale from New York to Los Angeles to Tokyo; from the beaches of Florida to the streets of Chicago to a hotel ballroom on a strange and sweltering summer night in Cedar Rapids. I have been able to go to those places because of the faith that has been placed in me by the Chicago *Tribune*, where I write my syndicated newspaper column; by *Esquire* magazine, where for nine years my "American Beat" column was anchored; and by "ABC News Nightline," where I have had the good fortune to tell many of my stories on television. The men and women I work for have encouraged me to wander anywhere that held out the promise of people to be met and experiences to be savored. I am grateful to my editors for that faith; the trip has been a long and wonderful one.

But I am still that kid; I have gone out to see some things, but part of me is still on Main Street. It's as if the kid on Main Street is always waiting for me to come back and tell him what I have found.

And I like that. There is a song by Bob Seger—another person who has roamed far from where he grew up in the center of the United States, but who always comes back—called "Hollywood Nights." The song is about the sense of wonder and quiet drama and secret disorientation that inevitably comes to a person who grew up in the middle of the country and who finds himself in places and situations he could never have imagined. There is a passage in that song that has provided me the title for this book:

> She stood there bright as the sun on that California coast,
> He was a Midwestern boy on his own.
> She looked at him with those soft eyes so innocent and blue,
> He knew right then he was too far from home . . .

The secret, of course, is that even on the nights when it seems that you are too far from home, your home is still inside you. It travels with you everywhere, and because of it you are the person you are, and the stories that you find in your travels are stories you might not have noticed had you been one of those people at the Broadway openings and the nightclub parties and the senatorial receptions. The kid on Main Street still waits for you, and you do your best not to let him down when you return to tell him about what you have seen.

Those are the stories in this book. Thanks for coming along on the journey with me.

Bob Greene

## He Was a Midwestern Boy
## On His Own

# The Man Who Wrote "Louie Louie"

**A** woman with a son in high school wrote me a letter. She said that her son was studying the history of popular culture, and that the current class discussion was about the song "Louie Louie."

Her son had come home and told her that there had been an animated conversation in the class about the lyrics of "Louie Louie." Were the lyrics dirty or not? The teacher had played the song over and over, but no consensus had been reached.

The woman thought that I might be able to come up with the definitive answer to this historical quandary. Was "Louie Louie" a dirty song? My assistance would be greatly appreciated.

(Do you think George Will gets mail like this?)

The "Louie Louie" argument, of course, has been going on for years. The song, as recorded by the Kingsmen, became a nationwide hit in the autumn of 1963. Almost immediately rumors started to circulate: the lyrics were dirty. Because the vocals were just about impossible to decipher, no one could be absolutely sure. Virtually every kid in America, though, knew that something was going on in that song. Among the lines reputed to be included on the record: *Every night at ten I lay her again. . . . She's the girl I've got to lay. . . . I tell her I'll never lay her again. . . .*

And now they are studying "Louie Louie" in high school classes. I thought it would be relatively simple to find the answer.

1

\* \* \*

I was wrong. I had always assumed that the Kingsmen had written "Louie Louie." It turns out that they didn't.

I won't bore you with the details of how I found the man who did write "Louie Louie"; suffice it to say that I did find him, and his name is Richard Berry. He is fifty-three years old and lives in Los Angeles with his mother and the youngest of his six children, a nineteen-year-old daughter.

Berry said that he wrote "Louie Louie" in 1955. "I was performing with a Latin group in Anaheim," he said. "They were called the Rhythm Rockers. They were a full Latin band—twelve or thirteen pieces.

"I was back in the dressing room waiting to go on, and I heard the Rhythm Rockers playing an instrumental. I heard the congas and everything, and I thought that I could write a really interesting song to go with that kind of music. The title 'Louie Louie' just kind of fell out of the sky. I didn't have anything to write the words down on, so I took a piece of toilet paper and wrote the lyrics on the toilet paper.

"The whole idea was that Louie was the guy the singer was talking to—the singer wasn't Louie. It's like that song 'One for My Baby (and One More for the Road).' In that song, 'Joe' is the bartender. You know—'Set 'em up, Joe. . . .' Joe is the star, but the singer is not Joe. The same with 'Louie Louie.' The singer is a sailor, and he's talking to Louie. Louie could be a bartender, a streetcar driver, a barber . . . anybody."

Berry saw "Louie Louie" as a love song. He recorded it on a local label called Flip in 1956. "Actually, it was the B side of the record," he said. "The A side was 'You Are My Sunshine,' which of course I did not write. I sang 'You Are My Sunshine' in a combination country/rhythm-and-blues style."

In 1957 Berry was getting tired of the music business—too much work, too little money. He wanted to get married, but he needed some cash. So he sold the rights to "Louie Louie" to a record-company owner. The price was $750. "Actually, the $750 was for the rights to 'Louie Louie' and four other songs," Berry said. "The deal was that I would sell the rights to five songs for the $750."

\* \* \*

Six years passed. Then Berry started hearing people say that "Louie Louie" had been recorded by a rock group up in Oregon.

"Some of my black friends had heard it, and they said, 'These white guys recorded your song, and it's awful. They really messed it up.' I didn't care at the time. I thought it was kind of interesting that 'Louie Louie' had become a white kids' record, but I wasn't curious enough to go out and buy it.

"It wasn't until about eight months later that I heard the Kingsmen's version. It was . . . different. The Kingsmen sang it raggedy and real funky. If you listened to mine, mine was real smooth. But as to the Kingsmen's record, I didn't have any negative or positive feelings about it either way."

Berry was told that the Kingsmen had found a copy of "Louie Louie" in a record bin in the Portland area and had decided to perform it. Before long the rumors about the dirty lyrics began to circulate, and "Louie Louie" quickly moved toward the top of the record charts.

"No one really contacted me about it," Berry said. "I suppose when people saw the 'Richard Berry' writer's credit on the record label, they assumed that Richard Berry was one of the Kingsmen. I couldn't get too interested because I realized that I had made all the money I would ever make off 'Louie Louie' back in 1957 when I had sold the rights."

Finally, though, when he kept hearing the dirty-lyrics rumors, he got hold of a copy of the Kingsmen's record and played it.

"They were singing the same words exactly the way I wrote them," Berry said. "And they were not dirty lyrics. There was not one dirty word or suggestive phrase in that song."

This, of course, is the nugget of information that a nation has wondered about for a quarter of a century. I asked Berry if he would mind singing "Louie Louie" for me—very slowly, so I could write it all down. He said he would be more than happy to, just to set the record straight once and for all.

Here are the lyrics to "Louie Louie":

> *Louie Louie, me gotta go*
> *Louie Louie, me gotta go*
>
> *Fine little girl she waits for me*
> *Me catch the ship for cross the sea*

*Me sail the ship all alone*
*Me never think me make it home*

*Louie Louie, me gotta go*
*Louie Louie, me gotta go*

*Three nights and days me sail the sea*
*Me think of girl constantly*
*On the ship I dream she there*
*I smell the rose in her hair*

*Louie Louie, me gotta go*
*Louie Louie, me gotta go*

*Me see Jamaica moon above*
*It won't be long, me see my love*
*I take her in my arms and then*
*Me tell her I never leave again*

*Louie Louie, me gotta go*
*Louie Louie, me gotta go*

In listening to the Kingsmen's "Louie Louie" after it was first released, Berry was absolutely convinced that the band had remained faithful to his lyrics. But no one wanted to believe it.

"A couple of radio stations banned the song," he said. "I even heard that the FBI wanted to get involved. It was ridiculous."

And something started to happen. "Louie Louie," because of the rumors, became more than a pop song. It became a cultural phenomenon.

"When the movie *Animal House* came out in 1978, 'Louie Louie' took on a whole new life," Berry said. "John Belushi and the guys who played his fraternity brothers sang it at that toga party in the movie, and all of a sudden at every university in the country kids were having toga parties and singing 'Louie Louie.' There is a whole generation of kids who probably think that 'Louie Louie' first appeared in *Animal House*."

Berry said that more than four hundred versions of "Louie Louie" have been recorded; some music authorities place the figure closer to a thousand. "It's been sung by everybody from Julie London to Rod McKuen," he said. "I have been told that the Kingsmen have sold more than twelve million copies of their version over the years. And someone told me that there have been an estimated three hundred million copies of 'Louie Louie' sold worldwide by different artists.

"I never could understand the popularity of it. It was a song with three stupid guitar-chord changes in it. Every young musician I have ever met has told me that 'Louie Louie' was the first song that he ever learned. I can believe that; it's such an easy song to play.

"The marching band at my daughter's high school even plays it at half time of the football games."

It wasn't until twenty years after the Kingsmen's release of "Louie Louie" that Berry met one of the Kingsmen.

"I met the lead singer, Jack Ely, in 1983," Berry said. "I asked him why everyone thought it was a dirty song. He said that the Kingsmen had recorded it in this little fifty-dollar studio. The microphone was way up in the ceiling. So Ely's vocals couldn't be heard very clearly. When people couldn't understand the vocals, the rumors started. And then it snowballed."

Several years ago Berry received some legal help and was able to win back some of the rights to "Louie Louie." He is far from wealthy, but he says he is satisfied.

"Sometimes people will introduce me to their friends and say that I am the man who wrote 'Louie Louie,'" Berry said. "At first no one believes it. But then they start asking about the lyrics. When I explain to them that the words were clean, and I say, 'Yeah, the Kingsmen sang my straight lyrics,' they don't want to accept it. It takes away the mystery. They shake their heads and walk away disappointed."

I thanked Berry for his time and for the information, and I said that I had to bother him with one more detail. I told him that *Esquire* has a research department that fact-checks everything that goes into the magazine. So I asked if he could help me out with a seemingly minor question: Was there a comma in "Louie Louie"?

"A comma?" Berry said.

"Yeah," I said. "Is it 'Louie, Louie,' or is it 'Louie Louie'?"

"I don't know," Berry said. "I never thought about it."

"They're going to want to know, and they're going to drive you crazy until they find out," I said. "Could you look on the original song?"

Berry laughed.

"You must be kidding," he said. "That piece of toilet paper that I wrote 'Louie Louie' on fell apart many years ago."

That made sense. "Could you make a decision, then?" I said.

"Okay," Berry said. " 'Louie Louie.' No comma."

# The Linda Hop

Here was the dilemma: Since 1968, I have been going to the national political conventions. Chicago, Miami, Detroit, Kansas City, New York, Dallas . . . the convention sites seem to blend together. The problem was, as a twenty-one-year-old in 1968, I thought that a national political convention was just about the most exciting place a person could ever be. By now, though . . . well, who in their right mind would want to go?

It wasn't the idea of conventions per se that I had turned against. It was just the idea of the Republican and Democratic national conventions. So, with a convention year coming up, my task was to find one that I considered significant and historic, yet to avoid the pair of political conventions.

If you put your faith in the stars, all good things will come to you. Just as I was beginning to believe that there was no answer to this quandary, I heard about the Linda convention.

The Linda convention was the brainchild of Linda Pasvogel, thirty-eight, of Fenton, Illinois. The concept was fairly simple. The convention was open to all women named Linda. "It's a gathering of Lindas for the purpose of having fun, celebrating our names, and sharing our interests," Linda Pasvogel announced.

According to Linda Pasvogel, the most popular name for girl babies born in 1948 was Linda. But since then, she said, the popularity of the name has declined dramatically. To be honest, I had not noticed this, but Linda Pasvogel said that if you check out elementary schools and high schools these days, you will find a definite dearth of Lindas.

Thus, the Linda convention. Almost as soon as Linda Pasvogel announced the event, controversy reared its ugly head. Linda Pasvogel had decreed that only Lindas who spelled their names *L-i-n-d-a* would be allowed to attend. No Lyndas. This caused something of an outcry.

"Did I make a mistake?" Linda Pasvogel said to me on the eve of the convention. "Perhaps I did. There are some Lyndas who are saying that my decision is unfair. But once you make a ruling, you stand by it. Lindas only. No Lyndas."

The Linda convention was scheduled to be held at the Sheraton Inn in Cedar Rapids, Iowa. Cedar Rapids is a lovely and friendly town, but it is not exactly the most convenient convention center in the United States in terms of transportation. So why had Linda Pasvogel chosen Cedar Rapids?

She said it was because she had once stayed at the Sheraton Inn there and had discovered that two of the motel's front-office staff members were named Linda. This sounded a little unlikely, so I checked. The assistant manager of the Sheraton Inn in Cedar Rapids is Linda Cue. The head of the banquet sales department is Linda Lovell.

The Linda convention was due to start at 4:00 on a Saturday afternoon and to end late that evening. The registration fee was twenty-seven dollars per Linda. This included dinner, but not motel rooms. Approximately 160 Lindas had made reservations for the convention; they came from various parts of the United States, but because of the Cedar Rapids location, most of them were from Iowa and surrounding states.

By 3:30 P.M., many of the Lindas were gathered in the motel bar, which was adjacent to the banquet room. On the door of the banquet room was a hand-lettered sign: CLOSED UNTIL 4:00 P.M.—THEN OPEN TO "LINDAS"! THANK YOU. Thus, the Lindas—who ranged in age from twenty-three to seventy-three—passed the time in the bar.

Linda Zylstra, twenty-eight, a housewife from Sully, Iowa, drank a Fuzzy Navel and said, "My aunt read about this convention in the paper, and she volunteered to baby-sit with my two-year-old and four-year-old so I could come." A few feet down from her, Linda Knoche, thirty-nine, of De Witt, Iowa, held a Miller Lite and said, "When I was younger, I hated the name. So many girls were named Linda that you never got called by your first name." Knoche, a customer-service representative for the First National Bank of Grand Mound, Iowa, which is a neighboring town to De Witt, said, "I'm not kidding. When I was in school there were three Lindas on my softball team. We'd have to use last names in order to make it clear who we were talking to."

Linda Gallagher, thirty-nine, a secretary in Cedar Rapids, said, "My father was so proud of my name because he named me after Linda Darnell, the actress. Whenever Linda Darnell would come on TV, he would make me watch the movie with him. He thought that Linda Darnell was just gorgeous."


It was warm in the corridor outside the banquet room, and the 160 Lindas were becoming restless when 4:00 came, and then 4:10, and then 4:15, and the doors were still not open. Linda Pasvogel, it seemed, had been so busy with last-minute preparations that she was still upstairs changing for the event.

At 4:20 she arrived. The doors were flung open. On one wall was a script LINDA written with pink balloons. The Lindas entered, one by one, to register and receive their name tags. Fortunately, this was a fairly speedy process; the tags had been prestamped HELLO, MY NAME IS LINDA, and each Linda had only to write in her last name.

Silk-flower corsages were presented to each Linda; the flowers bore white tags with LINDA inscribed in pink lettering. A man named Ray Meier, sixty-five, of Lowden, Iowa, sat at a Kimball organ and played the song "Linda" over and over.

(Now, you may think that "Linda" was first recorded by Jan and Dean in the 1960s: "Li-Li-Li-Li-Li, Li-Li-Li-Li-Linda." In fact, the Jan and Dean version, which was rather peppy, was a knockoff of the more leisurely paced original, written in 1946 by a composer named Jack Lawrence. The opening words: "When I go to sleep, I never count sheep, I count all the charms about Linda. . . ." It is said that the success of Lawrence's "Linda," combined with the popularity of the aforementioned Linda Darnell, is what made Linda the most popular name for American newborn girls by 1948.)

Linda Van Oort, thirty-five, a housewife from Des Moines, stuck her Linda name tag to her dress and pinned on her Linda corsage. "When I was little, everyone was Linda," she said. "Now I'm sad that the name has gone out of favor. But everything changes. Even Kimberlys are out now."

Kimberlys are out?

"Yes," Linda Van Oort said. "Kimberlys were very popular for a while, but the name seems to have peaked. Today I believe there is a surge in Carries and Jennifers."

Linda Pasvogel had ordered that, for purposes of decorum, there would be no alcohol at the banquet, so the Lindas sipped on soft drinks and introduced themselves. Linda Van Oort continued to seem somewhat wistful. "My husband said, 'You paid twenty-seven dollars to go to a Linda convention?'" she said. As if to provide a silent answer to the question, she handed me a color photograph that had been taken during a family vacation to Daytona Beach when she was in the eighth grade. In the photograph it was sunset, and with her feet she had carved LINDA in the sand.

Linda Teague, thirty-five, a direct-mail sales representative from Louisville, Kentucky, had driven nine straight hours to the Linda convention. "Usually conventions are for big wheels," she said. "You know—business executives. I thought it was nice that all you needed to get into this convention was to be named Linda. My dad was a news anchor in Louisville for more than twenty years. He was a celebrity in town, and he got all the attention. This is for me." Linda Minssen, twenty-five, an employee at a coupon clearinghouse in Fulton, Illinois, echoed this sentiment: "I was shopping at the Target store when someone told me about this. I've never been invited to a convention before, so I thought I'd come."

Linda Veit, forty-four, whose husband runs a security firm in Davenport, Iowa, said, "I go to his conventions all the time. He's at home with our boys tonight. He didn't say a word as I left. He was mowing the lawn. No good-bye or anything. I got in the car and called out that I was leaving for the Linda convention. He kind of acknowledged it: 'Okay.'"

*    *    *

The Lindas were instructed to gather on a grassy area outside the hotel. The idea was that they were to form a human L, and a photographer, perched on a ladder, would shoot a group picture.

But there was a problem. A dented black Camaro with Johnson County, Iowa, license plates was parked in an adjacent driveway. No driver was in the car. The car was in the photographer's shot, and would have ruined the picture. So about a dozen Lindas, in their party dresses, jogged over to the Camaro, put it in neutral, and shoved it out of the way.

When the picture had been shot and the Lindas had returned to the banquet room, I asked around and thought that I had discovered something amazing—even newsworthy. There were two Linda Lee Loves present—one forty-six years old, from Cedar Falls, Iowa, the other forty-two years old, from Rochester, New York.

Soon, though, I found out that this was no big deal. There were three Linda Lynches at the convention. There were two Linda Andersons. There were two Linda Geisherts. There were two Linda Webers.

A television reporter named Linda Shinn, of station KIMT in Mason City, Iowa, had driven to Cedar Rapids to do a piece on the convention—based, of course, on her own name. I was used to seeing network crews travel with producers, cameramen, sound engineers, lighting technicians, correspondents . . . but Linda Shinn, who was five feet two and weighed 110 pounds, was responsible for lugging all her own equipment, shooting all her own footage, then taking it back to Mason City and editing it.

"But how do you do your stand-ups?" I said. A stand-up is the part of a television story during which the reporter is seen on the screen.

"I just aim the camera at where I'll be standing, turn it on, step into the right place, and do it," she said.

"That's crazy," I said. "Let me shoot it."

So she showed me how to operate the Sony DXC-3000 camera, and I told her when she was standing in a spot with good background visuals. Peering into the lens, she said, "I'm Linda Shinn, for Eyewitness News."

"Punch it a little bit more," I said.

She looked at me quizzically. But she did it again, this time with more enthusiasm: "I'm Linda Shinn, for Eyewitness News."

"Once more," I said. "Hit the *I'm* a little bit harder."

We made eye contact again. She seemed ready to fire me from my new job. But she did it one more time.

"That's a keeper," I said.

She checked me out and shook her head.


I went out into the hallway to get some air. Linda Socha, thirty-two, a sales representative from Cedar Rapids, was on the pay phone to her boyfriend.

"Linda Ellerbee didn't show up," she was saying into the receiver.

I waited until she hung up.

"Linda Ellerbee didn't show up?" I said.

"Yeah," she said. "They said there were going to be all kinds of celebrity Lindas. Linda Evans, Linda Blair . . . but it's just us."


When I returned to the banquet room, dinner was being served. Simultaneously, Linda Pasvogel, on the dais, was giving away Linda-related door prizes. Linda Sinclair, forty-two, of Carlisle, Iowa, an exercise-class instructor, found out that she had won a paperback book titled *Alyssa* —written by an author named Linda Lang Bartell. She accepted the book from Linda Pasvogel. The cover copy said: "Caught in a web of treachery, only love's surrender can set her free."


A man wearing a black hat and a red mask entered the banquet room. He identified himself as a "Kissing Bandit" and said he had been hired by Linda Pasvogel to provide entertainment. But none of the Lindas seemed to take any note of him, and he ended up standing around the back of the room, waiting for instructions that never came.


A Linda at one of the tables said that she had skipped her twenty-fifth high school reunion to attend the Linda convention. "This just seemed more important to me," she said. Meanwhile, on the dais, Linda Pasvogel was still doling out the door prizes.

"This is a very important announcement," she said. "Our next prize is four pairs of panty hose that have been sent to us from thirty thousand feet in the air." She said that a United Airlines flight attendant named Linda Schmidt had gotten the idea to send the panty hose while working a flight the day before, and had sent them via Express Mail to Cedar Rapids. They had arrived just prior to the beginning of the banquet.

The winner of the panty hose rushed to the front of the room to accept her prize. I sat with a tableful of Lindas and thought: Another night in the only life I'll ever lead.

Dinner ended. A band went into a spirited rendition of "I Saw Linda Yesterday," and the Lindas formed a long line, each Linda holding on to the shoulders or hips of the Linda in front of her. They hopped through the banquet room.

Then the lights were dimmed. Linda Pasvogel asked all the Lindas to return to their seats.

A color slide of Jack Lawrence—the man who wrote the song "Linda" in 1946—was projected onto a screen. Linda Pasvogel turned on an audiocassette player.

Jack Lawrence's voice echoed through the room. He said that he was sorry he could not be in attendance, but he wanted to greet the Lindas and wish them well. He told the story of how he had come to write "Linda"—how a friend of his had said that all of the friend's other children had names about which songs had been written, but how his daughter Linda had never heard a song with her name in it. Lawrence's tape-recorded voice said that, as a favor to his friend, he had written "Linda." To his surprise, it quickly became the number-one-selling record in the country. And within a couple of years, more and more parents were naming their daughters Linda.

The taped speech concluded. The Lindas started to get up. But Jack Lawrence was not finished.

He said he wanted to do one more thing for the Lindas at the convention. He wanted to sing them his song.

And so, in the darkness, his voice filled the room:

"When I go to sleep, I never count sheep, I count all the charms about Linda. . . ."

# Dad's Girl

There is this photograph of my father; in the photograph he is wearing bathing trunks and is sitting with a beautiful woman who is not my mother. The woman is wearing a swimsuit, too. Both my father and the woman are smiling. They are obviously very close. The day is bright and sunny.

The photograph was taken in 1940, and the way I came to see it is sort of extraordinary. A while back, I wrote a column about the word "elderly," and about who qualifies to be described by that word. The column was syndicated to newspapers around the country. One of the papers that printed it was in San Diego.

A woman in San Diego read the column and decided to clip it out. Her reason for doing this was that her mother-in-law had recently come for a visit, on the occasion of the mother-in-law's seventieth birthday. The woman in San Diego thought that her mother-in-law might get a kick out of reading the column about elderly people.

So she clipped it and sent it to her mother-in-law. Soon after, a large envelope arrived in the mailbox of the woman in San Diego. The envelope had been sent by the mother-in-law.

The mother-in-law said that she had enjoyed reading the column. And she said something else: She said that she had once dated the father of the person who wrote the column. In fact, they had enjoyed a rather torrid romance. She had a picture of the two of them, which she was enclosing in the envelope.

So it came to be that the woman in San Diego sent me the photograph of her mother-in-law and my father, having a day in the sun in 1940.

My father, like the woman's mother-in-law, is now in his seventies. I sent him the photograph and an explanation of how I happened to have it. To say he was startled is an understatement; how would you like to unexpectedly see a photo of yourself and the person you had gone with half a century ago?

But I kind of wish I had kept the photograph for myself. It brought forth a number of complex feelings inside of me, and I was surprised to see that they were there.

You never think of your father as being twenty-five years old and going out with a gorgeous woman. By the time you know your father, he has taken on the dad's role; the fact that he was once a young, single man is something you can accept intellectually, but that is hard to deal with viscerally.

There he was, though, squinting in the sunlight with his girlfriend. In the picture my father looks a lot like me; but of course, on the day the picture was snapped, he had no idea that I would ever exist. When I look at the picture I see my dad, and I see a premonition of myself. He could have had no premonition of me on that day.

The other thing I think about when I see the picture is a little trickier. I had never thought about my father being with any woman other than my mother. They have had a long and happy marriage, and this bathing suit photograph was taken several years before they wed. Still, it's strange for a son to see a picture of his dad enjoying the company of anyone but his mom.

I was so mixed up about that aspect of the photograph that I almost didn't send it to my father. I was worried that when my mother saw the photo, she might be hurt—at least in a small way. Yes, the photograph is ancient history; yes, it was taken well before their wedding. But my concern was that the photo might be the catalyst for involuntary jealousy on my mother's part, all these years later.

I called my brother and my sister to ask them what they thought. They felt I was being silly; they said that of course my mother would approve of my sending the photograph to my dad. It would bring him a rush of warm nostalgia, and she would be grateful that I had caused him to have that feeling.

I remained hesitant, but in the end I sent the photograph. My dad loved it, and couldn't get over the bizarre chain of events that had brought it to us. My mom said she thought it was great; she sensed my misgivings, and laughed as she said, "Did you think you were going to cause us to have a divorce after forty-three years?"

I don't know what my father is going to do with the photo; I guess it would be a little inappropriate to put it on display in their house. It must be a weird feeling to be in your seventies and to be confronted by a picture of yourself on a date when you were twenty-five; it must feel even weirder to consider that the pretty woman sitting in her bathing suit next to you is now also in her seventies.

My father must look at the picture and think about all that has happened in the half a century since it was taken. There have been wars and recessions and fads and spaceshots; there have been ten presidents and the introduction of television and a full career and retirement. There have been children and grandchildren and the loss of both his parents. All of that since the photograph was snapped.

He couldn't have been thinking about any of that on the sunny day when he smiled for the camera, and the young woman next to him smiled, too. But I'm thinking about it; I'm thinking about it right now.

# A Moment to Care

Douglas Maurer, fifteen, of Creve Coeur, Missouri, had been feeling bad for several days. His temperature was ranging between 103 and 105 degrees, and he was suffering from severe flulike symptoms. Finally his mother, Donna Maurer, took him to the emergency room of Children's Hospital at Washington University Medical Center in St. Louis.

The blood tests revealed one of the most agonizing things a parent can learn about a child. Douglas Maurer was diagnosed as having leukemia.

During the next forty-eight hours, Douglas endured blood transfusions, spinal and bone marrow tests and chemotherapy. He developed pneumonia. For five days his mother stayed in his hospital room. One night Douglas, afraid, asked her to sleep in his bed by his side. Through her tears, she had to tell him that she couldn't; IV tubes and monitor cords were attached to his body, the bed was small, and there was no room for her without the danger of dislodging the medical equipment.

The doctors told him in frank terms about his disease. They said that for the next three years he would have to undergo chemotherapy. They did not sugarcoat the side effects. They told Douglas that he would go bald, and that his body would most likely bloat. Upon learning this, he went into a deep depression; although he was told that there was a good chance for the disease to go into remission, he was smart enough to know that the unspoken truth was that leukemia is often a fatal disease.

On the day he had been admitted, he had opened his eyes, looked around his room, and said to his mother, "I thought you get flowers when you're in the hospital." This was his first time in a hospital.

One of Douglas's aunts, hearing this, called a floral shop to send Douglas an arrangement of flowers. The flower shop was Brix Florist, in St. Louis.

As the aunt placed her telephone order, she was unsure that the salesclerk would do a conscientious job. The voice of the salesclerk, a woman, was high-pitched, and she sounded young. The aunt imagined an inexperienced clerk who would be unaware of the flower arrangement's significance.

So the aunt said, "I want the planter especially attractive. It's for my teenage nephew who has leukemia."

"Oh," said the salesclerk. "Let's add some fresh-cut flowers to brighten it up."

"Fine," said the aunt.

When the floral arrangement arrived at the hospital, it was beautiful. Douglas was feeling strong enough to sit up; he opened the envelope and read the card from his aunt.

Then he saw that, in the envelope, was another card. His mother said that the second card must have been placed in the envelope by mistake; it must have been meant for another floral arrangement, for another person.

But Douglas removed the card from the envelope anyway.

The card said:

> Douglas—I took your order. I work at Brix Florist. I had leukemia when I was 7 years old. I'm 22 years old now. Good luck. My heart goes out to you.
>
> Sincerely,
> Laura Bradley

According to his mother, Douglas's face lit up. He said, "Oh!"

His mother said, "For the first time since he had been in the hospital, he had gotten some inspiration. He had talked to so many doctors and nurses. But this one card, from the woman at the florist's who had survived leukemia, was the thing that made him believe he might beat the disease."

I called Brix Florist, and asked to speak with Laura Bradley. At first she was unsettled by hearing from a newspaperman; she thought she might have done something wrong. But I explained why I was getting in touch.

"When the woman on the phone told me that the boy had leukemia, my head dropped into my hands," Laura Bradley said. "I felt tears coming into my eyes. It reminded me of when I first learned that I had it.

"I realized what the boy must be going through. I wanted him to know that you really can get better. So I wrote the card and slipped it into the envelope. I didn't tell anyone at the shop that I did it. I haven't been working here very long, and I was afraid I might get in trouble."

I told her that I doubted if she would get in trouble; I told her what her card had done for Douglas Maurer and his family. She said thank you, and there was an awkward silence, and then we said good-bye.

It's funny; Douglas Maurer was in a hospital filled with millions of dollars of the most sophisticated medical equipment. He was being treated by expert doctors and nurses with medical training totaling in the hundreds of years.

But it was a salesclerk in a flower shop, a woman making $170 a week, who—by taking the time to care, and by being willing to go with what her heart told her to do—gave Douglas hope and the will to carry on. The human spirit can be an amazing thing, and sometimes you encounter it at its very best when you aren't even looking.

# Lost Love

The call came in to my office at the Chicago *Tribune*. I was out on a story. The caller identified himself to my secretary, Julie Herbick; he said his name was Tony Leotta. She had him repeat the spelling. She always does.

He said that his fiancée, Theresa Sielicky, had been missing for four days. He said that they had had an argument late at night. They lived together in an apartment complex called the Pavilion, on the Northwest Side of Chicago; they had recently moved to Chicago from Oregon. Tony Leotta said that after the argument he had gone out to sleep on the couch in their living room. She had slept in the bedroom. When he woke up around 7:00 A.M., he said, she was gone. She had packed most of her clothes and makeup.

Tony Leotta said that he and Theresa worked for the same company—Information Resources Inc., a market-research firm with headquarters in downtown Chicago. Tony Leotta, twenty-seven, was a technical support supervisor; Theresa Sielicky, twenty-two, was a receptionist/switchboard operator.

In the four days since Theresa had disappeared, she had not shown up for work, had not called any of her friends, and had not called her mother back in Oregon. This was highly unusual, Leotta said; Theresa called her mother quite often. He was afraid that something bad had happened to her.

"She reads Bob's newspaper column every morning," Leotta said to my secretary. "If he wrote something in the column about her, I know that she would see it. If he could just tell her to call her family and friends, and let us know she's all right."

He said that she had walked out on him before, but had come back a few days later. This time, though, he was really worried.

Later that day, Julie told me about the phone call.

"I don't know," I said. "If she's done it before, she may have just taken off on him. Let's wait a few days."

Four days later, Tony Leotta called again. Again, I was out of the office.

"I still haven't heard from her," he told Julie. "I've reported her missing to the police, but I think they're regarding it as just a domestic quarrel. This doesn't make any sense. She still hasn't come to work. She hasn't called her friends, her parents—no one."

He filled in their history a little bit. He said that they had met in Salem, Oregon—Theresa's hometown—where he was stationed at a branch office of Information Resources. She was working at a shoe store at the time. They had fallen in love. They became engaged, and when he was promoted to the Chicago office, she came with him. For a while she had worked in a Chicago-area shoe store, but then she had obtained the receptionist job at Information Resources. They liked being able to work in the same office.

"I know she'd see it if Bob wrote about her," Leotta said.

Julie said she would pass the message on to me.

Later that day, when I checked in, Julie reviewed my calls, including the one from Tony Leotta.

"Call him back," I said. "Ask if he has a picture of his fiancée. Maybe I'll run it with the column."

Julie called Leotta. Leotta said he had a photograph of Theresa Sielicky. He would bring it in the next morning.

*   *   *

When he showed up with the photograph, I was out again. Julie said he was well dressed and well groomed, and that he appeared upset and nervous. He handed her the picture. It was a color snapshot; in the photograph, Theresa Sielicky was wearing a Chicago Cubs baseball cap and clutching a teddy bear.

Tony Leotta told Julie that the police had asked him to take a lie-detector test, just to rule him out as a suspect. He said he was more than willing to take the test, if only to persuade the police to run their investigation more aggressively. Then, out of nowhere, he said to Julie, "I talked to some of her friends. I guess she was planning on leaving me."

He also said that she had left him before, "for several weeks," but had come back.

Julie recalled that, during the first phone conversation, Leotta had said that Theresa had left him for several days, not weeks.

In Salem, Oregon, Theresa's mother—Kay Rogers, fifty, the co-owner of an insurance agency and former president of the Salem Chamber of Commerce—was getting phone calls from Tony Leotta several times a day.

"Tony had met Theresa here in Salem, at a Halloween party at a bar called O'Callahan's," Kay Rogers said. "He really pursued her. After they became engaged, and they were preparing to leave for Chicago, we made a videotape of them. They told me about the first night at O'Callahan's. They were joking about it—they said that Theresa would never let anyone pick her up at a bar, and so the day after the Halloween party Tony had sent her flowers at Connie's shoe shop, where she was working. The point of the videotape was that they could add to it through the years—on their wedding day, when they had their first child, et cetera."

Some days Tony Leotta would call Kay Rogers two times. Some days he would call her three times. Some days he would call her only once. But each time his question was the same: "Have you heard from Theresa?"

The first time he called Theresa's mother, he asked her, "Are you familiar with a columnist named Bob Greene?" He said that Theresa read my column every morning "over coffee," and that he was trying to persuade me to write about her. "He said he was sure that was the way to find her," Kay Rogers said.

During one of the calls, Tony Leotta had another question for Theresa's mother.

"Did you know that she was going to leave me?" Leotta said.

In fact, Kay Rogers was, indeed, aware that her daughter had grown somewhat disenchanted with Tony Leotta. That was why she was not overly surprised that Theresa had left the apartment.


In Tigard, Oregon, a suburb of Portland, Theresa's father, Roger M. Sielicky, fifty-one, manager of natural-gas marketing for the Northwest Natural Gas Company, was growing increasingly alarmed. He was divorced from Kay Rogers, but they remained friendly. With each passing day, his panic grew.

"I didn't know what to do," Sielicky said. "I called the police in Chicago, and I got the Yellow Pages and started calling hospitals. But I felt helpless, all those miles away."

So Theresa's father decided to fly to Chicago. He arrived at O'Hare International Airport late at night. "I had never been to Chicago before," he said. "There were some pretty disreputable-looking people hanging around the outside of the airport. It wasn't like Oregon."

Sielicky rented a Chevrolet Celebrity from Hertz and drove downtown to the Congress Hotel, where he registered in room 4401. He did not sleep during the night.

"I had told Tony that I would meet him the next day," Roger Sielicky said. "I had always liked him a lot. Back in Oregon, I found him to be very charming, and my belief was that he was a very serious young man who would become quite successful in business. Like most parents, I guess, I wasn't thrilled with the idea of my daughter living with someone before they got married. But they were engaged, and she was determined to do it. As they left for Chicago I told Tony that I expected him to take care of my daughter, and he said he would."

In the morning, Sielicky met with Chicago police officers, who updated him on their investigation. He was supposed to get together with Tony Leotta at a Bennigan's restaurant near O'Hare between 1:00 P.M. and 1:15 P.M.

"Tony was an hour late," Sielicky said. "He walked into the restaurant a little after 2:00." The two men ordered a plate of fried zucchini, and when it arrived they shared it.

"Tony was crying and saying how worried he was about Theresa," Sielicky said. "He said that he had done everything he could to find her, but that he wasn't getting anywhere. He told me that there was this newspaper columnist named Bob Greene, and that his last hope was to get a message to Theresa through the newspaper column."

Sielicky noticed something unusual about Tony Leotta: Leotta's right arm was in a cast almost up to the elbow. When Sielicky asked about it, Leotta said that he had broken his finger when the lid of a washing machine had inadvertently dropped on it. When Leotta had visited the newspaper office to drop off the snapshot of Theresa, Julie had noticed the same thing. Julie's husband is a physician; when she had told him about it that night, he had said that there is something known as a boxer's fracture —a break in the finger that often occurs when a person strikes someone.

"Tony seemed as distraught as I was," Roger Sielicky said. "He asked me to drive him back to the Pavilion apartment complex, where he and Theresa had their place. So I drove him there, but I didn't go in."

Sielicky was carrying a photograph of his daughter with him. He took it to restaurants, bars, and hotels in the area, asking if anyone had seen her. He had no luck. He knew that his daughter loved being tan, so he tried local tanning parlors, too. "I kept getting this sinking feeling," he said. "The city is just so large."

Late that night, Sielicky drove back to O'Hare for the return flight to Oregon—"just absolutely in total despair," in his words. Before he departed, he left with the police a wallet-sized photograph of Theresa. On the back of the photograph she had written:

> Daddy—You're my father & I thank God for that over & over again—I love you & am so proud to say "He's my Dad!"
> Love forever, your daughter

Greg Masonick, thirty-nine, an eighteen-year veteran of the Chicago Police Department, had been assigned the file of Theresa Sielicky, who was being classified as a missing person.

At Information Resources, Masonick found out that both Tony Leotta and Theresa Sielicky were considered good employees. Their romantic relationship was common knowledge. But Masonick talked to one female

employee to whom Theresa had confided that she was becoming unhappy living with Leotta; Theresa had inquired if she might move in
temporarily with the woman, but nothing came of it.

At the Pavilion apartment complex, Masonick was told that the two
were referred to as the "Ken and Barbie" of the development, because
they were attractive and always appeared so upbeat and happy.

Masonick learned something else, too. Two months before, Theresa
had been taken by Tony Leotta to the emergency room of Westlake
Community Hospital in suburban Melrose Park, where she was treated
for contusions of the face. The couple had told hospital personnel that
Theresa had had a household accident. But Masonick learned from other
sources that Theresa had said that Leotta had taken her face and hit it
several times against the bathroom floor in their apartment.

Masonick confronted Leotta with this.

According to Masonick, Leotta admitted, "I did have a fight with
Theresa, and I physically hurt her. I took her to the hospital." Leotta
said that after that fight they had patched up their differences.

Masonick learned that, on the evening prior to Theresa Sielicky's dis-
appearance, Theresa, Tony Leotta, and a group of friends went out on
Lake Michigan on a large boat, where there was a party. After the party
the group went to a downtown Chicago restaurant and bar called At the
Tracks. They were known at the bar; many employees from Information
Resources often went there after work.

On this particular night, though, things were different. Carl Berman,
the owner of the bar, said that Tony Leotta was drinking wine coolers
all evening, and that it was apparent that he and Theresa Sielicky were
not getting along.

"They didn't want to be with each other particularly," Berman would
recall later. "She was pretty weepy. There was no physical violence—it
was more verbal. But you could tell there was a real problem going on.
You just got the feeling there was going to be trouble. She was very,
very upset."

Katie Baer, the waitress who was serving their table, said she remembered Tony and Theresa from previous visits as "a neat couple . . . a lot
of fun . . . never a problem." But on this night, as she told Masonick,
she grew concerned.

"Tony really seemed angry," she would recall later. "He kept losing
his temper. This other couple was trying to calm him down. Tony and
Theresa had to be physically separated several times. At one time, this

other woman at the table said to one of the men, 'We have to do something, he's going crazy.' There was one point when they were standing
outside on the sidewalk together, arguing. She was crying. I just assumed
they were breaking up. She looked really sad and upset. One of the
employees in here said to one of the other employees, 'Uh oh, trouble
in paradise.' "

Both Carl Berman and Katie Baer told Officer Masonick that Tony Leotta and Theresa Sielicky had left At the Tracks together just after midnight.
The next morning is when Leotta said that Theresa had disappeared.

Greg Masonick asked Tony Leotta if he would take a polygraph test.
Leotta agreed. In areas of questioning regarding whether Leotta knew
Theresa Sielicky's whereabouts and whether he had knowledge of the
transportation of her from one area to another, the examiner concluded
that Leotta's responses were "not truthful."

Masonick informed Leotta of the results.

"Well, I'm telling the truth," Leotta said.

Greg Masonick drove out to the Pavilion apartment complex. Police
technicians had already examined the apartment where the couple lived
and had found nothing out of the ordinary. Now Masonick checked the
mailbox assigned to Tony Leotta and Theresa Sielicky. There was a letter
that had been sent to the couple by Theresa's father just before her
disappearance. It said, in part:

> Hi, you two—
> . . . We are really happy and proud of you. We miss you a lot and
> are trying to find a way to see you.
>
> Love,
> Dad

The police had not been able to come up with any criminal record for
Tony Leotta. One afternoon, though, Greg Masonick began to "play
around," in his words, with a police computer, trying different per-
mutations of Tony Leotta's name.

There was no Anthony Leotta. But there was an Anthony Liotta who had outstanding warrants in Pennsylvania for burglary, theft, receiving stolen property, and criminal conspiracy. On his Chicago employment records, the man calling himself Tony Leotta had listed his birth date as October 23, 1959. The Anthony Liotta who was wanted in Pennsylvania had a birth date of October 29, 1959. Similarly, the social security numbers had been changed only slightly.

Greg Masonick presented this information to Tony Leotta—who he now suspected was Tony Liotta. According to Masonick, Liotta admitted that he was the person, and said that approximately two years earlier he had stolen $100,000 from an employer in Pittsburgh. He said he had fled to the Bahamas and had then ended up in Salem, Oregon, where he met Theresa Sielicky. However, Liotta still denied having anything to do with Theresa's disappearance.

Liotta was arrested on the Pennsylvania charges and taken to the Cook County Jail. He said he wished to waive extradition: he wanted to leave Chicago and be turned over to Pennsylvania authorities.

I was working in my office on a Saturday morning when the phone rang. The caller identified himself as Officer Greg Masonick of the Chicago Police Department.

"I understand you might be working on a story about a guy who's trying to find his missing fiancée," Masonick said.

I told him that I was considering writing such a story.

"I wouldn't," Masonick said.

Masonick and I made an appointment to meet. He told me that, just before Tony Liotta was scheduled to be transferred to a prison in Pennsylvania, Masonick and Chicago police officer Kenneth Winkie went to see him in the Cook County Jail. Officially, Theresa Sielicky was still a missing person. The police officers realized that if Liotta left Chicago, the case might never be resolved.

"We knew he was lying," Masonick told me. "We sat there with him for an hour, and he kept telling us that he knew nothing about how Theresa had disappeared. He maintained his story that she had walked out on him while he was sleeping in the middle of the night.

"For almost an hour he kept repeating that story. So we tried to appeal to him as a human being. At one point I said to him, 'Tony, you know about the families of veterans who are missing in action? They'll never know what happened to their sons. Theresa's mother and father love their daughter. At least give them the peace of knowing what happened to her.'

"It still didn't look as if he was going to break. But then, suddenly, he burst into tears. He said, 'I've got to tell you how it happened.' "

The following is Officer Masonick's account of what Tony Liotta told him:

After their argument at the At the Tracks bar, Liotta and Theresa drove home to their apartment—apartment 915 in one of the Pavilion complex buildings. Liotta received a telephone call from his mother in Pittsburgh. Theresa listened in on the other line.

After Liotta had hung up, Theresa made some disparaging comments about his family. This was the point at which Liotta realized that his fiancée really was going to leave him.

They began fighting in the kitchen. As the violence escalated, Liotta —using a knife with a three-inch blade that had been hanging on a magnetic bar mounted on the wall—stabbed Theresa once in the chest.

He carried her into the bedroom, put her on the bed, then returned to the living room and went to sleep on the couch. This was at approximately 2:30 A.M. He woke up at 7:00, and his first thought was that it was "all a bad dream." But he went into the bedroom, and there was Theresa, dead.

He got dressed. He went out, got into a 1984 Mercury Capri hatchback that he had borrowed for the weekend from a friend, and drove to an automatic cash station, where he withdrew $300. He then drove to an Ace Hardware store, where he purchased a thirty-three-gallon plastic garbage can. He returned to the Pavilion complex, carried the garbage can up the elevator to apartment 915, and stuffed Theresa's body into the garbage can. Then he put the top on the garbage can and sealed it with masking tape.

He cleaned up the apartment, scrubbing the blood from the kitchen floor and carpeting. He removed the bloody sheets from the bed. He packed Theresa's suitcase with some of her clothing and cosmetics, and the sheets. He went to the elevator, carrying the suitcase and dragging the plastic garbage can. He rode down the main elevator, the suitcase and the garbage can beside him. Apparently either he was alone in the elevator, or no one questioned him about the garbage can.

He tried to put the garbage can in the car, and found it would fit only in the hatchback section. He stopped behind several stores and discarded Theresa's belongings in different dumpsters. He then drove to Busse Lake, a nearby body of water, with the intention of getting rid of the garbage can. But there were too many picnickers, so he rejected that idea.

He started driving south until he crossed the Indiana border. When he reached Hammond, he found a deserted area close to Lake Michigan. He carried the garbage can across the field. He punched holes in its bottom, so that it would sink more easily. Then—still wearing all his clothes—he walked into the water until he was waist-deep in it. He watched the garbage can submerge.

He drove back to Chicago and did a load of laundry. Then he began telling friends that Theresa had walked out on him.

"He related all this in a voice completely devoid of emotion," Greg Masonick said. "He had cried at first, but he told the story in a very dry manner. The fact is, her body had been in their apartment for twelve hours before he decided to remove it."

Masonick contacted Indiana law enforcement authorities and related Liotta's story. The Hammond Police Department was not surprised. Five days after the death of Theresa Sielicky, a man named Glenn A. Gray was walking along the Indiana lakefront when he saw the nude body of a female lying face-down, straddling a boulder, partially in the water and partially on the rocky shoreline. Gray called the police. When officers arrived, they determined that the body had decomposed so badly that no positive identification was possible. The woman was, however, wearing a ring on her right hand. She had been stabbed once in the chest.

It was one of those police situations that sometimes happen: the Chicago police had a missing person, but no body. The police in Indiana had a body on the shoreline of Lake Michigan, but no report of a missing person. Somehow, the information had never been exchanged. With Greg Masonick's phone call, it all fit together.

Officers Masonick and Winkie arranged to have Tony Liotta temporarily released from the Cook County Jail, in their custody. They followed Liotta's directions to Indiana. He led them to the spot in Lake Michigan where he said he had dumped the garbage can holding the body of his fiancée. It was less than one hundred yards from where the body of the woman had washed up onshore.

The ring on the woman's finger matched exactly the description of a ring that had been given to Theresa Sielicky by her brother.

Later that night, Greg Masonick called Theresa's father in Oregon. He made sure that Mr. Sielicky was sitting down. Then, as gently as he could, Masonick said, "Tony has confessed to killing your daughter."

A period of eleven days passed between the time Theresa Sielicky was killed and Greg Masonick discovered that Tony Liotta was wanted on the charges in Pennsylvania. During that time Liotta reported for work regularly at Information Resources, telling his fellow employees how his fiancée had walked out on him and how worried he was about her whereabouts. He made several visits to the At the Tracks bar. He called Theresa's mother every day, asking if she had heard from her daughter. He shared the appetizers at Bennigan's with Theresa's father. He contacted my office repeatedly, trying to solicit my help in finding his fiancée.

"He was trying to set us all up," Greg Masonick said. "He figured if you wrote a column about this man who was desperately trying to locate the woman who had left him, it would take the heat off him. It would make it appear as if a third person had harmed her. The thing is, it almost worked."

Tony Liotta was charged with first-degree murder and concealment of a homicide. He pleaded guilty and is currently serving a twenty-year prison term.

# The Nixon-Presley Papers

$\mathbf{F}$irst of all, I am not making this up.

I realize that is a strange phrase with which to begin a column. But once you read on, you will understand its necessity.

By now, many people are aware of the fact that in December 1970, Elvis Presley visited President Richard Nixon in the Oval Office. A White House photographer was present and snapped twenty-eight shots during that meeting. When a syndicated newspaper columnist, who shall remain nameless, reported recently that the government was offering the Nixon-Presley pictures for sale to the public, they immediately became the most requested photographs in the history of the National Archives, far outdistancing a rare portrait of Abraham Lincoln.

The details of how that meeting came about, though, are less well known. The National Archives and Records Administration in Washington has more than forty million pages of documents from the Nixon administration in storage—including all the paperwork related to the Nixon-Presley visit.

I requested a set of that paperwork. I present the documents here with a minimum of editorial comment.

Again—this is not satire. This is real; these are the real documents on file with the government.

It started with a letter written by Presley to Nixon. The letter covered five pages of American Airlines stationery. Presley's handwriting resembled that of a second- or third-grade student.

Dear Mr. President:

First I would like to introduce myself. I am Elvis Presley and admire you and Have Great Respect for your office. I talked to Vice President Agnew in Palm Springs 3 weeks ago and expressed my concern for our country. The Drug Culture, the Hippie Elements, the SDS, Black Panthers, etc, do *not* consider me as their enemy or as they call it the Establishment. *I call it America* and I Love it. Sir I can and Will be of any Service that I can to help the country out. I have no concern or motives other than helping the country out. So I wish not to be given a title or an appointed position. I can and will do more good if I were made a Federal Agent at Large, and I will help best by doing it my way through my communications with people of all ages. First and Foremost I am an entertainer but all I need is the Federal Credentials. I am on the Plane with Sen. George Murphy and We have been discussing the problems that our Country is faced with. So I am Staying at the Washington hotel Room 505-506-507—I have 2 men who work with me by the name of Jerry Schilling and Sonny West. I am registered under the name of Jon Burrows. I will be here for as long as it takes to get the credentials of a Federal Agent. I have done an in depth study of Drug Abuse and Communist Brainwashing Techniques and I am right in the middle of the whole thing, where I can and will do the most good. I am Glad to help just so long as it is kept very Private. You can have your staff or whomever call me anytime today tonight or To-morrow. I was nominated the coming year one of America's Ten most outstanding young men. That will be in January 18 in My Home Town of Memphis Tenn. I am sending you the short auto-biography about myself so you can better understand This ap-proach. I would Love to meet you just to say hello if you're not to Busy.

Respectfully,
Elvis Presley

P.S. I believe that you Sir were one of the Top Ten Outstanding Men of America also.

I have a personal gift for you also which I would like to present to you and you can accept it or I will keep it for you until you can take it.

* * *

On December 21, 1970, Nixon assistant Dwight L. Chapin sent a memo, on White House stationery, to Chief of Staff H. R. Haldeman. In his memo, Chapin explained the proposed visit.

MEMORANDUM FOR: MR. H. R. HALDEMAN

FROM: DWIGHT L. CHAPIN

SUBJECT: Elvis Presley

Attached you will find a letter to the President from Elvis Presley. As you are aware, Presley showed up here this morning and has requested an appointment with the President. He states that he knows the President is very busy, but he would just like to say hello and present the President with a gift.

As you are well aware, Presley was voted one of the ten out-standing young men for next year and this was based upon his work in the field of drugs. The thrust of Presley's letter is that he wants to become a "Federal agent at large" to work against the drug problem by communicating with people of all ages. He says that he is not a member of the establishment and that drug culture types, the hippie elements, the SDS, and the Black Panthers are people with whom he can communicate since he is not part of the establishment.

I suggest that we do the following: This morning Bud Krogh will have Mr. Presley in and talk to him about drugs and about what Presley can do. Bud will also check to see if there is some kind of an honorary agent at large or credential of some sort that we can provide for Presley. After Bud has met with Presley, it is recom-mended that we have Bud bring Presley in during the Open Hour to meet briefly with the President. You know that several people have mentioned over the past few months that Presley is very pro the President. He wants to keep everything private and I think we should honor his request.

I have talked to Bud Krogh about this whole matter, and we both think that it would be wrong to push Presley off on the Vice Pres-ident since it will take very little of the President's time and it can be extremely beneficial for the President to build some rapport with Presley.

In addition, if the President wants to meet with some bright young people outside of the Government, Presley might be a perfect one to start with.

In the margin next to the advice Chapin offered in that last paragraph, Haldeman scrawled: "You must be kidding."

But he initialed his approval for the visit.

A second memorandum was prepared for Nixon, to get him ready for his meeting with Presley. Included in this memo were some "talking points"—suggestions for what Nixon might say to Presley.

MEMORANDUM FOR: THE PRESIDENT

SUBJECT: Meeting with Elvis Presley,
         December 21, 1970, 12:30 P.M.

I. PURPOSE

To thank Elvis Presley for his offer to help in trying to stop the drug epidemic in the country, and to ask him to work with us in bringing a more positive attitude to young people throughout the country.

In his letter to you, Elvis Presley offered to help as much as possible with the growing drug problem. He requested the meeting with you this morning when he presented himself to the guard at the Northwest Gate bearing a letter.

II. PARTICIPANTS

Elvis Presley; Bud Krogh (staff)

III. TALKING POINTS

A. We have asked the entertainment industry—both television and radio—to assist us in our drug fight.

B. You are aware that the average American family has 4 radio sets; 98% of the young people between 12 and 17 listen to radio. Between the time a child is born and he leaves high school, it is estimated he watches between 15,000 and 20,000 hours of television. That is more time than he spends in the classroom.

C. The problem is critical: As of December 4, 1970, 1,022 people died this year in New York alone from just narcotic related deaths. 208 of these were teenagers.

D. Two of youth's folk heroes, Jimi Hendrix and Janis Joplin, recently died within a period of two weeks reportedly from drug-related causes. Their deaths are a sharp reminder of how the rock music culture has been linked to the drug sub-culture. If our youth are going to emulate the rock music stars, from now on let those stars affirm their conviction that true and lasting talent is the result of self motivation and discipline and not artificial chemical euphoria.

E. Suggestions for Presley activities:

1. Work with White House Staff.

2. Cooperate with and encourage the creation of an hour Television Special in which Presley narrates as stars such as himself sing popular songs and interpret them for parents in order to show drug and other anti-establishment themes in rock music.

3. Encourage fellow artists to develop a new rock musical theme, "Get High on Life."

4. Record an album with the theme "Get High on Life" at the federal narcotic rehabilitation and research facility at Lexington, Kentucky.

5. Be a consultant to the Advertising Council on how to communicate anti-drug messages to youth.

The meeting took place. Nixon assistant Egil "Bud" Krogh was in the Oval Office, taking notes. When the meeting had ended he compiled them into yet another memo.

MEMORANDUM FOR: THE PRESIDENTS FILE
SUBJECT: Meeting with Elvis Presley,
         Monday, December 21, 1970, 12:30 P.M.

The meeting opened with pictures taken of the President and Elvis Presley.

Presley immediately began showing the President his law enforcement paraphernalia including badges from police departments in California, Colorado, and Tennessee. Presley indicated that he had been playing Las Vegas and the President indicated that he was aware of how difficult it is to perform in Las Vegas.

The President mentioned that he thought Presley could reach young people, and that it was important for Presley to retain his credibility. Presley responded that he did his thing by "just singing." He said that he could not get to the kids if he made a speech on the stage, that he had to reach them in his own way. The President nodded in agreement.

Presley indicated that he thought the Beatles had been a real force for anti-American spirit. He said that the Beatles came to this country, made their money, and then returned to England where they promoted an anti-American theme. The President nodded in agreement and expressed some surprise. The President then indicated that those who use drugs are also those in the vanguard of anti-American protest. Violence, drug usage, dissent, protest all seem to merge in generally the same group of young people.

Presley indicated to the President in a very emotional manner that he was "on your side." Presley kept repeating that he wanted to be helpful, that he wanted to restore some respect for the flag which was being lost. He mentioned that he was just a poor boy from Tennessee who had gotten a lot from his country, which in some way he wanted to repay. He also mentioned that he is studying Communist brainwashing and the drug culture for over ten years. He mentioned that he knew a lot about this and was accepted by the hippies. He said he could go right into a group of young people or hippies and be accepted which he felt could be helpful to him in his drug drive. The President indicated again his concern that Presley retain his credibility.

At the conclusion of the meeting, Presley again told the President how much he supported him, and then, in a surprising, spontaneous gesture, put his left arm around the President and hugged him.

In going out, Presley asked the President if he would see his two associates. The President agreed and they came over and shook hands with the President briefly. At this meeting, the President thanked them for their efforts and again mentioned his concern for Presley's credibility.

At some point after the meeting, one female White House staff member wrote a brief note to a female colleague.

Lucy:
Elvis Presley (believe it or not) was granted an appointment with the President on Monday, Dec. 21. He left these autographed photos with the President. I don't think any acknowledgement would be necessary. For your good disposition!

Bev

On December 31, 1970, President Nixon mailed the following letter to Elvis Presley:

Dear Mr. Presley:

It was a pleasure to meet with you in my office recently, and I want you to know once again how much I appreciate your thoughtfulness in giving me the commemorative World War II Colt .45 pistol, encased in the handsome wooden chest. You were particularly kind to remember me with this impressive gift, as well as your family photographs, and I am delighted to have them for my collection of special mementos.

With my best wishes to you, Mrs. Presley, and to your daughter, Lisa, for a happy and peaceful 1971,

Sincerely,
Richard Nixon

# Misty's Book

The big blockbuster books generally come from brand-name authors—Sidney Sheldon, Danielle Steel, Judith Krantz, Jackie Collins and the other popular novelists whose names on the jacket of a book guarantee its success.

But I have just read a book that has moved me as few books have ever moved me before. You probably have never heard of its author, and you may laugh at its title before you learn the story behind it. The book is called *Where's Chimpy?*

*Where's Chimpy?* is a children's book. The plot is simple. A little girl named Misty is ready to go to bed. Her father is reading her a story. She realizes that she has misplaced her toy monkey, Chimpy. Her father tells the girl that they will look for Chimpy in the morning. But the girl will not go to sleep without the toy monkey. She tries to remember where she has left it. She has a great deal of trouble finding Chimpy. With her father's assistance, she finally finds the toy monkey, and turns in for the night.

It's a pretty standard children's story, and very well-written.

But here's where the difference comes in. Most books like *Where's Chimpy?* feature artists' drawings to accompany the text. This book doesn't. The text is illustrated with color photographs—and the photographs are of a real girl and her real father.

The girl is Misty Spurlock, six, of Sleepy Hollow, Illinois. Misty was born with Down's syndrome, the chromosomal disorder that usually causes mental retardation and certain physical defects and disabilities. Misty is the daughter of Rick Spurlock, thirty-one, who owns a janitorial business, and his wife Barbara, twenty-nine. The Spurlocks also have a healthy eight-year-old son named Ty.

The Spurlocks's next-door-neighbor is Berniece Rabe, an author of children's books who has received numerous honors for her work. One day Rabe got the idea to write *Where's Chimpy?* and to invite the Spurlocks to let Misty and her toy monkey be the featured characters.

"Every child has a right to be a star at least once in his or her life," Rabe said the other day. "I wanted to give Misty the chance to be the star."

The Spurlocks agreed. "Misty and I always play together," her father said. "So it was just a matter of us playing in a way that would go along with the text of the book, while a photographer took pictures."

The color photographs in the book—and they are wonderful—were taken by prize-winning photojournalist Diane Schmidt. "We shot for two days," Schmidt said. "Misty worked so hard. She and her dad were just great. It was a long shooting schedule, but Misty never seemed to get tired. When we were finished, Misty gave me a big hug and kiss. I think this is probably the most personally satisfying thing I have ever done."

*Where's Chimpy?* is being published by Albert Whitman & Co., a small Illinois firm specializing in children's books. Most of the company's books have ended up being ordered by schools and libraries, instead of by large bookstores and bookstore chains. As I mentioned earlier, *Where's Chimpy?* is probably not destined to be a best-seller, even in the children's field.

But something rather remarkable happened the other evening. At the Spurlocks's home in Sleepy Hollow, one of the first copies of *Where's Chimpy?* was delivered.

Rick and Barbara Spurlock did not know how Misty would react. Because of Down's syndrome, her vocabulary and speaking skills are quite limited; she is small for her age.

Her parents and her brother showed her the book.

Misty looked at the cover and her eyes lit up.

She pointed at the photograph of herself and said, "Me!"

She began to turn the pages, seeing photo after photo of her father and her. She kept saying the same two words: "Oh, happy!"

Mr. and Mrs. Spurlock and their son Ty put their arms around Misty. As they all embraced, Misty's parents and her brother began to weep with joy. Misty, though, did not cry; the smile remained on her face.

That night she fell asleep on the living room floor. Her hands were still clutching the book.

# The Virgin

**H**e ordered blackened snapper.

"You have something else," he said to her. "We'll share."

She put her hand on his shoulder.

He is twenty-seven, an executive in the medical publishing field. He wore a gray business suit, but he had the handsome, sandy-haired good looks of a young major-league second baseman. She is thirty-seven, ten years older; she trains sales representatives for a manufacturing firm. Striking in a red dress with gold jewelry accenting her dark blond hair, she could pass for being in her twenties. She has been married and divorced. For the past year and a half, the two of them have been dating each other exclusively.

"I can't believe that radio station you listen to in your car," he said.

"I know," she said. "I keep it on the AM band automatically. For years I only had an AM radio in my car."

They looked at each other. She reached over and playfully touched his face.

He is a virgin.


In the days following the dinner, I spoke with each of them separately.

"I feel uncomfortable when people assume I have intercourse with my girlfriend, or when friends laugh at the quaintness of their parents going through life having 'gone all the way' with only the one they married," he said. "But I've never regretted my decision to wait, and I would guess that I'll appreciate it even more when I get married."

His decision to remain a virgin has nothing to do with the current national concern over sexually transmitted diseases. Indeed, he made the decision back in the days when free-wheeling sex was becoming the American norm.

"I was in high school in the mid-Seventies," he said. "I graduated in 'seventy-seven. There were a lot of sexual messages coming from magazines and movies and TV shows. I'm sure there was some fantasizing on my part, but I was by nature cautious. Some of the girls I hung around with virtually offered it. They'd say, 'We're going to corrupt you,' and they were kidding, but they weren't kidding, if you know what I mean.

"Then in college, even the 'good girls' were doing it. It was clear that it was available to me. That's when I realized it was a choice I had to make. It's a question of degree. Most people still have qualms about having intercourse with someone for whom they don't feel a great deal of affection, or even love. When you're a virgin, you simply carry this reasoning further. You can't feel right about doing that with someone unless you love them enough to *marry* them.

"At first, the risk of pregnancy was a big part of it. I would think, 'Oh, my God, what would I do if I got a girl pregnant?' I personally didn't know if I could have an abortion if I were a woman. As a man, I never wanted to have to face the dilemma of dealing with a woman who had to make that decision.

"Gradually, though, it just became a part of my moral stance. I work in my spare time with a couple of youth groups. We're always telling them to resist peer pressure. There are bumper stickers that say 'It's Okay Not to Drink' and 'Say No to Drugs.' Well, teen pregnancy is one of the worst crises in the United States today, and I feel good talking to the kids about that issue because I know that it's possible to resist the urge.

"There are a lot of myths about being a virgin. One is that you can't have a close, intimate relationship with a woman without sex. Or that you can't travel with a girlfriend—including sharing a hotel room or a camping tent—without sleeping with her. A corollary myth is that intercourse helps a couple determine whether they're 'compatible' for marriage. There are other ways of determining compatibility. And I highly doubt that the divorce rate among couples who, say, lived together before marriage is lower than the rate among those who didn't.

"Sexual restraint forces a couple to develop other aspects of their relationship. My friends wonder aloud sometimes if they're in a relationship only for the physical side of it. I'm certain I'm not. Staying a virgin helps one prepare for the inevitable day after a couple of years of marriage when you'll actually have to *talk* to each other."

He said that plenty of opportunities to lose his virginity have presented themselves during his adult life. "Women come on fairly strongly nowadays," he said. "I recently met a woman and we went out on a business dinner—not a date. I dropped her off at her apartment building, and she invited me in. I got up there and we started talking. She leaned over toward me and bumped against me. There's a look. You can tell. She was looking for fun. I kind of backed away. I said something like 'I have to be going,' and I left.

"Before my current relationship, there was a pattern. I'd go out with a woman a few times, and I wouldn't have to explain anything. But then, maybe on the fourth date, maybe on the sixth date, she'd start doing more than kissing, you might say. And that's when I'd have to say, 'I'd prefer not to go past a certain point.' If she'd ask me what I meant, I'd say, 'I don't feel comfortable going all the way.' And if she kept asking me why, I'd finally say, 'I've never done that.'

"I'd get some interesting answers. Some women would just say something like, 'I guess we feel differently' or 'I have different needs.' But one thing you've got to admit—it's distinctive. Regardless of what the women thought of my attitude, they certainly didn't come across it every day. Those women usually understood and respected my preference after we had talked about it. For every woman who has walked away when I made it clear what I wouldn't do, I'll bet there have been two who have stayed to hear a new perspective on the issue. No woman has ever called me weird to my face.

"Does it become more difficult with time? No, I'd say it becomes easier. There is a certain satisfaction in knowing that you have the strength to say no. There's a sense of, 'I've held out for this long—do I want to do it with this person if I'm not sure I'll marry her?'

"On my wedding night, I don't expect fireworks to go off in my ears. It will be more a feeling of quiet satisfaction. How can I explain this best to you? If I had a brooch from my grandmother, maybe it would bring five bucks at a garage sale. It wouldn't seem like it had any value.

"But if I gave it to someone I married, then it would take on a whole different significance. If someone were to find that brooch in the gutter, it might mean nothing. To my wife, though—well, I've been basing my life for a long time on the assumption that it would mean something very special."

The woman he is dating told me that her sexual history is probably like that of many females of her generation.

"In college I was living with four other women in an apartment," she said. "I met this guy on a Wednesday night in one of the campus bars. We started going out together. We'd sleep together every weekend. I went to the university infirmary and got birth control pills. I enjoyed what we were doing. He wasn't all that experienced a lover, and I had never slept with anyone before. But still, it was fun.

"We ended up getting married. I had the typical American girl's dream of what a wedding night should be like. But he was really tired from his bachelor party. We made love in our hotel room, and he fell asleep. I was awake. I was bored. I got dressed and got in the car and went out for a drive. I went to one of those silver diners. I was sitting at the counter in my jeans, and I ordered a Coke. Some guy started looking at me, so I went back to the hotel room. I didn't even wake my new husband. I still don't know whether he ever knew that I left the room that night.

"We were married for five years. I guess we had a pretty normal sex life. But then we separated and divorced. When I was thirty I started dating a man, and then sleeping with him, and then we started living together. He was much more experienced than I was. It was great. We did a lot of experimenting. It lasted three years, and I've never regretted it."

She said that she met her current boyfriend two years ago. "We were clicking pretty well," she said. "We had a couple of weekend dates. Nothing much was happening. I remember one night we were sitting on my couch. He was aware that I'd been married and divorced and had lived with a guy. And at one point he just said, 'I'm a virgin.' He used that term.

"My first thought was, 'Hold the phone. What am I dealing with here?' I wondered why a man his age would be a virgin. He started to explain himself. I said, 'In college, you didn't do that?' But at the same time it was kind of like, 'Is this any of my business?'

"He told me he had made this commitment to himself not to have intercourse before he was married. He said something like, 'That's how

I feel about it, and if it's a problem for the women I date, then I respect their feelings, but I'm not going to change my mind.'

"I think that there was a moment's fleeting thought in my mind that I would be different. That if he felt strongly enough about me, he'd change his attitude. Obviously, I thought it was really unusual. I had to ponder it. The idea that even if we got close and fell in love, we still wouldn't do it.

"And we did fall in love, and I told my friends that I was in love. But I didn't tell them that he was a virgin. I think they just assumed that the normal stuff was going on—of course they assumed it. I didn't want to talk about it.

"I did tell my mom about it. She'd known my husband and the man I had lived with. She asked me if my new boyfriend and I were going to get married. I said, 'Well, Mother, I don't know. There's another area of things to consider. I've experienced things he hasn't.' And she asked me what I was talking about. And I said, 'We haven't had intercourse. What do you think of that? He's a virgin.'

"Obviously, she was very surprised. But I had already told her that he was a man of principle, and her attitude was that if I could be happy with him, then I should stay with him.

"There are times when I think it would really be lovely to have inter-course with him. But do you know something? I would have a very difficult time at this stage if he came to me and told me he'd changed his mind. I would really question what was motivating him. I would be very hesitant. Not that there's a chance he would ever change his mind.

"For a while my mom continued to ask. And I would always say, 'No, Mom, we haven't. It's not in the cards here.' She hasn't asked lately.

"I'm out a lot on business. I see men every day. If I see a good-looking guy . . . sure, everyone has fantasies. But I don't do anything about it. There are times I'd like to be near the ocean, too, but I don't fly out to California."


On the night I joined them for dinner, they finished dessert, and we left the restaurant. I walked my way and they walked theirs. I looked back. She leaned up and kissed him on the cheek. He put his arm around her. It seemed that they were having a beautiful evening.

# At the Movies

I decided to go see the movie *Field of Dreams* because I'd heard it provides a deeply emotional experience. Little did I know just how emotional—and for a completely unexpected reason.

I got to the theater early. I was one of the first two or three people to take a seat. Slowly the auditorium began to fill up—this was a Saturday afternoon showing, the first of the day. Just before the lights were dimmed, an usher escorted a woman down the aisle.

The woman's left arm was hooked around the usher's right arm. She was feeling her way down the aisle with the assistance of a white cane with a red tip. She was well dressed, very pretty, and she was blind.

Three or four rows in front of me, the usher stopped. The woman, using her cane, moved in to select a seat. In the middle of the row were some other people. When her cane touched them, she smiled and took a step backward. Then she sat down.

The movie started. As I had heard, it was wonderful—but I must confess, at least half of my attention was on the blind woman. I know that blind people must go to movies, but in all my years of seeing films I didn't recall being in a theater with a blind man or a blind woman. And the fact that she was alone—that raised so many questions in my mind. What was it that compelled her to go to all the trouble of coming to a theater by herself? She had no one with her, no one to talk to before or after the movie—if this was going to be a solitary experience, would staying home and listening to the radio or listening to a television program not be easier? What was the attraction of traveling from wherever she lived so that she could sit in the movie theater all by herself?

Her presence caused me to watch the movie in a way I had never watched a movie before. So many things in a motion picture are purely visual—that seems obvious, but the dialogue and sound effects do a lot to explain the plot. Yet there are many parts of a movie that are driven by things that are seen and not heard. When those things occurred, I checked to see her reaction. Often there was none.

The people behind her were munching their popcorn loudly, and crumpling up the bag. An annoying enough thing under any circumstance—how must it have been affecting her enjoyment of the movie? When the film ended and everyone filed out, she waited in her seat for the usher.

He didn't come. I stood at the back of the theater. The usher still didn't come, and she was the only person left. I walked down and asked her if I could help her to the exit.

Her name was Emely Coleman. She is thirty-six; she was born in Anderson, Indiana, with congenital glaucoma. She was always legally blind; she told me that her mother died when she was five, and that she was sent away to live at the Indiana State School for the Blind. About ten years ago her vision became markedly worse. Now she cannot see at all out of one eye, and can make out some shapes and colors with the other.

"I felt like going to a movie," she told me. "A friend told me that this was a good one. It sounded like something I would enjoy. I was told that it was about fantasy. About someone's dreams."

Although she had gone to movies with friends before, this was the first time she had done it alone. "I just felt like going out rather than staying at home today," she said. "I thought it might be more fun to go to a theater than to turn the television set on. Being around the people. There's the smell of the popcorn, and even though I can't see the other people in the theater, I can sense their presence."

Once she had gotten to her seat, she said, she was a little nervous about what the experience was going to be like. "I asked myself, 'Now, am I really going to enjoy this?'" she said. "I wasn't sure what it was going to be like, without a friend sitting next to me. But by that time it was too late. The usher was gone, and the movie had begun."

She told me some more about her life. She said that she had moved to Chicago from Indiana and that she had received training at the Chicago Lighthouse for the Blind. Now, she said, she works as a receptionist and switchboard operator at the suburban Garrett-Evangelical Theological Seminary in Evanston. She lives alone; she gets up at 4 A.M. each day and takes two elevated trains to her job.

She said she had, indeed, enjoyed the movie. I asked her about the last scene; the climactic moment comes when the camera pulls back, and there is a dramatic and emotional sight on the roads around the farm/baseball diamond in the movie. She said she had been able to make out some of the things in the film, but not that one.

We were in the lobby. "I didn't have to see that scene to feel the impact of what the movie was all about," she said. "I felt like crying, but I thought I would be embarrassed if the other people saw my tears."

Me, too, I said. Me, too.

# So . . . We Meet at Last, Mr. Bond

**S**ometimes when I think back to the Sixties, and the heroes I grew up with, it seems that no one is left.

President Kennedy is dead. The Beatles can never sing together again. Martin Luther King is dead.

But then it occurs to me: one man remains. James Bond is still alive.

He is still alive in the person of Sean Connery. Connery no longer portrays Bond in the movies, but to a generation of Americans he was, and is, the only James Bond. His successors were merely imitations.

Connery made seven James Bond movies, beginning with *Doctor No* in 1962, and in so doing set the standard for everything that was daring and thrilling and cool. Was there an American boy who did not secretly want to grow up to be James Bond? Apparently, though, Connery himself wanted to grow out of being James Bond; he made it clear that he was tired of playing the role.

But Connery is still walking around, acting in other movies and living his life. The man who is James Bond remains among us.

"My knee had been hurting me for three or four years," Sean Connery said. "I hadn't been able to kneel on it. Then, whenever I had to do some running, it began to ache. Finally I had to do something about it."

We were in a car headed for Downers Grove, Illinois, where Connery had an appointment with the orthopedic surgeons who had recently operated on his knee. He was going in for a checkup.

"The doctors frightened me to death by asking me to watch a television tape of the operation," Connery said. "They used an instrument with a little camera attached when they went into my knee, and they made a tape of the whole thing.

"I have such an aversion to needles. That's putting it mildly. When I was a child in Scotland, all of the school pupils had to be inoculated because there was a diphtheria epidemic going around. We all had to stand in line. Standing right in front of me was this big, fat girl with great big arms. Her arm was directly at my eye level. They stuck her with the hypodermic needle, and I saw the whole thing. The fear of needles has been with me ever since."

The voice was hypnotic. The reality of the situation was that a fifty-six-year-old man was sitting in a car telling a story about something that had happened to him at the beginning of his life. But it was James Bond talking; whether Connery prefers it to be that way or not, it was James Bond talking.

"Do you want a piece of gum?" he said, offering me a stick of Juicy Fruit.


Thirty minutes before, we had been on Michigan Avenue in Chicago, where Connery had been rehearsing a scene for the movie *The Untouchables*. In the movie, Kevin Costner plays Eliot Ness, Robert De Niro plays Al Capone, and Connery plays Jimmy Malone, an old Chicago cop who shows Ness the way that the city operates.

The lobby of Roosevelt University had been turned into a replica of a Thirties hotel. Costner, De Niro, and Connery were supposed to run through their lines, but everything was behind schedule.

Connery had been wearing a blue hooded parka, a thick sweater, and running shoes. A production assistant had come up to him and said, "There's something on your face."

"What?" Connery had said.

"Something sparkling," the production assistant had said.

"Must have been from the tiara I was wearing," Connery had said.

He had stood there studying his script. I had made idle conversation with him, all the while doing my best to hide the fact that there was no one in the world that I had ever wanted to meet more.

\*    \*    \*

Now we were in the car heading for the doctors' offices in Downers Grove. I asked him how he would rate Ian Fleming's original James Bond novels.

"To tell you the truth, I never read them all," Connery said. "I read *Thunderball*, because initially that was supposed to be the first movie. But I was never all that crazy about the books.

"I liked Fleming. He was erudite—and a real snob. Being a genuine snob can be quite healthy. At least you know who you're dealing with.

"Fleming had approval over the casting of James Bond. He had wanted Cary Grant to play the role. But there was no money. The whole budget for *Doctor No* was $1 million. By the time we had had all the success with the movies and were shooting *You Only Live Twice*, one set alone cost more than the entirety of *Doctor No* had cost to film."

I asked if there had been any suppressed rivalry between Fleming and Connery. After all, Fleming had created James Bond. Until the novels were turned into movies, Fleming could pretty much pretend that he *was* James Bond. As soon as the movies came out, though, Connery was Bond forever.

"We got along rather well, surprisingly," Connery said. "We had both been in the Royal Navy—although he was a commander and I was an able-bodied seaman."

He said that he had no particular opinion about the news that Timothy Dalton will be the latest actor to portray Bond. "The guy should be young," Connery said. "Or at least under fifty."

Connery said that he had seen very few of the Roger Moore James Bond movies—"I think I saw two of them. I don't remember the one I saw first. I think it took place in New Orleans, with some black guys in a jazz band.

"I didn't particularly like what the movies had become. All the hardware, and people falling through the Eiffel Tower or something, and then getting up and walking away."


We pulled into the parking lot of the doctors' offices. Connery walked into the reception area and was immediately escorted back to an examining room.

Jo Ann Ready, a nurse, said, "You look like you're walking okay."

"It doesn't feel too bad," Connery said.

Dr. E. Thomas Marquardt and Dr. Timothy C. Payne came into the room. "Take off your pants and lie down," Dr. Marquardt said.

Connery removed his trousers and reclined on a couch that was in the room. Dr. Marquardt took one of Connery's legs and began to bend it.

"No pain here at all?" Dr. Marquardt said.

"Not really," Connery said.

"No catching sensation?" Dr. Marquardt said.

"I haven't really been trying anything fancy," Connery said. "I've been playing some golf. And I've been doing this business in the swimming pool." He lifted his leg several times to show the doctors what he meant.

"Well, you're coming along remarkably well," Dr. Marquardt said.

"But my shoulder has started to hurt," Connery said. "And my arm gets a little sore when I'm playing golf."

Dr. Marquardt laughed. "That's what usually happens," he said. "We alleviate one thing, and then the other parts of the body start acting up. Let me take a look at the shoulder."

Connery stood up and stripped off his shirt. "You won't need a needle to look at this, will you?" he said.

"No," Dr. Marquardt said. "Let's get some X rays taken, though."


Connery walked down a short hallway and then lay down on an X-ray table in a narrow room.

Vicki Kybartas, an X-ray technologist, said, "Do you want a lead shield?"

"What?" Connery said.

"Do you want an apron over you?" Kybartas said.

"Why?" Connery said.

"Some people prefer it when they're being X-rayed," Kybartas said.

So Connery let her put the apron over his chest.

"Roll over on your right side," Kybartas said. "And hold on to the table with both hands. I don't want to have to pick you up off the floor."

She took the X-ray.

"Now flat on your back," she said.

The X-ray machine hovered over Connery, pointing down at him. He seemed trapped, covered by the heavy apron, and the machine seemed somehow menacing. I was watching, and suddenly I realized what it reminded me of: a moment from a movie.

"The laser scene," I said to Connery.

"I know, I know," he said. *"Goldfinger."*

Back in the examining room, Dr. Marquardt and Dr. Payne took a look at the X rays.

"You've got a little arthritis in the shoulder joint, and a little rotator-cuff tear," Dr. Marquardt said.

"Can you fix it?" Connery said.

"It's a little bigger job than the knee," Dr. Marquardt said.

"I thought the knee was more serious," Connery said.

"On a scale of one to ten, the knee operation was a two," Dr. Marquardt said. "The shoulder would be a seven."

Connery, still in his shorts, went into a golf stance.

"If I swing correctly, the ball just flies," he said.

In the car on the way back downtown, Connery said, "I don't want you to think I go to doctors all the time, but if we've got some time before I'm due back on the set, there's a dermatologist I'd like to see. I've been having some trouble with my scalp."

I was already thinking about how I was going to bring up what I had in mind. It was totally immature, and I knew I would regret it, but I had to do it.

I took a deep breath.

"In every movie, there was sort of a signature line," I said. "There was a line you said every time."

"Yes, I know it," Connery said.

"I was just wondering . . . was there a certain way you said it?" I said.

"The reading of the line?" Connery said. "I suppose there was a way that I delivered it."

"There was a pause in it," I said.

"Yes," Connery said. "There was a pause in it."

"Was the pause built in?" I said.

"I don't know," Connery said. "I just put the pause there whenever I said it."

"So how did you say it?" I said.

He began to get what I was driving at. "I just said it," he said.

I had to go for it.

"Would you mind saying it?" I said.

Connery exhaled. He seemed to think about it for a moment.

Then, in the middle of traffic, he said:

"My name is Bond . . . James Bond."

"Thank you," I said.

In the waiting room of Dr. Keith M. Kozeny's office, the receptionist asked Connery to fill out a new-patient form.

He did, and in a moment Dr. Kozeny, the dermatologist, called Connery back to his examining room.

"I have these little pinpoints on my head that itch a little," Connery said. "I think I got them from being out in the sun."

Dr. Kozeny looked at Connery's scalp under a light. "I have a little cream I can give you," he said. "It should provide some relief. I've got some sample bottles in the back."

"Another thing," Connery said. "There's this little growth." He indicated a spot between his neck and his shoulder.

"That's nothing," Dr. Kozeny said. "We can take that right off. Let me give you a little novocain."

"Novocain?" Connery said. "Does that mean a needle?"

# Breaking Point

$S$EATTLE—The death of Billy Todd Jr., who was fifteen, did not make the national news.

That probably figures. The boy was not famous, and he did not have important friends, and when it was discovered that he had hanged himself there were few who could say that they really knew him.

Billy arrived in Port Orchard, Washington, with his mother and his younger brother, Joe. They had virtually nothing, and were placed in a Kitsap County shelter for the homeless.

"I think the first thing I noticed about Billy was how much he loved that cat," said Kathy Menz, the woman in charge of the shelter. "He held on to that cat as if it was the only thing he had in his life. In some ways, I guess, it probably was. He clutched the cat so close to him."

As luck would have it—and Billy's life was full of bad luck—no pets were allowed in the shelter for the homeless. So the cat had to go. Billy was assured that, if his mother was able to find housing outside the shelter, he could have the cat back. The cat was being placed somewhere temporarily, he was told.

Billy took it about as well as could be expected. "He never really had a home," Kathy Menz said. The family had constantly moved around the country. It was known that they had lived in Idaho, Oregon, California, Texas, Nevada, Arizona, and New Mexico. There may have been other places.

When Billy was six, his father deserted the family. "Billy blamed himself for his father having left," Kathy Menz said. "A lot of kids whose dads desert them do that. He felt responsible; he thought he must have done something wrong to make his dad run off. He hadn't, of course; it wasn't Billy's fault. But he felt it was."

It so happened that, living in the shelter in Port Orchard, was a man named Mack Litton whose wife and two children were with him. The Litton family befriended Billy, and Mack Litton—an out-of-work welder—treated him with kindness.

"Billy was a nice, quiet kid," said Litton, thirty-two. "He was a boy who worried whether other people would laugh at him. He didn't have nice clothes, and he had never had a father to teach him how to do things. He didn't know how to throw a baseball or a football right, for example. No one had ever showed him how."

So Mack Litton showed him. They played ball out behind the shelter, and Litton tried to persuade Billy that his life might not be destined to end up in despair. "I told him that things might eventually turn out all right," Litton said.

The effect of Litton's friendship on Billy was remarkable. "You could actually see it," said Kathy Menz. "The gloom lifted when Mack was playing sports with Billy or just talking to him." Reporter Caroline Young of the Seattle *Post-Intelligencer*, who covered the story of Billy's death, said: "I think for the first time in his life, Billy found someone who seemed like a father to him. It had never happened before. No one had even bothered to enroll Billy in kindergarten until he was seven years old."

Billy's mother had been told that the shelter wanted its residents to try to find outside housing within three weeks. That was a goal, not a requirement, but Billy's mother did her best. She found a house to live in with Billy and Billy's younger brother.

"When Billy heard he would be leaving the shelter, he was devastated," Kathy Menz said.

One does not usually think of people being dismayed at the thought of leaving a shelter for the homeless. But Kathy Menz thinks she understands what was going through Billy's mind.

"You take a boy who has never had anyone act like a father to him, and you let him know what that feels like, and then you tell him that he has to move on again. . . . It was more than Billy could bear," she said.

Mack Litton could sense Billy's unhappiness. "The house his mother had found was nothing more than a shack, really," Litton said. "Billy called it a 'raggedy house.' It was very close to the school where he had been enrolled. He was afraid that every time the other students would pass the house, they would laugh at him."

But Billy knew he would have to move. On a Sunday his little brother was downstairs in the shelter, waiting for lunch. When the meal was ready, he went upstairs to tell Billy.

In the closet, Billy had hanged himself.

"I just don't think he wanted to go on," said Kathy Menz. "When we put all of his possessions together, they didn't even fill up a plastic garbage bag."

When he had been asked to give up his cat—the cat he had taken from city to city with him—Billy saved the cat's leash. It was as if the leash was the one reminder of the cat he was allowed to hold on to.

That's what he used to hang himself. Looped around the neck of Billy Todd Jr. was his cat's nylon leash.

# Star Turn

The pursuit of the American Dream means something different to each of us. The story of John Searing is a case in point.

Searing, thirty-six, lives in New Jersey and is a salesman of art supplies. Since he was a child, he has had one goal in life: To yell "Here's Johnny!" at the beginning of "The Tonight Show."

"As a kid, I used to sit in front of the TV set and yell 'Here's Johnny!' along with Ed McMahon," he said. "Our family had a reel-to-reel tape recorder, and I would record 'The Tonight Show's' theme song and then I would yell 'Here's Johnny!' at the appropriate point."

In 1980, Searing wrote to "The Tonight Show" and asked if he could yell "Here's Johnny!" on the air some night.

In response, the show sent him an 8-by-10 glossy photograph of Johnny Carson.

Most people would have gotten the message. But Searing wrote another letter, and another letter after that. He got a form response from a "Tonight Show" staff member, thanking him for his proposal and saying that it would not be feasible to use it.

Did this stop John Searing?

No.

He wrote to Johnny Carson again. In fact, when it appeared that his letters were being totally ignored, he began writing to Johnny Carson every day.

"No matter what was happening in my life, I would write a letter every day and address it to Johnny Carson personally," Searing said. "Each letter asked if I could please yell 'Here's Johnny!' on the show."

In all, Searing wrote more than eight hundred letters to Johnny Carson. He also sent dozens of audio tapes, featuring himself doing imitations of Jimmy Stewart, Walter Brennan, Richard Nixon, and Elmer Fudd—all of the voices pleading with Carson to let John Searing go on the show and yell "Here's Johnny!"

Finally, after more than six years of letter-writing, Searing received a call at work from a "Tonight Show" staff member.

The staff member said, in a gentle voice: "John, why are you obsessed with doing this?"

And Searing replied that nothing in his life would mean more to him than getting to yell "Here's Johnny!" on the air.

The staff member said he would get back to Searing. And, a few days later, the word came: Searing would be allowed to do it.

What was the first thing to go through Searing's mind?

"The idea that I would be actually standing there, in the same spot where Ed McMahon usually stands, and that Johnny would be standing backstage behind the curtains, waiting for my signal to come on."

Searing flew to California. On a warm June day, an NBC limousine picked him up at his hotel and took him to "The Tonight Show" studios in Burbank for the late-afternoon taping. He was escorted to a dressing room with his name on the door. "Tonight Show" assistants asked him if he wanted his shoes shined, if he wanted anything to drink, if he would accompany them to the makeup room.

Then the show began. Ed McMahon did the regular introduction. Johnny Carson came out and did his monologue. There was a commercial. After the commercial, Johnny Carson explained to the audience about John Searing and his eight hundred letters. Searing then came out and sat on the famous couch next to Carson, and tried to explain why he had felt compelled to write all those letters.

The men talked for about six minutes. Then Carson directed Searing to go over to the microphone that Ed McMahon uses at the beginning of each show. Carson, meanwhile, went backstage.

Searing was handed the script that McMahon had used minutes before. He took a deep breath and started reading aloud:

"From Hollywood, 'The Tonight Show,' starring Johnny Carson! This is John Searing, along with Doc Severinsen and the NBC Orchestra, inviting you to join Johnny and his guests . . . Danny DeVito . . . from the San Diego Zoo, Joan Embery . . . letter-writer John Searing . . . and adventures in the kitchen with Doc!"

He then paused for a drum roll.

"And now, ladies and gentlemen," he yelled . . . "Here's Johnny!"

The band played "The Tonight Show" theme, and Johnny Carson came out from behind the curtains once again. The audience roared.

Carson called Searing over. They exchanged some banter, and then Carson said:

"Now go and write no more."

Searing went out to dinner with a friend, then watched the show in his hotel room as it was broadcast late that night on videotape.

"I was thinking, it's not real," he said. "It's not really 'The Tonight Show,' and that's not really me. It didn't really happen."

Searing is now back in New Jersey, selling art supplies again. He feels no irony when he talks about the experience.

"If you want to be a success at anything, you've got to have a goal," he said. "You can't let anybody stop you from that goal."

He says he wants to go into show business now.

# Jack's Here

MINNEAPOLIS—Jack's here tonight. We won't see each other, but Jack's in town.

It's just one of those coincidences. They've been happening to us forever. Jack is my best friend and he has been since we were five years old. No matter where I have traveled, I always have known that when I go back to the city where I grew up, Jack will be there.

That's about to end. Jack is going to leave our hometown—leave Ohio after all these years, and move to Minneapolis. He's got a great new job, and he seems excited about giving his life a new direction at the age of forty-two.

We talk just about every week. The other evening we were having our usual long-distance phone conversation, and he said, "So, are you traveling?"

I said yes—I said that lately I've been traveling more than I've truly wanted to. He asked me where I was headed next, and I said Minneapolis.

"What day?" he said.

I told him, and he said, "Me, too."

He was coming here to start preparing things so that his family can join him in a few months.

We compared itineraries—a little different than automatically meeting at the corner of Ardmore and Elm every Saturday morning, like we did when we were kids—and it turned out that when Jack's plane was due to arrive in Minneapolis, I'd already be at the appointment that had brought me here.

So we knew that even though we were both going to be in Minneapolis, the chances were pretty good that we wouldn't get together. It's happened before—it's happened in Chicago when Jack has passed through, and it's even happened in the town where we were born. The town that Jack is about to leave.

It's funny—I haven't talked much to Jack about what leaving that town is going to mean to him. First of all, he probably doesn't know—how do you know the answer to something like that before it's happened?

And second of all, he would sense automatically that my question was really a ruse. Sure, I'm interested in how he's going to feel after he moves away. But mainly I'm interested in how I'm going to feel after he moves. They could tear down City Hall in our hometown, they could tear down the police station, they could even tear down the pizza place—none of that would make the town seem as empty as it's going to seem after Jack moves away.

Last summer I was asked to write an essay for inclusion in a national magazine. I wrote on the topic of friendship. I quoted Jack in the essay. He was talking about his nine-year-old daughter:

"She's just starting to notice boys. There are these two boys in her class—and they're us. They spend all their time together, they run around on the playground together—they're us. They're not real big kids, and they're not tiny. They're a little bit bigger than small. They're us."

Tonight, packed in my suitcase, I have a letter that I received just before I got on the plane to Minneapolis.

"We heard that we were mentioned in *Time* magazine, so we read the article," the letter begins.

The letter was written by the two boys—the two boys in Jack's daughter's class. It turns out that their names are Max and Patrick.

"I love basketball and I enjoy watching it, too," Max informs me.

"I love all sports," Patrick informs me. "I'm about four feet, six inches, and Max is about four feet, five inches."

For a moment I wondered why they would think to write down their height. It's obvious, of course; Jack's words in the quote: "They're not real big kids, and they're not tiny. They're a little bit bigger than small. They're us." They were letting me know.

The boys ended their letter:

"We are best friends just like Jack and you." They signed it, "Your friends, Max and Patrick."

They had enclosed something in the envelope. It was a color snapshot. In the photo, the boys are smiling and holding baseball pennants made out of felt. One of the boys is holding a California Angels pennant; the other is holding a Seattle Mariners pennant. There is no writing on the back of the snapshot, so I don't know which boy is which.

I assume, though, that it's Patrick with the Mariners pennant. He's a little taller in the picture. About four foot six, I'd say. The fellow with the Angels pennant seems to be an inch or so shorter.

Hang on to the times you're having, Max and Patrick. If you're lucky, more than thirty years will pass and you'll still be best friends. Chances are you'll move away—at least one of you, and probably both. But hang on to that friendship. It may serve you well, in ways you can't even imagine now.

It's getting late in Minneapolis. I'm finished with my business for the evening.

Jack's here tonight. We won't see each other, but Jack's in town.

# The Children's Hour

Here is what I overheard:

Boy: "What's your name?"

Girl: "Playtoy."

Boy: "Why do you call yourself that?"

Girl: "You know how a dog is a man's best friend?"

Boy: "Yeah?"

Girl: "Well, I'm a boy's best toy."

In the metropolitan area where I live, there is a telephone service called Connections. It is one of those "party lines" that have received national publicity lately. Callers dial a certain phone number and can talk with other callers from all over the same area code. There is a fee, which appears on the next phone bill.

The regular Connections number is for people sixteen and older. The company that runs Connections instituted a separate line for youngsters up to fifteen years old—presumably in an effort to give younger boys and girls a chance to talk to one another without being exposed to "adult" topics. Undoubtedly the company's intentions were honorable.

Out of curiosity, I dialed into the junior version of Connections. I didn't say anything; I just wanted to see what kids these days have to say to one another. So I held the phone to my ear and listened.

What I heard . . . well, read on. I'll tell you what I heard. It was like being dropped, invisible, into an adolescent netherworld where the boys and girls don't know you're there. A thousand interviews with kids fifteen

**63**

and under couldn't elicit the information I gathered over two days and nights of listening silently and taking notes.

Girl: "My name is Sasha. What's yours?"
  Boy: "This is Mike."
  Girl: "Mike who?"
  Boy: "Mike from hell."

When you first dial into the line, a recording informs you that the price is twenty cents for the first minute and eight cents for each additional minute. No last names are permitted; no exchanging of phone numbers is permitted. The tape says that all calls are "moderated."

The "moderators" are people whose job it is to monitor the calls. They work in shifts during the twenty-four hours the phone service is open each day. All the male moderators are called Rick; all the female moderators are called Lucy. I was told by a spokesman for Connections that the derivations of the names came from the old "I Love Lucy" television show—that is, Lucy and Ricky Ricardo.

In theory, the Ricks and Lucys are supposed to listen to every conversation that is going on, to enforce the rules and keep things clean. In practice, though, hundreds of calls, distributed in clusters of ten over a multitude of lines, come in at the same time. Thus, the conversations often go unmonitored.

The first time I called, a girl was in midsentence:

". . . you know the girl in the video for that song? I look like her twin. So if you want to know what I look like, watch that video."

I was to learn that invariably the first thing the boys and girls asked —after first names—was for physical descriptions. Ninety percent of the girls seemed to say that they had long blond hair, blue eyes, were five feet five, and weighed 110 pounds. Ninety percent of the boys seemed to say that they had brown hair, lifted weights, were six feet tall, and weighed 170 pounds.

\*    \*    \*

Appearances—or the description of appearances—seemed to count for everything.

Boy: "Suck on your father's dick."

Girl: "What do you look like?"

Boy: "Like a cross between Sylvester Stallone and Rob Lowe."

Girl (with obvious interest): "That's cool!"

The Lucys and the Ricks achieved mythical status. Not only did they have the power to disconnect youngsters they caught using obscenities or trying to exchange phone numbers—they also had the power to transfer callers to other lines when the callers thought their current group of conversationalists was not exciting enough. The Ricks and Lucys, to judge by their voices, sounded as if they were in their twenties. The young callers treated them with the respect that children tradition-ally give to camp counselors. The callers could be fickle, though.

Girl: "Lucy? I want to be transferred. Lucy? Are you listening? I want to be transferred. Lucy? Lucy? Lucy, Lucy, Lucy? Lucy bitch. . . ."

There was a racial dynamic going on, too. Because youngsters could call from all over the area code, they could talk directly to people they would probably never meet in real life. The most telling examples of this took place when white suburban children (callers are allowed to mention their approximate neighborhoods) talked to blacks from the inner city. In-terestingly, rather than try to find common ground, each group seemed determined to behave according to stereotypes, no matter how ugly and negative.

Girl from suburbs: "My mom grounded me tonight."

Boy from inner city: "Do you want me to come over and shoot her? I've shot two people in my life."

Girl: "I don't know."

Boy: "Just give me your address and I'll shoot your mother."

Girl: "I can't. Ricky will hear, and he'll disconnect me."

Boy: "Well, maybe I'll call back later and see if you change your mind. I've got to go out and get some dope money."

\*    \*    \*

Many callers used nicknames, apparently invented for their Connections calls. There was Reebok; there was Terminator; there was Richie Bear. They seemed to feel that their nicknames magnified their stature.

Boy: "I'm Dream Commando."

Girl: "What do you look like?"

Boy: "I'm six feet tall, I weigh 170, my hair is like Brian Bosworth's, and I have a black Chevy."

Girl: "Neat! But if you're under sixteen, how can you have a car?"

Boy: "I'm really sixteen. I shouldn't be on this line."

Girl: "Stay on, Dream Commando. Where do you live?"

There was the sound of another telephone being picked up at Dream Commando's house. A voice—the voice of Dream Commando's little brother—came on the line.

Little brother: "First of all, he's not six feet tall. Second of all, his hair isn't like Brian Bosworth's. And third of all, he doesn't have a car."

The girl laughed. Dream Commando shouted at his brother, then hung up.


Sometimes the racial thing took on a melancholy aspect. One evening the line I was listening to was filled with white kids from affluent suburbs. A new caller came on—the voice was that of a black youngster who had trouble expressing himself, and who (to judge from the patterns of calls I had been hearing) lived in the inner city.

Girl: "I'm from Highland Park."

Second girl: "I'm from Winnetka."

New boy caller: "Hello?"

Girl: "Where are you from?"

There was a moment's silence. Then the boy spoke again:

"My neighborhood is very beautiful. There are trees and big front lawns. . . ."

Girl: "Yeah, but what suburb?"

The boy hung up.


The worst thing that could happen to a caller would be for other callers to tell him or her to "call Story Line." Story Line was a telephone service that played taped fairy tales and other wholesome things for children.

Boy: "So do you get high?"
Girl: "Yeah. Do you?"
Boy: "Yeah. How old are you?"
Girl: "Fifteen. How old are you?"
Boy: "Fifteen too."
New boy caller: "Hello? Hello?"
Boy: "How old are you, kid?"
New boy caller: "Twelve."
Girl: "Call Story Line."
Boy: "Yeah, call Story Line."


Girl: "I'm Barbie."
 Boy: "Hi, Barbie, I'm Danny."
 Girl: "So what's happening, Danny?"
 Boy: "I called the adult Connections line. Do you know what they were talking about? Station wagons!"
 All the other callers laughed uproariously.


Bullying and cruelty were as evident on the Connections line as in real life.
 Boy: "So where do you live?"
 Girl: "Cicero."
 Second boy, with high voice: "Hello?"
 First boy: "Are you a girl?"
 Second boy: "No, I'm a boy."
 Girl: "Well, you sound like a girl to me."
 Second boy: "But I'm not a girl. I'm a boy."
 First boy: "You sound like a girl to me, too."
 Second boy: "I am a boy."
 Girl: "Go break your neck."


Girl: "What are you doing now?"
 Boy: "I don't know. Being weird. Sitting in my closet."
 Girl: "You're sitting in your closet?"
 Boy: "Yes. I'm fourteen."

\*   \*   \*

Boy: "What's your name?"
  Girl: "Little Stoner."
  Boy: "Does Little Stoner get high?"
  Little Stoner: "Yeah."
  Boy: "That's cool. Is that how you got your name?"
  Little Stoner: "Yeah."
  Much younger girl: "We made snowmen at our school. . . ."
  Boy: "Little Stoner?"
  Little Stoner: "Yeah?"
  Boy: "Can I lick your pussy?"
  Little Stoner: "That's so sweet."
  Much younger boy: "Does anyone on the line play golf?"
  Little Stoner: "Call Story Line."
  Boy: "Hey, Little Stoner . . . have you ever given a blowjob?"
  Little Stoner: "I'm fifteen years old. What do you expect?"
  Boy: "Little Stoner?"
  Little Stoner: "Yeah?"
  Boy: "I want to fuck you."
  Much younger girl: "Go for it, Little Stoner!"


Dream Commando (the alleged Brain Bosworth look-alike with the alleged black Chevy, whose little brother had humiliated him) called back the Connections line later, and was telling every girl he spoke to that he was Dream Commando. Then a new caller came on the line.
  Dream Commando: "So who's the new caller?"
  Girl: "Jenny."
  Dream Commando: "Hey, Jenny, what's happening?"
  Jenny: "I just got home from Yale for vacation. I should be calling the line for older people, but I thought I'd try this line."
  Dream Commando: "You go to Yale?"
  Jenny: "Yes, I do. What's your name?"
  Dream Commando: "Jonathan."

\*   \*   \*

Apparently boys and girls can get "married" on the Connections line, although the specifics of how this was done and what it signified were lost on me.

Boy: "Rachel, are you married?"

Girl: "Married? I'm fourteen years old."

Boy: "I mean married Connections-wise."

And another exchange:

Boy: "Hello?"

Girl: "Who is this?"

Boy: "Exotic Taste."

Girl: "Oh, hi! The other night I was married to your friend Evil for maybe an hour."

In the cruelty category, many boys tried to belittle other boys in order to impress the girls on the line.

Girl: "What school do you go to?"

Boy: "Tinley."

Second boy: "Oh, nice school. I used to go there till my dad got a job and made enough money so we could move out of that neighborhood."

Girl: "I'm baby-sitting now. I might as well waste the people's phone bill. I'm like totally bored baby-sitting."

Boy: "Are you depressed? You sound depressed."

Girl: "It's my normal voice. I gotta go."

She hung up.

Girl: "Did you hear Star tried to kill himself?"

Second girl: "You're kidding."

First girl: "He tried to swallow mercury. I don't know where he got the mercury. Like in a thermometer or something. He bit the end off. I was so bummed. It was like the day before my birthday."

Boy: "Lucy? Lucy?"

Third girl: "Yeah, Lucy? Are you there? Switch us to another line, Lucy. This is boring."

* * *

Boy: "You got a nice voice."
   Girl: "What I got is a dork on the phone."


After midnight one evening, I heard this exchange.
   Boy: "Do you like to have three guys in the same bed with you?"
   Girl: "Yeah." There was a clicking sound. "Hold on a second. That's call-waiting." A few seconds passed. Her voice returned on the line. "Okay, I'm back."
   Boy: "How much can you bench press at least five times?"
   Girl: "Who are you talking to?"
   Boy: "This other dude."
   Second boy: "About 150 pounds."
   First boy: "I can do 180 pounds twelve times."
   Girl: "I can handle two guys in the same bed. Maybe three or four."
   First boy: "You'd get a little sore."
   Girl: "A little."
   Second boy: "What's your phone number?"
   Girl: "Is Ricky or Lucy listening?"
   First boy: "Just say it real quick."
   The girl said her number. The boys said they would call her. I thought—I wanted to believe—that she had given a fake number. I dialed it and it was busy for a few minutes—signifying that both her main line and her call-waitng line were in use. I tried again later. A girl—the same girl—answered. I hung up.


How to end this? One evening I listened to a boy and girl meet on the Connections line, introduce themselves, and then talk for maybe five minutes.
   Boy: "Amy, I have to hang up. I love you."
   Girl: "I love you too. . . . I guess."

# Above and Beyond

When Bernie Meyers, who was seventy years old and who lived in Wilmette, Illinois, went into the hospital last September, his family at first did not know how serious his illness was. Thus his ten-year-old granddaughter, Sarah Meyers, was not taken to see him.

"He hadn't been feeling well for some time," said Sarah's mother, Ann Meyers. "He went into the hospital for some tests. Just to find out what was wrong."

What was wrong was lymphoma—a cancer of the lymphatic system. In Bernie Meyers' case, the lymphoma was advanced and irreversible. He died within two weeks.

Sarah Meyers never got a chance to say good-bye to her grandfather.

"Sarah saw him regularly, because we live close to where he lived," her mother said. "This was her first experience with death. We could tell that, as upset as she was, she was additionally upset that she didn't see him in those days before he died. She didn't get to have one last talk with him."

Sarah didn't say much about what she was feeling. But in October she came home from a friend's birthday party. The other children at the party had been given helium balloons as favors. Sarah had hers with her—a bright red balloon.

"She went into the house," her mother said. "When she came back out, she was carrying the balloon—and an envelope."

Inside the envelope was a letter she had written to her grandfather. The envelope was addressed to "Grandpa Bernie, in Heaven Up High."

In the letter, Sarah wrote: "Hi, Grandpa. How are you? What's it like up there?" The letter ended with Sarah telling her grandfather that she loved him, and that she hoped somehow he could hear what she was telling him.

"I'm not sure what Sarah's concept of heaven is," her mother said. "But I do know that she printed our return address on the envelope. I didn't ask her about it. She punched a hole in the envelope, and tied the envelope to the balloon. Then she let it go.

"That balloon seemed so fragile to me. I didn't think it would even make it past the trees. But it did. We watched the balloon sail away, and then we went back inside."

Two months passed; the weather got cold. Then one day a letter arrived addressed to "Sarah Meyers + Family." The letter bore a York, Pennsylvania, postmark, and had been mailed by a man named Donald H. Kopp.

The letter began:

Dear Sarah, Family & Friends—
Your letter to Grandpa Bernie Meyers apparently reached its destination and was read by him. I understand they can't keep material things up there, so it drifted back to earth. They just keep thoughts, memories, love, and things like that.

Donald Kopp wrote that he had found the balloon and letter while hunting and hiking in a Pennsylvania state forest near the Maryland border. That is almost six hundred miles from Wilmette—the balloon had floated over Illinois, probably parts of Michigan and Indiana, Ohio, and all the way across Pennsylvania before settling in the forest.

Donald Kopp's letter to Sarah continued:

Whenever you think or talk about your grandpa, he knows and is very close by with overwhelming love. Sincerely, Don Kopp. (Also a grandpa.)

Sarah said that after she had tied her letter to the balloon and let it float away, "At night I would think about it. I just wanted to hear from Grandpa somehow. In a way, now I think that I have heard from him."

Donald Kopp, who is sixty-three and retired from his job as a receiving clerk, said the other day that the red balloon, which had almost completely deflated, was resting on a blueberry bush the afternoon he found it.

"That's pretty dense woods," he said. "It was cold and windy that day. I walked over to see what the balloon was. I could tell it was a child's handwriting on the envelope. I didn't have my reading glasses on, and I thought it was addressed to someone at 'Haven High.' A high school or something.

"I put it in my pocket. When I got back home, I saw that it wasn't addressed to Haven High. It was addressed to Sarah's grandfather, in 'Heaven Up High.' "

So he decided to write his letter to Sarah. "It was important to me that I write to her," he said. "But I'm not very good at writing; I don't do it that often. It took me a couple of days to think of what to put in the letter. Then I mailed it.

"Like I said in the letter—I'm a grandfather, too."

# On Board

TAMPA—The Great Baseball Debate can get pretty complicated at times.

Yes, it seems somehow wrong that players should charge money for signing their autographs. But no, you can't really blame them for earning whatever the market will bear—especially when it entails traveling half-way across the country for one of those two-day "fan fairs."

Yes, the social problems of modern life have crept into the game of baseball, making it seem much less pure than the baseball of fading memory. But no, baseball even in its early days was far from pristine—and whatever societal problems may have insinuated themselves into the game back then were probably reported on less candidly by the sports-writers of the day.

You can intellectualize the debate; you can ask yourself why mere humans are invested with a status more befitting deities, and whether mere humans are built to handle the pressures of such a status.

Then something happens that makes all the intellectualizing unnec-essary.

Waiting to get onto a plane bound for Florida, I sat back in the board-ing area, resigned myself to dealing with the now-customary delayed departure, and read a magazine.

Suddenly, though, I sensed a change in the air. Something was hap-pening; people were reacting to something that they deemed important.

They were all looking in the direction of a man who had just arrived at the check-in counter. He would be traveling on our flight. The males—especially the males over thirty-five—seemed particularly excited.

The object of this interest was Minnie Minoso.

Minoso stood waiting with the rest of us. Someone too young to remember him asked me who he was.

My answer was automatic:

"Orestes 'Minnie' Minoso."

I found myself smiling at that. How had I remembered that Minnie Minoso's real first name was "Orestes"? From baseball cards. That had to be it. So much for literature not sticking in the mind.

Minnie Minoso's profession was being a baseball star. Not merely a baseball player—a baseball star. He broke into the big leagues in 1949 and enjoyed a long and successful career, most notably with the Chicago White Sox. He never quite reached the level of idolatry attained by a Willie Mays or a Mickey Mantle or a Joe DiMaggio—but there can't be too many American men of a certain age who, challenged with the word "Minoso," fail to come up with "Minnie" as the other word.

(In case you're wondering . . . the reason I was sure that the man in the airport was Minnie Minoso was a mundane and simple one. It may make you smile, but I hope your smile is gentle. Stitched across the back of his jacket, in big capital letters, was "MINOSO." Hey, he's allowed.)

The other people in the boarding area clearly were assisted in their recollections by the letters on the back of the jacket, too. Minoso is sixty-six now. He must be warmed by the thought that every time he walks into a room, there is this sense that *Minnie Minoso is in the room.*

That's what makes our baseball stars—our sports stars—so special. The Great Baseball Debate—the salaries, the rumors of improprieties, the kids who are forced to borrow money from their parents to secure the autographs of their heroes—all of that is secondary. It must be something to be Minnie Minoso and walk into a room . . . and to have that simple fact matter. Even if you get just a little assist by having your name stitched onto your jacket.

Whether this will carry over into another era—whether today's sports stars will turn heads in their retirement the way Minoso's generation of stars turns heads today—is something no one can be sure of. The sports world has changed since the days when Minoso stood at the plate—quick, now: Can you name all of the baseball teams in the Major Leagues?

What won't change is the inherent specialness of Minoso and his contemporaries. My father was in Florida when I arrived. He asked me how the flight was. I'm sure my answer was an echo of the words being spoken by just about every other passenger getting off that plane:

"The flight was fine. Minnie Minoso was on board."

# Double Your Fun

$A$ concept that seems to have all but disappeared from the American social landscape is that of the "dream date." Young American males used to fantasize about going on a date with the girl of their dreams. Sometimes it was a movie star; sometimes it was merely the beautiful girl who lived at the end of the block. But it was a constant in the male imagination—a date with a perfect, unreachable woman.

Every American boy, every American college man—even, or so I seem to recall, a certain American men's magazine—would ponder the wondrous possibilities of such a date.

I certainly was no exception; there was definitely one date that I had always dreamed about. This dream date was not with an actress or a *Sports Illustrated* swimsuit model, but in my imagination it was potentially even more exciting. Then, not so long ago, it occurred to me: Why not make it come true?

So it was that I shined my shoes, put on my tie, and got ready for a date with the Doublemint Twins.

I refer not to the Doublemint Twins you see in commercials today—you probably can't even fix a clear picture of them in your mind. There have been many pairs of Doublemint Twins over the years, but the ones you remember were the very first. They were the ones I wanted to take on a date.

Beginning in the 1930s, the manufacturers of Wrigley's chewing gum used the idea of twins to promote the Doublemint brand. The twins

**77**

were never real, though, until 1960. That's when they changed from artists' drawings on billboards and in store displays and came to life as Joan and Jayne Boyd, two twenty-one-year-olds from Indiana.

The Doublemint Twins were so pretty and so wholesome and so pure—yet there was something about them that . . . oh, I think you understand. Let's not get into it.

I tracked them down. The Boyd girls are fifty-one now. Joan is divorced and the mother of three daughters; she works in a clothing store in the Midwest. Jayne is married to a show-business executive; she is the mother of two daughters and a son, and lives in southern California.

Their own mother was in ill health, and Jayne was going to visit Joan so that they could both see their mom. I asked if they would perhaps have time to go on a date with me. They said yes.

I named a place for us to meet. "The restaurant may be crowded," I said. "How will I recognize you?"

"Believe me," Joan said, "you'll recognize us."

And indeed I did. At fifty-one, Joan and Jayne still look exactly alike. We sat down at a table, and as we waited to order they told me the story of how they achieved their little bit of history.

"We were starting a career as a singing duet," Jayne said. "A radio executive had heard that Mr. Wrigley was considering using real girls as the Doublemint Twins instead of using the drawings. He asked us if we were interested."

"I think they must have narrowed down the field before we were ever taken to see Mr. Wrigley," Joan said. "Because when we did see him, it couldn't have been for more than five minutes. And that's the last time we saw him in our lives."

They said that they were escorted into the office of Philip K. Wrigley. They were intensely nervous.

"All I can remember is that the office was huge and dark," Joan said. "Mr. Wrigley sat behind an enormous desk. He hardly said anything. Really—five minutes at the most. And then we were led out."

"But he must have approved of us," Jayne said.

"Because a few days later we were informed that we got the job," Joan said.

"We wore little white gloves, our mother was a widow and we lived with her. . . . I think we fit Mr. Wrigley's image of what the Doublemint Twins should be," Jayne said.

Before long, they were international superstars. "It was a miracle come true," Jayne said. "One day we were two nice little Catholic girls from Indiana, and the next thing we knew we were staying at the fanciest hotel in Paris, and American tourists were coming up to us and saying, 'You're the Doublemint Twins!' "

"And everyone always asked us for gum," Joan said.

"But we never got a free pack of chewing gum in our lives," Jayne said.

"Don't say that," Joan said.

"Oh, it wasn't Mr. Wrigley's fault," Jayne said. "I'm sure that if we had asked him, he would have given us all the gum we wanted. But we never saw him after that first time, and I think the advertising men were too scared to approach him and ask him for gum."

"So we'd buy our own gum to give to people on the street," Joan said.

"You know what else was strange?" Jayne said. "We were never allowed to chew gum in the commercials."

"That's right," Joan said. "We were told that Mr. Wrigley had ordered a directive. He had said, 'I never want to see gum in the mouths of the Doublemint Twins. My girls do not chew gum on-camera.' "

"We never quite understood that," Jayne said. "After all, we were promoting chewing gum. But we weren't supposed to be seen chewing it."

The service at the restaurant was a little slow. I asked the waitress if she could hurry things up. I also managed to tell her who my dates were.

"No," she said.

"Yes," I said.

"No," she said.

"It's true," I said.

She disappeared for a moment, and came back with the manager.

"Come on," he said.

"It's them," I said.

"Not really," he said.

I turned to Joan and Jayne.

"Do it," I said.

"Right here?" Joan said.

"You can do it softly," I said.

"Please?" the manager said.

"Okay," Jayne said.

The Boyd sisters put their heads together and, in the quietest of voices, sang:

"Double your pleasure, double your fun, with double-good, double-good, Doublemint gum."

After the manager had reeled away, his eyes spinning, I asked the Boyds what the biggest misconceptions about the Doublemint Twins had been.

"Well," Jayne said, "if you'll recall, the Doublemint Twins were always playing tennis or riding bikes or things like that. The idea was that the Doublemint Twins were very active, outdoor types."

"But we were never very athletic girls," Joan said.

"We would do our best to ride the bikes and all that stuff, but we were always black-and-blue afterward," Jayne said. "We just weren't very good at it."

"We always tried," Joan said. "We really did."

"They'd say, 'Go down that hill on that toboggan,' " Jayne said. "We did what we were told."

And did men ever become aggressive with them?

"You mean ask us on dates?" Joan said.

"Well . . ." I said.

I explained that I had once known a rock and roll singer who had a reputation as one of the world's most debauched and hedonistic men. Every conceivable fantasy a man could have, he had realized. Yet, he had once confided in me, there was one fantasy he could not shake from his mind.

"What fantasy was that?" Jayne said.

"You know," I said.

"No, what?" Joan said.

"You," I said.

"Us?" Jayne said.

"Yes," I said. "His fantasy was the Doublemint Twins."

"You mean to ask one of us to dinner or something?" Joan said.

"Uh . . . not exactly," I said.

"You mean something *nasty*?" Jayne said.

"I don't know," I said. "Let's change the subject."

"We were ladies!" Joan said. "We acted like ladies and we were treated like ladies!"

"I probably shouldn't have brought it up," I said.

"We were such good little girls!" Jayne said.

"No one even talked dirty in front of us!" Joan said. "If we walked into a room and men were talking dirty, they would stop!"

"I may have misunderstood this person," I said.

"I'm not saying we were perfect," Jayne said. "I'm sure that if we were in the car with a great date, we got in a few kisses."

"Really, let's drop it," I said.

"Sure, we kissed," Joan said. "We did that."

"I don't think it was like we were Marilyn Monroe, for gosh sake," Jayne said.

"Of course not," Joan said. "Men knew what kind of girls we were, and treated us with the utmost respect."


There was a clause in the Boyd sisters' contract with Wrigley: if either of them was to become pregnant, the deal was off. Marriage was okay; pregnancy, though, was out. The Wrigley company did not want to deal with a pregnant Doublemint Twin.

"I got married in 1962," Joan said.

"And I got married in 1963," Jayne said.

It was also in 1963 that Joan became pregnant. "I wrote a letter to the Wrigley company and told them," she said.

Both Joan and Jayne knew that this would mean the end, and it did. They were finished as Doublemint Twins. The Wrigley company hired a replacement pair of twins; there have been eleven more over the years.

"I was empty," Jayne said.

"Jayne and I had never been separated in our lives," Joan said. "Now we were both married, and I was pregnant, and the Doublemint days were over."

"It was quite an adjustment for us both," Jayne said. "It had all happened so fast, and now it was gone."

"It all went away so quickly," Joan said.

"I was in therapy for a while," Jayne said. "The doctor said that I had never really dealt with the death of the Doublemint Twins."

The two sisters held hands.

"But, of course, we're still here," Joan said.

"And we love each other very much," Jayne said.


I paid the check and said good-bye. Most people would have left it right there. The date was over, and it had been great. Most people would be content to bask in the warm afterglow.

I am a person who needs more.


"I'm not sure why you wanted to get together with us," said Alice Anderson Carmichael, fifty-eight.

"I just did," I said.

"But why?" said her sister, Alva Anderson Nelson, also fifty-eight.

"You were the Toni Twins, right?" I said.

"Yes," Alice said. "Back in 1947. We were seventeen. It was the 'Which Twin Has the Toni?' promotion."

"So," I said, settling back at the table, "you hungry or anything?"

# Twenty Years

**I**'d like to say thank you to Sylvia Dozer and Mac Albin and Sandy Erkis and John Forman. Also to Tom Hill and Nancy Schoedinger and Ed Klopfer and Debby Kayne. Might as well mention John Hagler and Cathy Holt and Gary Herwald and Karen Birch.

I'm feeling the best I've felt in years, and it's all because of one simple event: the twentieth reunion of my high school graduating class. I've just returned from central Ohio, where our graduating class gathered for the reunion; those people in the first paragraph, along with more than one hundred other men and women, showed up, and it was . . . well, it was amazing.

I had my trepidations about the reunion. Twenty years is a long time, and like most high school classes, we were not all that united back when we were in school. There were cliques and in-groups and people who were left out; there was a lot of meanness in high school, and we all ran in our own little circles. I was afraid that twenty years later, the smallness that was always a part of high school might make itself shown and might ruin the reunion; I was afraid that all of us would come to town looking for warm, nostalgic memories, and walk away with stark reminders that things had not been so perfect back in 'sixty-five after all.

But it didn't work out that way. From the moment the four-day re-union began, it was apparent that things were going to be a smashing success. Simply put, people had grown up; they had had their triumphs and their failures, their exultations and their miseries, and they were ready to touch base with the one group of people who knew them best: the people with whom they had gone to high school for four years.

We all walk around every day pretending to be the characters we have invented for ourselves during our adult years. But we can't fool our high school friends; they know who we really are, and from the first minutes of the reunion that knowledge provided a feeling of warmth and security that I could not have predicted. There were name tags, but we didn't need them; twenty years later everyone seemed to know everyone else on sight. We were older and unquestionably the worse for wear, but we were there.

Of course the roles had changed; back in 'sixty-five we were all the same thing: We were high school seniors. Now we had different functions in the real world. It was weird to consider it: Bill Salt was a gastroenterologist, and Dan Vogel was an FBI agent, and Bill Meeks was an attorney and Diane Mathless ran her own delicatessen. What were we doing, having real jobs like that? We were still kids, weren't we?

Clearly we weren't, but you wouldn't have known it at the reunion. The nicest thing was the attitude everyone was showing toward everyone else—the unspoken truth was that we realized that there was unpleasantness and narrow-mindedness back in high school, but that we all wanted to get past that, at least for the course of the reunion.

People sat and talked who hadn't spent fifteen minutes together in the whole four years of high school. People danced together who in high school barely spoke. And when the class photograph was taken, it wasn't like in a high school picture—when people used to be afraid to stand next to anyone other than the ones they considered to be cool enough. For the reunion picture everyone stood together at random, laughing and joking and enjoying the fact that we all were here.

There was such kindness, such friendliness—that's what struck me. Perhaps if the reunion would have stretched into weeks or months, the pettiness and bickering that we all deal with in the real world would have made itself evident. It didn't, though; it was as if everyone at the reunion realized that something very precious—our memories—was at stake here, and if we screwed it up we would be screwing it up for all time.

I hadn't been at my class's ten-year reunion; the people who had been there told me that it couldn't compare with the twenty-year. They said that at the ten-year the men and women were too intent on impressing each other with what they had accomplished out in the world—were too nervous about making sure that everyone knew just how well they were doing.

There wasn't a lot of that this time. Everyone seemed to realize it: We have pretty much become what we are going to be. There will be more happiness and more heartache along the way, but by and large this is it. This is who we are. Accept it and embrace it.

And we did; we did. The band played songs from our years in school, and we danced and looked into each others' faces. The world of business and ambition and ego waited for us on the other side of the reunion, but there would be time enough for that. For now there was only one word for what was going on, and it was a word as old-fashioned and full of childhood as we were on this night: magic.

# Japanese Beat

$\mathbf{F}$or all the years that American Beat has been appearing in *Esquire*, the column has never ventured outside the United States. That's the point. You call a feature American Beat, you'd better keep it in America.

But this funny thing happened. A Japanese edition of *Esquire* was launched. The businessmen and editors behind Japanese *Esquire* asked me to come to Tokyo to make some appearances and help get the magazine off the ground. I argued that this might be a disaster for the new project. When my potential hosts from Japan tried to get me to explain why this was, I fumbled around for several minutes and then gave them the truest and most direct answer I could come up with: "I have a bad personality."

Apparently it didn't translate. I watched *Adventures in Babysitting* on the movie screen of the airplane and wondered what might lie ahead.

Thirteen and a half hours and fourteen time zones from my home, I stumbled off the plane. A delegation from Japanese *Esquire* was waiting just beyond the customs area.

"We have a meeting planned in your hotel room," one of the welcoming party said.

"You've got to be kidding," I said. I get jet lag flying from Chicago to Ohio. I felt as if I had been beaten with logs for the past half day.

"No," the person said. "The people are waiting for you."

"I have to sleep," I said. "Let's do this tomorrow."

"Please," the person said. "For you to refuse to do this would be very insulting."

We sat in my room, the welcoming party and I. The person in charge made a call to another room in the hotel. Soon there was a knock at the door.

Four Japanese men walked in. I shook hands with each of them. Behind them was a Japanese woman. I shook her hand, too. This seemed to embarrass her.

We spoke for maybe fifteen minutes, with the people who understood both languages doing their best to translate. The meeting seemed to be over. I glanced longingly in the direction of the bed.

"We have a surprise for you," one of my hosts said.

"What's that?" I said.

"The hotel has decided to name a drink the American Beat, in honor of your visit," he said.

"You're joking," I said.

"Oh, no," my host said. "The hotel wants to add the drink to its menu, as a permanent item."

"Well, that's really nice," I said. "Tell them thanks very much. This is really something. I'll thank them in person tomorrow, after I get some sleep."

"You don't understand," my host said. "The hotel has come up with four different recipes for the American Beat drink. They want you to choose one."

"Okay," I said. "Do you have a copy of the recipes?"

"I'm afraid you still don't understand," my host said. "The management of the hotel would like to come to the room and mix all four versions of the American Beat, and then have you taste all four and select your favorite."

"I can't tell you how flattering this is," I said. "But I've been up for more than twenty-four hours. Could we do this tomorrow?"

"That would be very insulting," my host said.

Fifteen minutes later one of the members of the welcoming party shook me awake. The drink team from the hotel had arrived. There were two management people, and a bartender in a tuxedo. A table on wheels, covered with bottles of liquor and mixing utensils, had been rolled into the room.

The bartender in the tuxedo, working somberly, mixed the first version of the American Beat. He shook it vigorously in a metal container. He poured the drink into glasses—one for each person in the room. When he presented me with mine, he bowed deeply.

I took a sip. "This is great," I said, my eyes drooping.

The bartender bowed again. He immediately went to work on the second version. He shook. He poured. He bowed.

"Real good," I said, on the verge of total collapse.

He prepared the third version, and then the fourth. All eyes were on me.

"They would like to know which one you have chosen," one of my hosts said.

"I don't know," I said. "You choose."

"Please," my host said. "That would be very insulting."

"I lost track," I said.

"Please," my host said. "If you could just choose one."

I looked at all of the half-empty glasses that covered every flat surface in the room.

"The green one," I said.

This was translated to the hotel people. The bartender bowed. Everyone left.


Well, actually, everyone didn't leave. One of the members of the welcoming party was a young woman named Riki Ninomiya, who spoke fluent English. My hosts from Japanese *Esquire* had reserved a room for her just down the hall from me. She would be staying in the hotel for the length of my visit, just in case I needed her to help me deal with a foreign land and a foreign language.

Riki waited behind. "If you have any questions at all, just call me," she said.

"I have one question already," I said. "When the four men came into the room and I shook their hands, it seemed like it was okay. But when I shook the woman's hand, she seemed a little bothered by it."

"The custom here is not to shake the hand of a woman," Riki said.

"The custom is to bow your head to a woman. But don't worry about it. They know that you are from the United States."

Riki said that she was sure I needed my sleep. She left me in the room. I looked out the window. Below and to my right was one of the headquarters buildings of the Sony Corporation. Below and to my left was a Kentucky Fried Chicken restaurant.

I fell into bed. I don't know how long I slept—probably just a few hours. I woke up, disoriented, and started flipping through the channels on my TV.

Most of the shows were normal Japanese programs. But suddenly, on the TV, two Japanese women were having sex with each other. In the middle of having sex, they started burning each other with lighted cigarettes.

This I had never seen. I dialed Riki's room.

"Hey, Riki," I said. "You tell me that I'm supposed to bow my head to Japanese women. But I just turned on the TV, and there are two naked Japanese women burning each other with cigarettes. What's the deal? Are you supposed to bow your head to them, or are you supposed to burn them with cigarettes?"

"Bob, you're watching a porno movie," Riki said. "You've got a pay channel. Go back to sleep."

But I couldn't. The time-zone changes had screwed me up. I picked up the phone and made a call back to the United States. My friend John Walter is an editor at *USA Today*, and I wanted to know if I could get a copy of his paper in Japan. He assured me I could.

"John, the screwiest thing just happened," I said. "First these people came to my room, and I shook hands with the men and it was all right. But I shook hands with this woman, and I was told you're supposed to bow your head to Japanese women. Then I turned on the TV—and there are these two naked Japanese women burning each other with cigarettes."

"Yes," John said. "But when they get finished, they'll probably bow their heads to each other."

\*   \*   \*

I was wide awake. The clock meant nothing. I was like a madman. I kept making calls to the United States. It was so easy; it was as simple as dialing direct from L.A. to New York. I made about fifteen calls, then drifted back to sleep.

When I woke up again, I saw that there was a little cardboard notice on the night table, and that the notice said that there was an access charge for all international calls. My eyes were bleary, but I was shocked by what I saw.

I dialed Riki's room.

"Riki, I'm in terrible trouble," I said. "You know that card by the bed? It says that there's a surcharge of a thousand dollars for every international phone call. I've made fifteen calls already. What am I going to do, Riki? I haven't even been here for one day yet, and I've spent fifteen thousand dollars on phone access charges."

"It's not a thousand dollars, Bob," Riki said. "It's a thousand yen. Go back to sleep."

Which I did, for a while. When I woke up this time, it was still dark outside. But a Tokyo newspaper had been slipped under my door—an English-language publication called the *Mainichi Daily News*.

I turned on the light and started flipping the pages. I found an intriguing story.

It seemed that the president of a Japanese company was attending a business convention in Kochi City. The president of the company was sitting in a bar along with other men at the convention. The president of the company said "what beautiful teeth" the man sitting next to him had. He then "innocently slipped his forefinger" into the man's mouth.

The man with the beautiful teeth "chomped down on the offending fingertip so hard that it was left dangling." The company president was rushed to a nearby hospital, but the fingertip had to be amputated.

The man with the beautiful teeth said that he had mistakenly believed it was "a peanut" that the company president was putting in his mouth, rather than the president's finger.

But the company president said that the man with the beautiful teeth bit him on purpose, "out of intercompany rivalry."

The company president was suing the biter. He said he was bringing suit not just because of "the physical inconvenience I suffer," but because his missing fingertip might be interpreted "the wrong way."

The newspaper account said that "cutting off the last joint of a finger is a practice of the *yakuza*."

I dialed Riki's room.

"Hey, Riki," I said. "What's the *yakuza*?"

"Please, Bob," she said through a fog. "It's 5:oo in the morning. The *yakuza* is the Japanese Mafia. Go back to sleep."

This time I did, and for a long while. When I woke up it was the middle of the day. There was a little refrigerator in my room. I was thirsty, so I looked in it for something to drink. I pulled out a blue-and-white can, read the label, and felt myself begin to gag. The beverage was called "Pocari Sweat."

The time difference was really beginning to get to me. Riki called and invited me to dinner. It was 6:oo P.M. in Tokyo—4:oo A.M. in the midwestern United States. I sat at the table like a zombie. When we had finished our meal we went to the top-floor barroom of the hotel.

We were shown to a table. A Japanese musical group—the male musicians in black tuxedoes, the female vocalist in a long white gown—prepared to do its show.

At last, I thought, a genuine touch of the Far East.

The group went into its first number. It was "La Bamba."

The next day was a blur; I kept trying to figure out what time it really was. In the evening a reception sponsored by Japanese *Esquire* was scheduled, and I was supposed to make a few remarks.

There had been a minor controversy over my attire. At first my hosts had requested that I wear a black suit, out of respect for the others at the reception. When I had explained that I did not own a black suit, my hosts had offered to have one made for me in my hotel room.

But then, at the last minute, my hosts had changed their minds. They said that they wanted me to wear blue jeans and a loosened tie. I said that I was in favor of informality, but jeans were too informal. No, they said—jeans would be perfect.

The reception was to take place in the hotel, and at the appointed hour Riki escorted me to an anteroom where I was supposed to wait until I was introduced. My understanding had been that I would be in the anteroom alone. But when Riki and I walked through the door, there were about a dozen gray-haired Japanese men, all of them fifty and over, all of them in black suits, sitting stiffly around a long table. Riki and I immediately assumed that these men were the board of directors of the parent company of Japanese *Esquire*.

"Riki, we've got to do something," I whispered. I looked as if I had been milking cows. "Can you do simultaneous translation?"

"Not very well," she whispered back.

"Well, go find someone who can," I said.

Minutes passed; it seemed like hours. I smiled broadly at the men, who stared back with apparent curiosity. Finally Riki reentered the room with a female translator.

My smile grew crazed. "See, gentlemen, I was supposed to wear a black suit, just like you're wearing," I said.

I waited while the translator repeated the words in Japanese.

"But then they told me to dress like this."

The translator translated. The men showed no reaction. I felt like a Catskills comic on the unfunniest night of his life.

"The thing is, I don't want to make a bad impression," I said. I waited for the translation. "Up in my room, I have a pair of brown corduroy slacks I can change into."

Nothing—absolutely nothing—from the men in the black suits.

"I realize that brown corduroy isn't perfect," I said. "But maybe you think it would be better than this."

I went on for about five more minutes. When it was clear that I was finished, there was a slight pause. Then, in unison, the men smiled and began to clap their hands.

The translator said to me, "That means that they approve of the way you are dressed."

And then . . . the men stood up, bowed their heads, and left. We watched them walk away.

It turned out that they were not the board of directors of Japanese *Esquire*'s parent company after all. We had been in the wrong room.

*   *   *

After that, the reception was a breeze. Each person was handed an American Beat drink. Food was served. Copies of Japanese *Esquire* were passed out.

A Japanese woman came up and asked me to sign her Japanese *Esquire*. I asked her to tell me her name, which she did.

"You'd better spell that," I said.

"Here," she said. "Just copy it off this."

She opened her wallet and showed me her American Express Gold Card.

That kind of thing kept happening. Everything was so Western. When you placed a local call in Tokyo and were put on hold, you heard music-box renditions of "Greensleeves" and "Home on the Range." When you turned on the television, in addition to Japanese programs you could watch "St. Elsewhere," "Knots Landing," "The Jeffersons," or Larry King interviewing George C. Scott. Even the commercials for Japanese home-protection devices featured something referred to as the "Beverly Hills Security System."

So it was almost a shock when you encountered something that made you realize that you were not, indeed, in Tulsa.

The morning after the reception, I called room service for breakfast.

"Do you have muffins?" I said.

The woman in the kitchen made it clear she did not understand. The room-service menu was printed in both Japanese and English, and the hotel kitchen staff recognized the English words for the items on the menu. Muffins were not on the menu. Still, I thought, they must have them.

"Muffins," I said.

The woman said something back to me in Japanese.

I thought I would be helpful and spell it.

"Just a muffin," I said. "M-U-F-F-I-N."

The woman said she would get her supervisor.

The supervisor came on the line.

"Yes, Mr. Muffin?" she said.

\*     \*     \*

That night was my last official function in Tokyo—a speech at the Kinokuniya Hall. The audience would be listening to the translation through headsets. About an hour before the doors opened, I was brought onto the stage to test the sound system.

The seats were empty. The only people in the cavernous auditorium were audio and lighting technicians, who spoke only Japanese. I was motioned toward the lectern.

I stood there. I looked around me. I had given up trying to figure out what time it was in the United States.

One of the technicians motioned at me again. He wanted me to speak.

I leaned close to the microphone. The words came out automatically: "Elvis . . . has left the building."

I heard my voice echo off the walls. Why was I saying this? I knew this was the phrase the public-address announcer always used to intone at the end of every Elvis Presley concert, but why was I standing here in Tokyo saying it? The Japanese technicians looked totally perplexed. I changed my inflection slightly:

"*Elvis* . . . has left the building."

I was beginning to like this.

"Elvis . . . has *left* the building."


I looked over to my right. Riki was standing there with her arms crossed.

"I think it's about time for you to go back home," she said.

And the next day I did. And here I am.

# Orator

**S**ometimes the dramas of life are played out in unexpected ways; sometimes the lessons to be learned are just beneath the surface.

The event was a panel discussion in a medium-sized auditorium in Miami. About two hundred people had turned out to hear the speakers. For about forty minutes the speakers orated on the assigned topic; then they turned to the audience for questions. Men and women stood and asked whatever was on their minds, and the speakers answered.

It had been a pleasant hour, but it was clearly time for the panel discussion to end. The moderator asked if there was one final question; a man in the front row stood up.

He appeared to be in his seventies. He began to speak. He said he did not have a question; instead he had a story to tell. He turned around so that he was facing back toward the audience.

And he started to talk. His story was a disjointed, anecdotal one, and it became immediately obvious that it would not be brief. The man was not an accomplished public speaker; he began losing his audience within the first thirty seconds of the story. But on he went.

He appeared to be a likeable fellow; he was not drunk and he was not boisterous and he was not obnoxious. He merely had a story he wanted to tell, and there was an audience present, and he was going to stand up and talk.

There was an uncomfortable feeling in the room. It was one of those moments when everyone wants someone else to do something, but no one wants to be the one to do it. How to handle this? The audience had not come to hear this man talk, and the hour was over, and people wanted to go home.

The man was well into his story:

". . . and there was a large clock on the outside of the store," he said, looking out at the audience.

Up on the podium, the speakers were not sure what to do. They were equipped with live microphones, which they had used to answer the previous questions from the audience. They could have said something to cut the man off. But it would have seemed terribly rude; the man who was speaking was much their senior, and he seemed so earnest about what he was trying to express.

Still, there was the question of what the audience was going to do. Already five or six people had stood up and departed—simply walking out on the man in the middle of his story. Others were shifting in their seats. No one knew how long the man intended to continue, and there was always the unhappy chance that people might start laughing aloud at him, or leaving in greater numbers.

If the man was aware of any of this, he didn't show it. He continued:

". . . so someone asked the person in the store what he did for a living."

The moderator seemed perplexed, too. He had not anticipated this situation; how could he have? He did not want to cut the man off— what person with any kindness in his heart would want to do such a thing—but people in the audience were looking toward the front of the room, waiting for someone to take charge.

And the man stood and talked.

Sitting in a front-row chair next to the one where the man had been perched was a woman, also appearing to be in her seventies. The assumption was that this was the man's wife; perhaps she would gently touch his sleeve and urge him to sit down? But to gaze into her eyes was to know that she realized this was important for the man; it was important that he say what he had to say to this audience, and she couldn't bring herself to signal him that the audience might not want him.

If the man realized that any of this push-and-pull was taking place, it was not apparent. He began to embellish his story with details, gesturing with his hands. Another person got up and left.

It was not the most vital or noteworthy thing that was happening in the country. This was one room in one building in one city; no matter what happened, the course of human events would not be changed. But somehow it was important: A man, for whatever reason, needed to speak in public in front of other humans, and even though he was violating social protocol by taking over the program, that need seemed to be recognized by most of the people in the room. If he were to be hooted down, no one outside the room would ever know about it. If everyone were to walk out en masse, leaving him standing there, no one outside the room would ever know about it. In the global scheme of things, it didn't matter.

In the one room, though, it mattered. The speakers on the podium looked at each other; what to do? The members of the audience continued to move in their seats; what to do?

And then, as abruptly as he had started, the man finished. He came to the end of his tale, summed it up, and nodded toward his audience.

For a moment there was silence. Then the speakers up on the podium, as if getting the same idea at the same time, began to applaud for the man. The audience picked up on their signal; in a moment everyone was applauding for him, and he basked in it, and his wife smiled.

There was a shuffling of chairs. The program was over. The people headed for home. One small moment in the stageplay of life that never ends.

# Poem for a Cop

Cops cry.

Years of watching movies and television shows featuring actors portraying unemotional, hardened police officers have managed to convince the public otherwise. But cops cry. Cops cry.

In Chicago recently, off-duty police officer John Matthews was brutally beaten to death, allegedly by five men who had been holding an outdoor "beer party" that Matthews and other officers had earlier broken up. He was attacked so savagely that it took nearly seven hours to identify his body.

Police officers sometimes die in the line of duty; they know that when they apply for the job. On September 22, 1986, Jay Brunkella, a tactical officer in the Rogers Park District, was killed during a drug arrest.

I was thinking about Officer Brunkella's death when I heard about this latest killing of an officer—I was thinking about it because I know what happened in the aftermath of Officer Brunkella's death. It says a lot about what goes on inside of all police officers, and inside the members of their families.

Shortly after Officer Brunkella's death, one of his fellow members of the Rogers Park District tactical unit—Officer Ken Knapcik—returned home after his shift to find a note addressed to him on the dining room table.

Dad—

This poem came directly from my heart. . . . I love you so much it scares and amazes me that you go out every day and risk everything to provide us with all that we have.

I didn't write this poem to scare you or Mom, I just wrote to express how much I love you and how lost I'd be without you!

I love you, Dad!

It was signed by his fifteen-year-old daughter, Laura. Laura added a P.S.:

"Hey, let's be careful out there."

With the note was a poem that Laura Knapcik had written. Titled "The Ultimate Cop," it was dedicated "To all the cops in the world who have daughters who love them with all their hearts. And especially my Dad."

The poem, crafted with care, is about a police officer's daughter who sees on the 10 P.M. news that her father has been shot. The poem is too long to reproduce in its entirety here; it ends with the lines "Daddy, my Daddy, can you hear me cry? Oh God, I need my Daddy, please don't let him die!!!"

That night Ken Knapcik stood alone in his house as he read his daughter's note and her poem. He is forty years old, a twenty-year veteran of the Chicago police department.

"I started to read it," he said the other day. "It took me several minutes. I would get through a part of it, and then I would have to stop and wait awhile before I could go on. I was weeping.

"She had never told me that she was scared for me. She had told me she was proud of me—but she had never told me she was scared. I have three daughters, and I don't recall any of them ever telling me that they were scared.

"I took the poem to work with me the next day and showed it to my fellow officers. I've never seen so many grown men weep. Some couldn't even finish it."

Laura Knapcik told me, "I never told my dad how scared I was, because I didn't want him to feel guilty for being a policeman. One night when I was about eleven, I had a dream that he had been killed. He was working midnights when I had that dream, so I got into bed with my Mom. I was still crying; she asked me what was the matter. I told her. She said, 'It is scary.' She said that she gets scared, too."

Laura said that ever since she and her sisters were small, her dad had told them that he wished he could carry them around with him. She used to laugh at that, thinking her dad was joking—the image of him carrying the family with him seemed sort of funny to her.

"Then when I was a little older, he and I were having an argument," Laura said. "He said, 'Don't you understand that I'm serious? I wish I could carry you and your sisters and your Mom with me every moment. I wish I could have you with me all the time, so I could always be there to protect you.'" That night it was Laura who cried.

The poem, by the way, is not framed in the Knapciks' house, and it is not taped onto a page in a scrapbook.

It is in the pocket of Officer Knapcik's police jacket. He carries it with him every time he leaves the house for a new shift.

"I don't want to be out there without it," he said. "I'll probably carry it with me forever."

# A School of One's Own

$\mathbf{F}$or those of us who happily accept our state of arrested emotional and social development, it was a dream come true. You people who smugly categorize yourselves as "normal" might not even have noticed the news item. For me, though . . . well, the report that the high school was for sale leapt out of the paper as if propelled by a suddenly uncoiled spring.

The news report was fairly straightforward. In the middle of the United States—specifically, in Maine Township, Illinois—sat a high school that had been closed since 1981. This wasn't some ancient, crumbling structure. Maine North High School had first opened its doors in 1970. The anticipation then was that it would serve a rapidly expanding population of youngsters. Within eleven years, though, falling enrollment made it apparent that the school was not needed. Other high schools in the area had sufficient classroom space for the children of local residents. So Maine North was shut down.

Now, the news report said, a commercial real estate auction house had been retained to sell Maine North to the highest bidder. Sitting vacant, the school complex was costing $600,000 a year just to maintain. Clearly, the school district had to get rid of it.

This seemed to be a buyer's market. The school district had been attempting to unload the building since 1983, with no success. My decision was instantaneous: I would purchase it. I was prepared to pay $10,000 to take the white elephant off the school district's hands. I could expense-account it, I figured.

Perhaps you can identify with the appeal of this; sadly, perhaps you

**101**

can't. You may have a summer home or a rental cottage to which you escape on weekends. After a hard day of work, you may repair to a favorite tavern. For me, though, the prospect of having an entire high school of my own—to be able to wander the hallways of my personal school, to hang around the gym, to guzzle a bottle of soda pop in the parking lot on a warm afternoon—well, heaven could wait.

I ordered a copy of the auction catalog and prepared a speech for my editor: "I have some good news and some bad news. The good news is that we've just purchased a beautiful high school, and for only ten thousand dollars. The bad news is that we've got to come up with six hundred thousand dollars a year for upkeep."

I'm not a details man. I just wanted the school.


When the catalog arrived from Sheldon Good & Company, real estate brokers, it was not a letdown. Most of the catalog consisted of descriptions of conventional properties—apartment buildings, office complexes, retail centers. But then there was that one page: "Parcel 61—Modern 379,000 Sq. Foot High School."

The specifics were enticing: "96 classrooms" . . . "8 science labs" . . . "full size 75 foot competitive swimming pool" . . . "2 story library facility with dumbwaiter" . . . "art classrooms with kilns" . . . "full kitchen and cafeteria."

I think that's what cemented the deal in my head: the vision of possessing my own school cafeteria. I headed out to Maine North to make an inspection tour.


Maine North was in the middle of a suburban residential area, several miles from the nearest expressway. At first glance, the school seemed in remarkably good shape for having been closed for more than seven years.

The corridors where 1,600 students once hurried to classes were painted orange and white. It felt sort of eerie, walking those deserted hallways; I kept half-expecting a ghostly principal to materialize and demand to know where my rest-room pass was.

All along the hallways there were metal frames for clocks—the clocks that at one point determined the parameters of those 1,600 students' daily schedules—but the clocks themselves had been removed. The clock frames looked like basketball hoops—basketball hoops turned perpendicular to the floor, and with no nets. There must have been a time when the clocks inside those frames held the answer to that most vital of all questions: Is there one minute until third-period Biology starts, or do we have two minutes?

All of the lockers seemed to have been wired shut—tight little strands of metal had been snaked through the holes where combination locks once did their duty, and the metal strands made it impossible to open the locker doors and look inside. Somehow, though, the school district authorities had neglected to secure locker number 1730. On the floor of number 1730 was a remnant of a previous civilization: a crumpled potato-chip bag.

I passed the auditorium, left the main building, and strolled over to the football stadium. The gate was sealed. But there were bleachers on both sides of the grass field, yellow goalposts, and a running track. Up at the top of the bleachers on the home team's side of the stadium—on the back of what must have once served as the "press box"—was a painting of a Viking ship, the symbol of the Maine North Norsemen.

The real estate auction was scheduled to be held in the ballroom of a large hotel. I arrived early, and was surprised to find hundreds of people there. Eavesdropping, I learned that most were seeking to bid on the other buildings and parcels of land that had been described in the catalog.

We each registered at a central desk and were given numbered auction paddles to be raised when making our bids. In the auction room we took our seats. Inexplicably, a musical combo had been hired, and was playing background tunes: "Baby Love," "My Guy." The bidders—and their eyes did seem a bit hard—paid little apparent attention to the singer or the instrumentalists.

Steve Good—who with his father ran Sheldon Good & Company—made the opening announcements. He said that he wanted to review the bidding procedures thoroughly: "You're not buying a machine or a car. You're buying an expensive piece of real estate. This is not a game. You've got to know the rules."

From a typed list, he read a litany of items that were on the premises of the various properties in the catalog, but that were not, in fact, a part of what was for sale. When he got to the high school, he said that the organ in the auditorium would not be included in the purchase price.

This annoyed me—I had liked that organ very much—and for a moment I considered lowering my bid. But just as quickly I decided to stick with my original figure.

Sheldon Good himself stepped up to the auctioneer's lectern. He said that there would be a minimum bid on each property. For Maine North High School, he said, the minimum bid that would be considered was $2 million.

I was expecting this. I felt it was an obvious bluff. If no one had been willing to purchase the high school during all the years it had been closed, surely no one was going to come up with $2 million now. My plan was to sit patiently while Good lowered and lowered and lowered the minimum bid, and then to make my offer.

The moment arrived. Sheldon Good said the high school was now on the block. He repeated the $2 million minimum figure, slammed down the gavel, and asked for an opening bid.

Within a fraction of a second, a voice from the chairs far off to my left shouted out: "Two million dollars!"

I was stunned. Sheldon Good rapidly called, "We have two million dollars. Two million dollars." He waited for a higher bid.

As if in a daze, I stood up. I waved my auction paddle at Good. He hurriedly pointed his finger at me.

I just stood there.

The room, which had been buzzing with noise, became noticeably quieter.

"Do you have a bid, sir?" Good said.

I could hear my voice saying it:

"I would like to bid ten thousand dollars."

Now the room was totally silent.

"What did you say your bid was?" Sheldon Good said.

"Ten thousand dollars," I said.

I could feel hundreds of pairs of eyes boring in on me.

"Sir, we have a bid of two million dollars," Good said.

"I bid ten thousand dollars," I said.

If there is a sound more silent than silence itself, that is the sound that filled the room.

All of the normal bustle of an auction had come to a complete halt. Good said, "Sir, do you understand how an auction works?"

"What do you mean?" I said.

"When there is a bid," Good said, "the next bid is supposed to be a higher bid. You can't offer a lower bid. The gentleman over there has bid two million dollars."

I had to think quickly.

"I don't think he has the money," I said.

Now there was a buzz of conversation in the room again. Good clearly wanted to be done with this. He resorted to a loophole. According to auction rules, all potential bidders were required to be carrying a certified or cashier's check in the amount of 10 percent of the suggested opening bid.

"Sir, the minimum opening bid on this property was announced as two million dollars," Good said. "Do you have two hundred thousand dollars with you?"

I opened my wallet. "I'll have to look. . . ." I said.

From the corner of my eye, I could see security guards walking up the aisle toward me.

"We're going to have to move on," Good said from behind his lectern. "Is there anything else from you?"

I gazed around at my fellow bidders.

"I would just like to say that I would really like to own this high school."

I was told to sit down, and the bidding continued. Two million, 3 million, 4 million, 4.75 million, 5.25 million, 5.8 million, 6 million, 6.4 million, 6.7 million, 6.75 million, 7 million, 7.1 million . . .

The high school was finally won by a real estate developer who bid $7.75 million. He explained that his company wanted to use the forty-eight acres of property to construct 960 condominiums and townhouses. His bid was contingent on two factors: that the land be rezoned to permit residential buildings, and that the school board itself approve the price.

If both of those conditions were met, it was expected that Maine North High School would be torn down so that the condos and town houses could go up.

I walked out of the auction room. A man stopped me and said, "Were you serious?"

"Yes," I said. "I was serious."

"But why would anybody want to own a high school?" he said.

I just looked at him. I guess he truly didn't understand.

# With This Ring

**A**ppearing in classified advertising sections of several newspapers around the country is this small ad:

Super Bowl Ring, #1. Best offer.
Write: P.O. Box 8116, Fort Collins, Colo. 80526.

When I saw the ad, my imagination shifted into overdrive. I envisioned a former football pro, a star from the first Super Bowl, now destitute and down on his luck. As a final desperate gesture, he was ready to sell his championship ring. What a story. The ultimate tearjerker.

I immediately wrote to the post office box number in Colorado, and asked the person who placed the ad to call me. Within a week, he did.

He said his name was Bill. "Did you play in the first Super Bowl?" I asked.

"Nah," he said. "See, I was living in Green Bay, Wisconsin, in the late Sixties. At the end of 'sixty-eight or the beginning of 'sixty-nine, there was this Mexican fellow who was in trouble with the law. He needed some money. He had the Super Bowl ring. He sold it to me for $75."

I asked Bill if he knew where the man had gotten the ring.

"He got it from a guy whose mother cleaned the Tropics Bar in Green Bay after the bar closed at night," Bill said. "The mother found the ring on the floor after closing time. She gave it to her son. He kept it for a while, and then the Mexican guy wanted it so much that the Mexican guy gave the cleaning lady's son his car in exchange for the ring."

I asked if he had any idea whose ring it was.

"Sure," Bill said. "It belonged to Tommy Joe Crutcher. His name is engraved on the band. Tommy Joe Crutcher was a second-string linebacker with the Packers. The ring is made of gold, with a miniature Green Bay helmet. Then there is a football with Tommy Joe Crutcher's number on it—No. 56. It has the score of the first Super Bowl game— Green Bay 35, Kansas City 10. Then there's a diamond. And there are the words 'Harmony, Courage and Valor.' I understand that the ring was personally designed by Vince Lombardi."

I asked Bill why he was selling the ring.

"I figure if I sell the ring, I can get a pretty good down payment on a house," he said.

When I thought about it, I decided he was probably right. To many Americans, a Super Bowl championship ring—especially a championship ring from the first Super Bowl in 1967—is probably worth more money than the original Declaration of Independence. I asked Bill how the responses were going.

"The biggest offer I've had so far is $18,000," he said. "But I'm going to hold out. I think I may be able to do much better."

My next task was to find Tommy Joe Crutcher, the Green Bay linebacker whose ring Bill allegedly had. I located Crutcher at the Southwest Grain Co. in McCook, Texas, where he is a co-owner. The business is a prosperous one, and Tommy Joe Crutcher, now forty-seven, also owns a twenty-four thousand-acre ranch near the Mexican border.

"Mr. Crutcher," I said, "I have to ask you a weird question."

"What's that?" he said.

"Back in the late Sixties, did you by any chance happen to misplace your first Super Bowl ring?"

"As a matter of fact I did," he said. "Why?"

"Well, I think I've located it," I said.

"You're kidding me," Crutcher said. "Where is it?"

"First let me ask you a few questions," I said. "Do you remember how you lost it?"

"Yeah, I do," Crutcher said. "But I'm not sure I want to talk about it. Where's the ring?"

"You first," I said. "Tell me how you lost it, and then I'll tell you where it is."

He sighed. "All right," he said. "I was in a bar in Green Bay one night. At the time, I was living in the Downtowner Motel. I was leaving the bar, and a couple of ladies volunteered to come home to the motel with me. They were married ladies. I knew them. Then a third one said she'd like to join us, so I said okay."

"You took three women back to your motel room?" I said.

"I suppose I did," Crutcher said. "And when I woke up in the morning, the women were gone, and so was my Super Bowl ring. I called the two married ladies, and they said that it was the third one who had taken it. If I had reported it to the police, their husbands would have found out where they had been. So I got in touch with the ring company and ordered another one—it cost me $700. I've worn it ever since. I never told anyone it wasn't the original until now."

I told him about Bill in Colorado, and his attempts to sell the ring. Crutcher said that the third woman from the motel had probably been drunk in the Tropics Bar one night, and had probably dropped the ring on the floor. Thus had started the path that brought it to Bill.

I asked Tommy Joe Crutcher if he was interested in buying the ring back from Bill.

"How much is he asking?"

I said that the top offer so far was $18,000.

Tommy Joe Crutcher laughed. "Hell," he said, "I'm nostalgic, but I ain't $18,000 worth of nostalgic. Tell him I'm not a buyer, but good luck in selling it."

# All the News

I read a lot of publications in the course of my job, but I have found one that I like the best.

It is called *The Family News,* and its editor is Heather Cook, eight, of Lisle, Illinois. I found out about *The Family News* from Heather's mother, Jeanne Altendorf, and now I am hooked on it.

The idea behind the newspaper is that Heather thinks that all of her relatives should keep up with what everyone else is doing. So, every month, Heather prepares *The Family News* and then mails it out.

"Heather has been doing this for over a year," her mother said. "The thirty-five copies of *The Family News* are read by seventy-three people in nine states who range in age from 6 to 102."

I guess the reason I like *The Family News* so much is the tone of its subject matter. It seems that every other publication I read depresses me, with stories about the cruelty and meanness of mankind. *The Family News*, on the other hand, never fails to bring a smile to my face. I am not a part of Heather Cook's family, but somehow the things she writes make me feel good.

Here is a sampling of some items from recent issues of *The Family News*:

- "Kevin is in first place in his conference in golf. He is glad!"
- "Annette and Larry joined a Bottle Club and they spend a lot of weekends going to Bottle Shows. Larry collects antique ginger beer bottles, Annette collects old glass candy jars, and they both collect all kinds of stoneware."

**109**

- "Matt got his second tooth. He scoots around the floor to get where he wants to go. If you hold his hands, he will move his legs like he is going to walk."
- "Mike went to California on a business trip."
- "Aunt Lenore broke her right arm. We hope it is healing well."
- "Grandma, Heather, and Kevin raked leaves and burned them in the back yard. It smoked so much it was up the street!"
- "Steve got a new van! It is dark blue, and you could almost even live in it! He got it because Steve and Scott spend a lot of weekends working at car races. It is very nice."
- "Anne is taking driver's education. She can only practice with her parents."

Now . . . obviously, that is not the kind of news that you would find in a metropolitan newspaper. But Heather's mother thinks that is precisely the reason *The Family News* has such an avid audience.

"I don't know whether Heather is a budding journalist or not," her mother said. "When she started putting *The Family News* out, I didn't expect it to last. She's a very quiet kid. But obviously it means a lot to her.

"I run the paper off on our copying machine at work. Then Heather colors in the drawings by hand. Everyone in our family likes it so much—my brother-in-law Tom donated the money to buy the stamps for us to send it out. And my Uncle Frank, who writes to no one, wrote Heather a letter asking her to keep *The Family News* going—he said that it's the most important news he gets."

I spoke with Heather; I told her that it was pretty impressive, being a newspaper editor at the age of eight.

"I think *The Family News* kind of keeps our family together," Heather said. "Every month I call people up to see what's new—if they went to a party or something. When they tell me what they've been doing, I write it all down as notes. Then I put it in the next issue.

"I don't think there's any comparison between *The Family News* and a real newspaper. A real newspaper is all about the city and the world, and my newspaper is just about my family. I know that nothing that I put in *The Family News* would ever qualify to get printed in a [major newspaper], for example, but all my uncles and aunts and cousins tell me to keep putting it out, so I do."

Heather said that she doesn't look upon the job of editing *The Family*

*News* as a chore. "I look forward to it," she said. "I think it's fun. The best thing about it is hearing how much it means to the people in my family. Our family keeps getting bigger, and I plan on doing this until I get really old, like eighteen."

Heather's mother said that, because of *The Family News*, her family is joined together in a way that most families aren't. "It serves as a kind of bonding," she said. "Heather wouldn't use that word, but that's how I think of it."

Heather's mother said that sometimes she will offer her daughter advice on what to put in the newspaper.

"I'll say, 'Heather, why don't you write such-and-such or such-and-such.' And she'll say, 'Mom . . . who's the editor of this newspaper, anyway?' "

I reiterated to Heather's mother how much I liked *The Family News*.

"I'll tell you what I think it is," she said. "A metropolitan newspaper, as big and complete as it is, you know that nobody's reading every word of it. But with *The Family News*, every subscriber is reading every word of every issue."

# Take a Wire

The idea seemed simple enough: I wanted to send a telegram.

I haven't sent a telegram in years—come to think of it, I don't know if I've *ever* sent a telegram—but on this particular Sunday I wanted to. It was part of a joke.

See, I have this female relative. She's twenty-five years old, she's single, she lives in Falls Church, Virginia, and she is absolutely gorgeous. I had found out that she had met a young man from out of town, they had hit it off and she had invited him to visit her at her apartment for the weekend.

My feelings were that the young man's intentions were not strictly honorable. For one thing, his name was Rocky. (I should break in here for a second and explain a few things. No. 1: The guy's name really is Rocky. No. 2: I know him, and he's a nice guy. As I said, this whole idea started as a gag.)

Anyway . . . I wanted to send my twenty-five-year-old gorgeous female relative a telegram. The message was going to be simple—three words:

"Just Say No."

All right, all right . . . maybe it's not the most hilarious joke in the world. But I get bored on Sundays, and I wanted to do it.

So I called my local Western Union office. I said I wanted to send a telegram.

"Where to?" the Western Union woman said.

"Falls Church, Virginia," I said.

"Let me check and see if we have service there," she said. (At this point I should have known I was in trouble.)

112

A few seconds passed. Then her voice returned to the line.

"The computer says we don't have agents there, but I don't believe that," the Western Union woman said. She promised to check further.

A couple of minutes later, she came back onto the line again. "We can't deliver a telegram to Falls Church on Sunday," she said.

This stunned me. I grew up with the traditional American vision of Western Union: A telegram could be delivered 24 hours a day, 365 days a year. A telegram could be the bearer of joyful news or terrible tidings—but a Western Union courier would always be ready to speed to anyone's doorstep.

"What do you mean you can't deliver a telegram to Falls Church on Sunday?" I said.

"We just can't," the Western Union woman said.

"Do you have any suggestions?" I said.

"Well, we could telephone it," the Western Union woman said.

"Telephone it?" I said.

"Yes," the Western Union woman said. "You could tell us the message you want to send, and we could telephone it to the person in Falls Church."

"If I wanted the message to be telephoned, why wouldn't I just telephone it myself?" I said.

"That's not a bad question," the Western Union woman said. And she was right. I can just imagine the reaction of my gorgeous twenty-five-year-old female relative if she answered the phone and heard: "This is Western Union. Just Say No."

I wasn't ready to give up, though. In addition to a local office, Western Union has a toll-free 800 number. I called that number, and again requested that a telegram be sent to my female relative in Falls Church, Virginia. Again, after a computer search, I was told that no telegram could be delivered on Sunday. The Western Union operator at the 800 number had a different suggestion, though.

"We could send a Mailgram," she said. "It would be delivered with the person's mail on Monday, or Tuesday at the very latest."

"Look," I said, "don't you have people who can just go out and deliver a telegram?"

The Western Union woman laughed. "If you're thinking of the Western Union boy on his bicycle, I don't think that's the way things work anymore," she said.

The next day, I looked up a newspaper clipping about telegrams. Back in 1929, Americans sent approximately 200 million telegrams. But by 1985, only 3 million telegrams a year were sent. People are finding that telephones, telexes and facsimile machines are more convenient. As one Western Union employee said: "It's like what happened to the 5-cent cup of coffee, the 10-cent cigar. We're a part of Americana."

I thought about making one more attempt at sending my "Just Say No" telegram to my gorgeous female relative.

But I decided against it. By that time, she'd probably already said yes.

# Loving Woody

There is a terrible phrase: "fly-over people." It refers to people who live in the middle of the country—the people whom entertainment and media leaders from New York, Washington, and Los Angeles fly over on their way back and forth between the East and West coasts.

When I was growing up in central Ohio, the term had not yet been coined. We knew instinctively, though, that because we were living in Columbus, we were not considered very important by the decision makers in the intellectual and show business capitals of the country. We didn't talk about it much, but we knew it—and I think knowing it is one of the things that made me start to love Woody Hayes so much.

The national stereotype of Woody Hayes is negative. Pick your word: bully, Neanderthal, boor—that's what people called him all during his career. When he was fired as head football coach at Ohio State University in 1978 after slugging a Clemson player during the Gator Bowl, the cheers could be heard from all corners of the country.

I didn't feel that way then, and I don't feel that way now. For those of us who grew up in Columbus, Woody represented something: the idea that if we wanted people to pay any attention to us at all, we'd better be winners. We'd better be just a little better than if we lived in New York or L.A., because no one was going to come to Columbus looking for us. We'd better be so good that the rest of the world would have to pay attention almost in spite of itself.

In twenty-eight years as head coach at Ohio State, Woody Hayes won

205 football games, won thirteen Big 10 championships, took his team to the Rose Bowl eight times. But it is not the numbers that make Woody so important to me; it is the lessons he taught me just by being there in Columbus when I was a boy.

And every time I go home now, I find myself seeking him out.


Woody is seventy-two now. He waited for me by the hostess's desk of a restaurant called the Jai Lai, just a few blocks from Ohio Stadium. I had tried to be early so that I wouldn't make him wait, but he was even earlier. I apologized.

"That's all right," he said. "I've been coming to this restaurant for more than thirty years. I feel comfortable here."

He rose from the chair where he had been sitting. He was wearing a gray herringbone jacket and dark slacks; we moved toward the back of the restaurant and chose a booth. We started to talk—he has a slight lisp that always surprises people who have not met him—and I asked him if there had ever been a point during his long career when he had considered looking for a job somewhere other than Columbus.

"No, because there wasn't any better job," he said. "There is no better job than head football coach at the Ohio State University. Now Bear Bryant, down at Alabama, he was a better football coach than I was. . . ."

"Why do you say that?" I said.

"Because he won more games," Woody said.

"That doesn't necessarily mean that he was a better coach," I said.

"Oh, sure he was," Woody said. "He won more games."

I asked him if staying in Columbus had anything to do with feeling he wouldn't have fit in in a bigger city.

"Well, I'm glad that I didn't grow up in New York, if that's what you mean," he said. "If I had grown up in New York City, I think I would have been much more impersonal. I wouldn't have had so many people in the community looking after me. I grew up in Newcomerstown, Ohio, and when you grow up in a community like that, they know what you're doing. They know when you do something wrong.

"They know everything about you. They know your feelings, your responses . . . they'll see you doing something, and they'll say, 'Now, I know you. You're the Hayes's little boy, Woodrow, aren't you?' They might not tell your parents on you, but they'll let you know that they've seen you're up to no good. And it's good for you, to have people watching like that.

"And in a community like that, a boy gets to know the old people. Do you know who lived seven miles down the road from me, in Peoli? Cy Young, the greatest baseball pitcher who ever lived. He was in his sixties by the time I was a boy, and he would come into town smoking that doggone corncob pipe, and he walked down the main street like his foot was in a furrow. As great an athlete as he had been, he never bragged about himself.

"Did Cy Young go to New York or Hollywood? He could have, you know. But the thing that made him great is that he knew where he belonged. When he pitched for Boston they loved him in Boston, and do you know why? Because he was just Cy Young, the farmer boy from Ohio, and people knew that he wasn't trying to be something he wasn't.

"Now Thomas Wolfe, he may have been the greatest writer of all, he was the one who said that you can't go home again because it's changed and you've changed. But I'll never forget what it was like in my home-town. We never locked the door. We would come home and there would be a cake on the table—Mrs. Burris or Mrs. House would have brought it over and left it for us. If it was Mrs. Burris there was a picture of William Howard Taft on the plate, and if it was Mrs. House there was a picture of Woodrow Wilson. On a blue plate. And we would return it with another cake on it.

"And I may never have become very sophisticated, but the idea that education is important was literally hammered into me. My father never went to high school, but he attended seven colleges and finally became superintendent of a school system. He didn't graduate from college until he was thirty-eight years old. I saw him do it. I was seven. He had earned his diploma at Wittenberg, and he needed ten dollars for a cap and gown. He told my mother that he didn't think he could go, because he didn't have the money.

"And my mother said that he was going—we were all going. She had a white pitcher with a red tulip painted on it, and she had been saving the money in that pitcher. And she said the money was for his cap and gown, and we all watched him graduate."

A television set in the corner of the restaurant was tuned to "Enter-tainment Tonight." I asked Woody if he had really meant that he was not a sophisticated man.

"You know, a sophisticated person can argue a good case for just about anything, but that thing may not be right," he said. "I think that the word *sophistication* carries something of an evil tone to it. I think that sophistication is a quality to be careful of.

"I've heard people from Harvard speak about certain authors, and they say, 'I cahn't read him.' They put you down with everything they say. I always used to tell my football players—the only way to lick people like that is to outwork 'em. They may be smarter than you, so you work harder. Yessir.

"I remember, during the Vietnam War, there was that time in 1970 when some students were trying to close the campus down. They knew that I was sort of a conservative guy, but I think they still liked me. Some of them were throwing rocks, but I walked out there across the campus to talk to them, and I turned my back on the rocks. They didn't hurt me. And they listened to me. You know, I think that deep down in their hearts they wanted some older people they could listen to. And we got the campus reopened.

"You've always got to remember that every kid comes out of one kind of family environment or another. When I was coaching, I always recruited heavily in the home. I knew that when you got a kid from a good home, then that kid was going to listen to you. And when you go into the home you're going to see some things that you didn't see in the high school.

"What you do is, you watch the relationship between the kid and his mom and dad, and with his brothers and sisters. Because if there is love and respect in that home, then you know that the kid has played on a great team before he ever gets to your football team. And if you see a kid at loggerheads with his parents when you visit in the home, you'd better watch out."

I told Woody that I had heard a story about him and that I always wondered whether it was true. In the story, Woody's physician had warned him that he might be on the verge of a heart attack and should check into a hospital. Woody waved the warning off. That night, at home in bed, he suffered the heart attack. Because the doctor had been right and Woody had been wrong, he lay in bed with the heart attack all night rather than call the doctor. He did not feel that he had the right to disturb him. At least that's how the story went.

"Well, I knew I'd had one," Woody said. "Yes, I just lay there. I didn't want to bother him. I told my wife, but I didn't want to bother the doctor until the morning.

"My health isn't quite as good as it used to be. I used to eat a lot of red meat—roast beef, steaks. Nowadays I can't handle heavy food in the evening. I can't sleep worth a dime. I used to read more, but I can't do it as much now because of my eyes.

"My wife and I have lived in the same house for thirty-four years. At the restaurant here, while I was waiting for you, everyone who came in, I knew them. But several times I had to ask myself, 'Who the dickens was that fella?' I'm afraid I don't remember names as well as I used to.

"I walk down the street in this city and everyone says hello. Everyone I see speaks to me, and I certainly want to speak back. And I honestly believe that my wife knows more people in this town than I do. I decided right after I was retired that no matter what happened to me, this was the town where I belonged for the rest of my life."

I told Woody that if he had ever had any dominant reputation, it was for being tough. How important was toughness in a person's life?

"It's very important," he said. "When you get knocked down, you get right back up again. You'd better learn it early—some things in this life are going to be hard. When things are going well, that's when you've got to ask yourself: 'What am I going to do when things get bad?'

"People talk about being tough as if it's a negative thing. But I'll tell you this: in all of my years of coaching football, I never saw a man make a tackle with a smile on his face."

As famous as he is, he talked about a recent speaking trip he had made as if he were still the boy from Newcomerstown on his first journey away from home.

"I went down to Memphis State University the other night," he said. "They had made my reservations, because they were sponsoring the speech. They had a very nice room for me at the hotel. And then I opened up a door in the room—and there was a whole big other room from here to there! And there was a platter with more fruit and cheese than I could eat in ten days."

I said that I had read hundreds of quotes attributed to him, but the one that always stuck with me was something he had allegedly said back in the midst of his coaching career. Someone had asked him if emphasizing winning so much wasn't basically an uncivilized attitude to take. And Woody had supposedly answered: "Without winners there wouldn't even be any goddamn civilization."

Sitting across the table, Woody said, "Well, when I lost a football game, I let down everyone."

"Don't you think they would have forgiven you?" I said.

"I had to forgive myself for it first, and that was hard enough," he said.

"But you're asking me if there is anything that is as important as winning. And I think the answer is yes. There's something that's even more important than winning."

I asked him what that was. He hesitated for a moment, then said, "There are some lines by a great orator—my dad used to quote him. He said it better than I ever could:

" 'In the night of death, hope sees a star, and listening love hears the rustle of a wing.' "

The tough guy was speaking softly.

"You see," he said, "the important thing is not always to win. The important thing is always to hope."

# Beach Party

Denise Stanfa, twenty-seven, who is a sales representative for a corrugated box company in Dallas, describes herself as a "fun addict."

"My life is devoted to thinking up ways to pursue different avenues that will provide me with fun activities," she said.

So last summer, before a vacation trip with seven women friends, she came up with an idea.

"We were going to a place in Delaware called Dewey Beach," she said. "Dewey Beach is always covered with some of the most beautiful men you would ever want to see in your life. I'm not an ugly person, but I'm not a knockout, either. Normally I would never have a chance to meet men like that."

Thus, before leaving Dallas for Delaware, Stanfa went to a company that makes business cards.

"It was just the local Quick-Print shop," she said. "I had them print up business cards that said my name was Muffin Hardgrove, and that I was vice president of the talent division of *Gentlemen's Quarterly* magazine."

The minimum order was 250 cards for $25, so Stanfa left the shop with 250 cards.

"There had been several times in the past when I had posed as being someone I wasn't," she said. "Once I said I was a stand-up comic. Once my sister said she was a criminal lawyer. Once my friend Sue said that she was an artist. It's kind of fun, stepping into another role for a few days."

121

On the plane ride north, Stanfa handed her new business card to the two men sitting next to her.

"They were pretty impressed," she said. "That helped me make up my mind that when I got to Dewey Beach, I really was going to be Muffin Hardgrove of *GQ*."

Stanfa and her seven friends arrived at Dewey Beach, and immediately began searching for the best-looking men they could find.

"I would walk up to the men," she said. "I would hand them my card, and say that *GQ* was planning a spread on the handsomest men on the beaches of the East Coast. One of my friends would have a camera set up on a tripod, and I would ask these men to come with me and pose."

Without exception, they did.

"Some of these men were absolute tens," Stanfa said. "I had no illusions—they would never have looked at me in any other situation. But because they thought I had the power to get them into *GQ*, they would do anything I said.

"It was really something. These were very macho, beautiful, gorgeous hunks of men who were as egotistical as they were good-looking. The kinds of men who would never let themselves be seen on the beach with anyone less than a bronzed blonde sex goddess.

"Sometimes, in fact, a man would be sitting with a woman. And I would walk up and give the man my *GQ* card. As soon as the woman saw what was going on, she would say to the man, 'Do it! Do it!' And the man would walk off with me."

Before too long, Stanfa and her entourage had become the center of attention at Dewey Beach.

"We would be walking to our cars at the end of the day, and guys would yell at us, 'Hey, there's the women from *GQ*.' There's a bar there called the Rusty Rudder, and men actually started coming up to us, to see if we wanted them to pose."

Stanfa began to wonder exactly why she was doing this. "I guess it mainly had to do with just seeing what would happen," she said. "The men treated me like I was a celebrity, and I have to admit, that felt good. I'm humble enough to know that most of the men we photographed were way out of my reach. I felt slightly deceitful. But then we'd see another gorgeous man across the beach, and we'd say, 'Let's go get him.' "

Stanfa and her friends took down the names, addresses and phone numbers of each of the men they photographed. "We told the men that our editors were going to decide which men to use in the magazine,"

Stanfa said. "We said that if they were selected, they'd get a call or a letter."

She told herself that there was a valid reason for what she was doing:

"I've always been interested in the psychology of what goes on in men's minds," she said. "What makes them tick. So part of me was thinking that this was a legitimate way to find out.

"But mostly, I think, I believe that life should be one big beach party movie. Life doesn't usually happen that way, and just this once I wanted it to."

Stanfa and her friends photographed more than thirty men at Dewey Beach. "Did we really hurt anybody?" she said. "I don't think so. Are their feelings going to be hurt? I don't think so.

"The pictures are great. I look at them now and say, 'Remember that guy? Wasn't he cute?'

"I've thought about the moral to all of this.

"The best I can come up with is, 'A picture is worth a thousand nerds.' "

# Barbecue King

The National Rib Cook-Off is scheduled to be held in downtown Cleveland. The contest is designed to find the best ribs in America. But that is not the interesting part. The interesting part is the identity of one of the judges.

He is Bobby Seale, founder and former chairman of the Black Panther Party. Seale's greatest moment of fame probably came during the Chicago Conspiracy Trial when he was bound and gagged in his chair in the courtroom of Federal Judge Julius J. Hoffman. Time has passed, though, and today the organizers of the National Rib Cook-Off characterize Seale as "a militant barbecuer."

"It's true," said Seale. His current job is assistant to the dean of the College of Arts and Sciences at Temple University in Philadelphia. "I've been barbecuing since I was twelve years old. One of my teachers was my Uncle Tom Turner. I have a recipe of his that I call 'Uncle Tom's Barbecue Baste.' I barbecue with a baste, not a sauce. You can marinate with it."

Seale said that barbecuing has become one of the most important things in his life. He has written an unpublished manuscript titled "Barbequing With Bobby"; he insists that the first word be spelled with a "q." There are 150 recipes in the book, which he hopes to have released simultaneously with a barbecue videotape, starring him.

"I'd like to be to barbecuing what Jane Fonda is to exercise," Seale said. "If she can sell 750,000 copies of her exercise videotapes, I don't see why I can't sell 200,00 or 300,00 copies of my barbecue videotape."

He said that he thinks there is a natural constituency for his barbecue expertise. "There was a time when 20 million liberals and left-radicals across the country were saying, 'Free Bobby Seale,' " he said. "Now they're grown up and have their own barbecue grills and pits in their back yards."

He said that even though his national reputation was built upon his position as leader of the Black Panther Party, an organization that made many Americans a little nervous, the truth was that even back then he was an avid barbecuer.

"I barbecued all through the Black Panther Party days," Seale said. "Everyone knows that I was the organizer, chairman, and founder of the Black Panther Party. But no one knows that I was also the Black Panther Party's top cook. I was barbecuing for my fellow Black Panther Party members all the time."

Asked why the nation never became aware of this, Seale said:

"J. Edgar Hoover, rest his racist soul, was more interested in stereo-typing me as a threat to the internal security of America than letting people know that I was a barbecue expert."

When he talks about his barbecuing methods, Seale's phraseology still harbors echoes of his days as a Black Panther Party speechmaker: "See where I'm coming from? I pile my coal up in the pit in the morning. I let every charcoal get white hot. Got where I'm coming from?"

Although Seale was renowned as a political activist, he said that he "hasn't had the time" to watch the televised coverage of recent political events and congressional hearings.

"Watching the hearings isn't what would please me, anyway," he said. "I'd rather have me three or four slabs of ribs with some friends.

"I'm fifty years old. I have a wife and two kids. Barbecuing is No. 1 with me in terms of leisure time. My idea of a good time isn't watching televised congressional hearings. This is summertime. I get a six-pack of cold beer, I play pinochle or dominoes or chess with my friends while I'm cooking the meat. You're not a human being unless you're involved in something. I'm involved in ribs."

Seale said that he was looking forward to his job as a judge at the National Rib Cook-Off in Cleveland: "I'll have a little note pad with me. I'm going to look for good sauces and how well the meat slides off the bone and into your mouth."

And for his old followers who might not understand the passion he feels for barbecuing, Seale said:

"This is an American pastime. I love it. Barbecuing can change a grumpy attitude to a pleasant kind of sereneness."

# The Tryout

$A$t first I didn't notice him. There were about a dozen people in the hotel's third-floor hallway, and most of them were standing up. He was in his wheelchair. His head was down; he was studying the Continental Basketball Association's official guidebook.

The idea of the story was supposed to be sort of a joke. I had heard about this stunt that the Continental Basketball Association was staging. The CBA is a minor league; it is composed of teams with names such as the Albany Patroons, the Wyoming Wildcatters, and the Tampa Bay Thrillers. The goal for basketball players in the CBA is someday to make it to the National Basketball Association.

One CBA game each week of the season is telecast on a cable network. The league's executives had thought up a clever promotional idea: the play-by-play man on the cablecasts would be a broadcast professional—but for a color commentator, the CBA would conduct a "nationwide search" for a regular fan who could do the job. One fan would be chosen to be the CBA's color man for the entire season. The only requirement was that the fan must have had no prior broadcast experience.

I thought it might make a funny column. Apparently this was a common fantasy; the CBA color commentator tryouts were being held in cities all over the United States and were drawing big crowds of entrants. Today the tryouts were in Chicago, at the Westin Hotel; I thought I would drop by and watch.

* * *

It was just after 10:00 A.M. One hundred twenty-two contestants had been scheduled for tryouts, at five-minute intervals throughout the day. The ones who were waiting for their chance were kibitzing with one another in the corridor.

"I read about this in *USA Today,* and I thought I'd come down and give it a try," said Jim Lutz, twenty-four, a mechanical engineer. "I'm just doing this on a whim. I'd like to be a color man on TV. A lot of people kind of idolize color men."

Lutz's fiancée, Karen Schulz, twenty-two, said, "I hope he gets it, but if he wins I hope there aren't a lot of women around him."

David Schneider, twenty-one, a college student, said, "Everyone looks up to a good color man. Billy Packer is the best basketball color man on the networks, and everyone knows who he is. A color man can walk into any restaurant and have people say, 'Hey, there's Billy Packer.' 'Hey, there's Al McGuire.' I'd like that."

I noticed that the man in the wheelchair was still studying the CBA guidebook. But I didn't go up to him yet.


I went into the room where the tryouts were being held. Chris Tomasson, the basketball league's media information director, was seated next to a television monitor that was hooked up to a videotape recorder. Tomasson would do the play by play for the tryouts; there was an empty chair next to him, where the aspiring color commentators would sit. Two judges sat at another table across the room.

Tomasson explained the procedure to me. A videotape of a game from last season would be shown. The game was between the Sarasota Stingers and the Toronto Tornados; the first four and a half minutes of the fourth quarter would be shown on the TV monitor. The audio track was crowd noise: a mixture of applause and cheers. Over that, Tomasson would provide a description of the action, and each contestant would provide the color.

A labor-union official named George Poppers, fifty-four, entered the room. Tomasson outlined the setup to him. Then Tomasson pressed the play button on the VCR. The game came onto the screen.

"This is the CBA Game of the Week," Tomasson said. "I'm Chris Tomasson, along with George Poppers, and we're back at Varsity Arena

in Toronto, Canada. Sarasota leads Toronto 99–98 at the beginning of
the fourth quarter. George, what can we look for in this quarter?"

"Well," George Poppers said, "Sarasota hasn't done too well on the
road this season. Hopefully that will change tonight."

The two men watched the game on the screen, talking back and forth;
when the four and a half minutes were up, Tomasson thanked Poppers
and asked him to wait in the hallway. After every ten contestants, one
would be selected as a finalist for the day. At the end of the day the
finalists would compete, and one would be chosen to go to the national
finals in New York.

I sat and watched as the contestants each had their four and a half
minutes. Some were glib; some were nervous. All seemed to be doing
this as a lark. "Sarasota isn't using the ball as much as they should," said
Felix Rojas, thirty-seven, a probation officer. Jeff Carlson, twenty-eight,
a desk clerk, said, "That was a beautiful pass from perennial all-star
Robert Smith." The same four and a half minutes of the same game
kept flashing by; each new contestant gave his own commentary.

I kept half-expecting the man in the wheelchair to be the next person
through the door. After about forty-five minutes, when he hadn't come
in, I went back into the hallway.


He was still studying the guidebook. When I got closer to the wheelchair
I saw that he had a Chicago Cubs bumper sticker applied to one side of
it. I noticed that his limbs were underdeveloped; he was bent over in
the wheelchair.

I introduced myself and said that he seemed to have been waiting a
long time.

"I'm not scheduled to go in until 1:00," he said. "They told me that
they'd had some cancellations, and that I can go earlier if I want. But
I'd rather study the statistics right up until my time comes."

He said that his name was Greg Talerico and that he was twenty-three
years old. When I asked him why he was trying out, his answer was
simple.

"If I could win, it would mean my entire life," he said.

He said that he had been born with hydrocephalus—commonly referred to as water on the brain. As he grew older he developed other
ailments. When he learned how to walk, it was with the aid of crutches.

"I read about this in *The Sporting News*," he said. "I love sports, but I never could play. When I was a little boy, I used to watch all the games on TV. I've never done anything like this before—tried out for anything.

"But if I could win—it would mean for the first time in my life that I was doing something productive. I honestly don't think I'm doing anything constructive with my life. But if I could win . . ."

He said that he lived in a center for handicapped adults. "It's clean," he said. "It's a comfortable place to sleep."

A young woman named Cindy Copp, who had been hired for the day to be secretary for the tryouts, came over and said, "We have some openings, if you'd like to go in before your scheduled time."

"No, thank you," Talerico said. "I'm just going to use all the time until 1:00 to study."

I had noticed a dignified-looking, gray-haired man standing in the vicinity of Talerico's wheelchair. I went over to say hello to him, and he said that he was Greg's father. His name was Patrick Talerico, forty-three, and he was a truck driver.

"I think it's good that he's attempting this," the father said. "He's been interested in sports since he was seven or eight. It was tough on him, never being able to play. Greg has had ten operations on his brain, starting when he was three years old, and it hasn't been easy."

He said that his son had traveled 150 miles from the center where he lived for today's tryouts. "If nothing else, at least he can say he tried," his father said.

I went back into the room where the tryouts were being held. Everyone was in high spirits. As the Sarasota-Toronto game flickered on the screen, sports clichés filled the air: "There's no love lost between these teams." "They're being very physical on the boards." "You can tell he's not happy about that call."

I found myself thinking about Greg Talerico, so I went back into the hallway to talk with him some more.

"I was on the crutches until I was fourteen," he said. "Then I began to fall down too many times, and I was told that I'd be in a wheelchair permanently.

"As I grow older I slow down more and more. They really don't know how long I'm going to live. I'm told that I've already lived longer than anyone thought I would."

He said he had made a point of arriving three hours early so that he would be sure to be prepared when his turn arrived.

"I've got butterflies," he said. "I'm trying to think positive, but that's hard to do sometimes."

Just before 1:00 I went into the room, so I would be seated when Greg came in. His father wheeled him through the door, and to the spot next to Chris Tomasson and the TV monitor. In a soft voice his father said, "Is there enough room under the table for your feet?"

Tomasson explained the procedure to him. He started the video recorder.

"This is the CBA Game of the Week," Tomasson said. "I'm Chris Tomasson, along with Greg Talerico, and we're back at Varsity Arena in Toronto, Canada. . . ." I could see Talerico's face light up at the sound of his words.

Tomasson turned to him and said, "Well, Greg, what can we expect in this fourth quarter?"

"Chris, we just saw some good play there from both sides," Talerico began. I realized that he was the only contestant I had seen so far who had bothered to remember Tomasson's name.

The four and a half minutes went quickly. During one play Talerico watched all of the superbly conditioned athletes race down the court; one of the players tried and failed to stop the basketball from going out of bounds. "He looks a little frustrated," Talerico said. "He feels he should have gotten the ball."

When the tape ended, Tomasson asked Talerico to wait in the hallway until a finalist from his group of ten contestants was chosen.

I walked back out into the hallway and asked Talerico what he had thought.

"It started up so fast," he said. "I was worried about saying a dumb thing.

"But I had fun. I don't know how I did, but I had a great time. It was great. It was everything that I hoped."

\*    \*    \*

Because Talerico had been one of the first of his group of ten to try out, he had to wait almost an hour for the others to have their turns. Then there was a brief delay while the judges made their decision.

Finally Cindy Copp, the secretary, walked up to people in the corridor who were milling around.

"First of all, I'd like to thank all of you for coming today, and for your great enthusiasm," she said. "You were all very good. We have picked one finalist. He is . . ."

I was looking at Greg Talerico's face.

". . . Al Pote."

Pote, a twenty-six-year-old civil engineer, broke into a wide grin and accepted everyone's applause and congratulations. Greg Talerico, still holding his Continental Basketball Association guidebook, joined the rest in wishing him well.

Talerico's father waited for the hallway to clear, then started to push the wheelchair toward the bank of elevators.

"I'm going to take this guidebook home with me tonight," Greg said to his dad. "It's really interesting, and I didn't get to finish it all."

"That's fine, Greg," his father said. We all have our dreams in this life. Some manage to attain glory. For others, at least there is a clean, comfortable place to sleep.

# Sequel

**R**ecently we told the story of Greg Talerico, a twenty-three-year-old man who had come to the Westin Hotel in Chicago to try out as a color commentator for the Continental Basketball Association. Greg didn't win. He didn't even make it to the finals of the tryouts.

But after the column about him appeared in *Esquire*, something remarkable happened. From all over the country, people called and wrote my office with messages of support for Greg, saying that his courage had inspired them.

The first letter, sent to Greg by a woman in Georgia, set the tone:

I just wanted to let you know how much the story about you meant to me. For some time now, I've had a secret dream to try to be a free-lance writer. I've just never had the nerve or the follow-through to go for it.

When I read your story, I made a promise to myself that I would at least give it a try. I just couldn't shake off the image of you sitting in that hallway, going over that guidebook until the last possible moment, putting in all the preparation you could. I thought, That's the kind of guts and persistence I need if I'm ever going to get anywhere.

I don't know whether or not I'll be successful, but at least now I know that I'll give it my best shot.

I hope this letter doesn't sound too corny. I really got a new sense of determination from reading [the column], and I just wanted to let you know that.

There was a letter from a banker in Denver:

Although I have made many presentations in my life, I cannot imagine doing anything as terrifying as being a sports commentator, and I really admire you for being a contestant.

Mr. Talerico, you were quoted as saying you had never done anything constructive in your life. [But] you had a very constructive effect on me and have made me reevaluate my current situation. You exhibited persistence and stamina by studying so hard and traveling so far for the audition, grace under pressure by perform-ing so well during the audition, and good sportsmanship by con-gratulating the winner. I wish that more of the people I worked with exhibited these qualities, and I wish that I exhibited them more often myself.

And then there was the letter from Olympic champion gymnast Bart Conner:

It seems every so often, perhaps not often enough, we are reminded of how fortunate we really are. Today I read [the column] about Greg Talerico's dream to be a TV color commentator. Thanks for helping me to remember that I am a very lucky man.

I happened to win a couple of gold medals in the Los Angeles Olympics. Because of that success plenty of opportunities have come my way—one of them being a spot as a CBS-TV commentator. And yet I only won the gold by .025 in parallel bars—it was very close! Just because I won by .025 points does it mean that my opinions carry any more weight than Greg Talerico's?

Life is strange and very unfair. The tears that welled in my eyes for Greg Talerico reminded me that I'm a very lucky man.

The most important response to the column, though, came from Salt Lake City.

Dave Blackwell, the sports director of KLUB radio, got in touch to say that he was the host of an evening talk show called "Sports Club Open Line." He wondered if Greg Talerico might want to become a part of the show.

"Broadcasting is such a tough business for anyone to get into," Black-well explained. "When I read the article, I realized that here was a guy who had more going against him than most. I have the forum to put Greg on the air. I went to the station manager, and if Greg would like the opportunity, we'd like to give it to him."

I put Blackwell in touch with Greg Talerico at Winning Wheels, the Prophetstown, Illinois, center where he lives. Blackwell talked to Talerico, and explained that he would like to make him a guest commentator on the program. Greg could simply prepare for the show during the day, and then talk on the telephone to Blackwell with his comments.

The results have been phenomenal. "The first couple of times he was a little nervous," Blackwell said. "But now he's fine. He's on the show at least once a week, and he's very good and very knowledgeable. At first I explained to the listeners about the *Esquire* column, and about Greg's handicap. But now I just say, 'Here's our friend Greg Talerico from Prophetstown, Illinois,' and there we go.

"I think he's developing a following on the station. What I'll do is call Winning Wheels at the beginning of the week and tell the nurse supervisor what nights the show is on that week. And then Greg will pick out a topic, and that night he'll call collect—he and my engineer are buddies by now, and the engineer knows to accept the call. Greg and I are very comfortable on the air together, and everything goes as smoothly as can be."

Greg Talerico himself feels overwhelmed by what has happened.

"It's great," he said. "For the first time in my life, I feel I'm doing something. I feel I'm important, at least a little bit. A lot of people around here say that I've changed 100 percent."

At first, he said, it was the letters that got to him. "Those people who told me that I had inspired them—I never thought that I could inspire anybody.

"Even my own little sister is proud of me. Her name is Amanda, and she's eight years old. She's crazy about me and I'm crazy about her. But you know how other kids can be to a little girl when they find out her brother is in a wheelchair.

"When *Esquire* came out, though, she took the magazine with my picture in it to school—and no one could believe that her big brother was actually in a national magazine! That was probably as important to me as anything that has happened—the fact that it helped make my little sister proud of me."

As for the show on KLUB, Greg said, "Dave Blackwell and I get along well on the air. He takes the time to listen to me and lead me through the conversations. On the day of the show, I start getting nervous. I look forward to it all week, and then on the day when I'm supposed to go on, I think about it all day. Being on the show really makes my week— it keeps me going from one week to the next. And now I'm taking classes at Sauk Valley College, in Dixon, Illinois. I'm studying composition and English."

People who are close to Greg have noticed the difference.

"You can hear it in his voice," said his father, Patrick Talerico. "It's more enthusiastic and full of life. You can tell from his voice that he's looking forward to some kind of a future now. He never was before. He didn't feel he had a future.

"When he first told me he wanted to go to Chicago for the color-commentator tryouts, I was a little apprehensive for him. I knew he wouldn't have much of a chance, but I thought he was brave for being willing to give it a try. Who could have known that all this would result from it?

"He always used to seem down all the time. Now, you can tell that he wants to live, where before he seemed willing to give up everything. I never dreamed that there would be a change like this."

Greg's mother, Mrs. Patricia Timke, said, "I guess this proves that the world is not all bad. Greg got sort of a rotten deal from life, but this whole thing has turned things around. It's clear to me that now Greg has something to live for. He feels that life is worth something.

"I remember the first time that I took him to a Chicago Cubs baseball game at Wrigley Field, he absolutely fell in love with the game. I felt so bad for him, knowing that he could never go out onto a field and play it. But he never wavered in his interest in sports. And now, finally, he is being rewarded."

At Winning Wheels, Paul Yackley, an administrator, said, "From the time Greg came here, he always felt he was inferior. He always felt he was a step below everyone else.

"This is the first time in his life that anything has happened to make him feel special. He gets tired awfully easily—as a person with his condition gets older, there is more and more loss of physical strength—but in spite of that, he is always excited and happy now. I don't think he ever dared dream of anything like this. Now he knows that, even if he never accomplishes anything else in his life, he has done this."

Joyce Gladhill, a nurse at Winning Wheels, said, "When the letters started coming in, they just put him on top of the world. The thought that his example could encourage someone made him feel, for the first time, that he was worth something.

"And now the radio show—Greg has a wonderful knowledge of sports. You can ask him anything about sports, and he knows it. On the nights that he's on the air, he uses the director of nursing's office, so that he has privacy. We never listen in, but we can tell when he comes out of the office that he's feeling terrific. There's a real pride there.

"He feels that they must really like him at the radio station, because they keep putting him back on. He tells me that he has to believe that he's doing something right, or they wouldn't have him back. And I can tell that he feels a sense of responsibility to keep coming up with fresh topics. I really like this change in him."


At KLUB, Dave Blackwell says that Greg is welcome to be a part of the radio show for as long as he wishes. "As far as I'm concerned, he has done a great job," Blackwell said. "It's really up to Greg, but from our end, he's a permanent member of the show."

And Greg himself sometimes ponders what that means. "I think about all the people who live in Salt Lake City," he said. "What do they think of me when they hear me on the air, and what do they say to each other? I never thought about having listeners before."

Dave Blackwell has sent me some audio tapes of Greg's appearances on the radio program. Sometimes, on those long, cold nights when you wonder why you do what you do, I'll get out of bed and go into the living room and put one of the cassettes on the tape player.

I'll sit back in the dark. There will be Dave Blackwell introducing Greg Talerico. And then there will be Greg's voice—strong and confident and full of enthusiasm, talking about sports with authority and insight. I'll listen for a while, and then I'll head back to bed. But the voice stays with me; the voice stays with me.

# On Lead Vocals . . .

LONGBOAT KEY, FLORIDA—We all have special entries in our own personalized Annals of Goondom—the times when we can truly say to ourselves, "Oh, I'm such a goon." On occasions when we feel especially goonish, we may find ourselves cringing for days afterward.

I'm still cringing.

On a recent evening I was walking along the beach, looking out at the Gulf of Mexico, when I noticed a band setting up under a thatched roof that is part of a resort complex. I wandered over to check it out.

One of the guitar players—his name is Andy Burr, and he is thirty-two—told me that the band was called the Shades, and that the Shades had been hired to play at a wedding. The layout was absolutely gorgeous; from the site of the wedding there was an unobstructed view of the beach and the water.

"I've always envied guys who do what you guys do," I said. Burr and the other members of the Shades have day jobs; they are grown men who make a living in offices while the sun is out, and then get together to play music after dark. You're seeing more and more of this—people who used to play in garage bands and who realize that there's no need for them to give up the pleasure, even if they never turned into Bruce Springsteen.

Burr told me that the band had been selected by the bride and groom—Jennifer Regan and Chris Bisby.

"What kind of music do they want you to play?" I said.

"Oldies," Burr said.

"Great!" I said. "What are you going to do . . . Beatles stuff? Beach Boys? Motown?"

"Reggae," Burr said.

"Huh?" I said.

"Bob, these people went to college in the Eighties," Burr said. "To them, reggae is oldies."

I stuck around, and Burr asked me if I had meant it when I had said that I envied bands like his.

"Absolutely," I said. "What you do really seems like fun to me."

"Well, feel free to sing with us on a song, if you want," he said.

"Are you serious?" I said.

"Sure," he said.

"But I don't know any reggae," I said.

"Name a song," he said. "Maybe we know it."

I thought for a moment.

" 'Under My Thumb,' " I said.

He looked at me quizzically. "Do you really think that's appropriate for a wedding?" he said.

"Maybe," I said.

He asked the rest of the band, and they said they could play the song, which was originally recorded by the Rolling Stones.

So for several hours after the wedding ceremony I listened to the Shades play their reggae music while the bride, the groom and the guests danced.

Then Andy Burr nodded to me as another guitarist hit the opening chords to "Under My Thumb": "Doo-doo-doo-doo-doo-doo, doo-doo-doo-doo-doo-doo. . . ."

I waited for Burr to tell me where to stand. I assumed that I was quietly going to sing backup, just to get the feel.

Instead, I saw Burr urgently motioning me to the main microphone.

"Come on!" he said.

"What?" I said.

"Come *on!*" he said.

The band did not know the words to "Under My Thumb." They had said that they could *play* "Under My Thumb," not sing it. There had been a terrible misunderstanding. I was expected to sing lead. Alone.

And I didn't know all of the words to "Under My Thumb," either.

But the wedding-party guests were dancing, and Andy Burr was turning purple because the instrumentalists were playing and there was no singer, and I stepped to the microphone and hissed to Burr: "You've got to help me."

He jerked the microphone toward me, and I heard the horrible sound of my voice coming out of the loudspeakers:

"Under my thumb, the girl who once had me down. . . ."

In those few moments I learned the first rule of being a successful singer: You've got to have complete confidence, or the audience will know it within seconds.

The audience knew it.

Thankfully, my memories of this are hazy. I recall turning to Andy Burr and, panic-stricken, asking him if he had any idea what the next words were.

" 'Siamese cat of a girl'?" I whispered to him frantically.

He nodded. Hell, he didn't know. I sang.

The people had stopped dancing. All of them. They stared with awful fascination.

" '. . . the difference in the clothes she wears'?" I whispered to Andy Burr.

He nodded. I sang.

The guests stared. Horror-struck.

It is over now. Chris Bisby and Jennifer Regan are husband and wife. The band is playing somewhere else in Florida.

In my personal Annals of Goondom, though, that one song will echo forever.

It's okay if you're cringing. Me too. I swear. It just happened again. There. Again.

Goon, goon, goon, goon. . . .

# Underground News

With the weather turning warm and the sun shining brightly, Beverly Arredondo would seem to have the perfect job. She works as a salesperson at Amling's Flowerland in Melrose Park, Illinois, and she gets to spend every day outdoors among thousands and thousands of beautiful, blooming flowers.

Much of the rest of the world spends its days in dingy factories or sterile office buildings. Not Beverly Arredondo. And what does she think about as she stands in the sunshine amid the gorgeous flowers that stretch almost as far as the eye can see?

"I get really nostalgic for the sewer," she said.

She doesn't seem to be kidding. Arredondo, thirty-two, came to the flower store after making her living in a totally different environment. Specifically, she worked in the sewers in Milwaukee.

"I did it for about a year and a half," she said. "Milwaukee was surveying its sewer lines, and I got a job with the subcontractor that was doing the work."

Arredondo was one of the few women on the sewer crews. Her duties consisted of opening manholes and lowering herself deep beneath the streets to check out the condition of the sewers.

Why would she want such a job?

"Dare me not to do something, and of course I'll do it," she said. "I was told that most women wouldn't want to go near a sewer. The dirt. The smell. Sewers are so 'untidy.' I loved it."

But wasn't it a little scary—the first time she found herself down in that dark hole?

140

"Scary?" she said. "Exciting was more like it. I mean, how many people get to do something like that? You're hooked onto a rope. You carry a gas detector and a flashlight. The depth of the sewers I worked in varied from eight feet to fifty feet. I always worked with a male partner, and we'd go into about thirty sewers a day, every day."

Arredondo said that she found it almost peaceful down in the sewers. "Boy, it was great," she said. "I found myself looking forward to each new sewer. It's not conventionally pretty down in the sewers, but it's . . . different. There were a lot of spiders, but not so many creatures—rats and stuff. They're mostly in the storm lines."

She found that, during the period she was working in the Milwaukee sewers, she stopped seeing her old friends so much.

"When you're a sewer person, most of your socializing is done with other sewer people," she said. "You sort of hang around with sewer guys, because you understand each other.

"Also, if you were to go into a singles bar with your friends, and if some guy were to ask you what you did for a living, you'd always have to deal with the 'What's a nice girl like you doing in a sewer?' remarks."

On the job, Arredondo quickly discovered the classic pet peeve of sewer workers:

"They hate Ed Norton jokes," she said.

Ed Norton, of course, was the sewer worker portrayed by Art Carney on "The Honeymooners" TV show. Norton was the upstairs neighbor and best friend of Ralph Kramden, who was played by Jackie Gleason.

"People assume that sewer workers will be flattered by the Ed Norton comparison," Arredondo said. "But most of the sewer guys I knew hated Ed Norton. They thought that Ed Norton acted goofy and stupid. When people mentioned Ed Norton to the sewer guys I worked with, they felt they were being laughed at. They thought that people were not taking their livelihood seriously. Sewer guys tend to be pretty macho and tough."

Did she ever worry that when she was thirty feet below the street in a sewer, her partner might put the manhole cover back on as a practical joke?

"No one would ever do that," she said. "Your partner knows that if he does that to you, the next time you can do it right back to him.

"And besides, I liked it down there. Yes, it's dark and it's dirty—hey, it's a sewer. What can I tell you? It's where I wanted to be."

And now she is surrounded by all those dazzlingly pretty flowers every day. Fresh air and sunshine and flowers—surely she can't be serious about longing for the sewers.

"I'm quite serious," she said. "Some days I'll be driving home from work, and I'll notice a manhole cover on the street, and I'll think to myself: 'I wonder what it's like down in that one?' "

# Bar Wars

**T**he continuing evolution of relationships between men and women can take us down a twisting and uncharted highway, with unexpected stops along the way. And so tonight we find ourselves in a bar called B.T.'s, in Dearborn, Michigan. It is nearing 11:00 P.M., and the crowd is getting restless.

There are approximately 150 men packed into the bar. For most of the evening, loud rock music has been playing. Now though, the music has been turned off, and the men are crowding toward the stage in anticipation.

"All right," yells Rick Salas, the bar's night manager, into a microphone. "We're loading up the guns and getting our ammo ready."

Silently, employees of the bar circulate through the crowd, handing black plastic miniature Uzi submachine guns to the men. The miniature Uzis are built not to fire bullets, but to emit hard streams of water.

"Remember," Salas shouts into the mike, "share the guns with the guys at your table."

A woman named Brandy climbs onto the stage. She is wearing a skimpy T-shirt and a bottom that is a cross between a G-string and a pair of bikini underpants.

A heavy-metal song begins to boom through the bar's speaker system. Brandy lifts her arms to cover her face. The men in the bar lean forward, taking aim with their miniature Uzis, and as Brandy stands stark still, they begin to shoot her in the crotch.

\*　　\*　　\*

143

The phenomenon started in the Detroit area last summer. Various bars promoted it with various names, but the one that stuck—the one that people used generically when discussing these evenings—was Rambo Wet-Panty Nights.

The concept was simple. The women would take to the stage, the music would start, and the men would aim and shoot between the women's legs. Tonight, seven women have been slated to be shot, one at a time. B.T.'s is a topless bar, and some of the women who will participate are among the bar's regular dancers. Others are "amateurs," who are here because of cash prizes that are given out for the women who do the best job of being shot at—a hundred dollars for first place, fifty for second, twenty-five for third.

The noise level of the bar rises dramatically as each new woman climbs up on the stage and the "open fire" command is given by Rick Salas. The men are whooping and screaming. They are leaning forward, in combat stances, looking down the barrels of the submachine guns and making sure that their aim is true.

From all directions, the streams of water converge on the women's crotches. It is impossible to tell their reactions from a seat in the audience; virtually every one of the women does what Brandy did: covers her face, partly to protect her eyes from errant shots, partly, one suspects, to avoid looking at what is happening out there.

When Rick Salas gives the "cease fire" order after each woman has been shot, the women are directed to dance and to roll around in the slop on the wet stage. Meanwhile, other female employees of the bar are on top of the customers' individual tables, providing more titillation for the already aroused men.

One woman, wearing only a G-string, is crouched atop a table that accommodates four customers. The men are watching the other men shooting at a woman on the stage. The woman crouched on the table takes a piece of ice from one of the customers' drinks and rubs it across her right nipple. At another table another woman is crouched and surrounded by men. The men are hooting as their compatriots fire the guns. One of the men, apparently overcome with excitement, takes his glass of beer and pours it on the bare chest of the woman who is crouching on top of his table. Seemingly unfazed, the woman uses both of her hands to massage the sticky liquid into her breasts.

"Come on!" exhorts Rick Salas into the microphone. "Shoot those guns! If you guys were like this in Vietnam, we would have won the war!"

The woman on the stage, her eyes covered with her hands, continues to be assaulted by the shots aimed between her legs. "Born in the U.S.A." is blasting through the speakers.

Out in the audience, a man named Rolf, who identifies himself as a computer-marketing specialist, leans forward and presses on the trigger of his Uzi.

"I got her," he yells above the bedlam. "I got her. She's hot; I know she likes it. She likes it, and she knows that I know she likes it."

A man named Ron, who says that he works for a plastics-manufacturing company, shouts, "You work hard all day, and this is a release. I worked twelve hours today, and this is a way to get some aggression out.

"There's a woman where I work who's about to get married. I keep asking her out, and she keeps saying no, because of the wedding. I know I could nail her, but she won't give me a chance. I think of her being up on that stage, so I could shoot at her."

A man named Dave, who identifies himself as an auto worker, says, "You don't get to do something like this every day. I've shot a .357, a shotgun, a .30-30, and a .44 Magnum. But how many times do you get to shoot a girl in the pussy? This is great."

Waitresses are circulating, saying in calm voices to the men with the guns, "Would anyone like another drink?"

A man named Jonathan, who says he is a batch processor in a chemical factory, says, "This gives you a great feeling of power and authority. The ultimate machoism. I'm aiming at her clitoris. She knows I'm shooting at her crotch and she knows it's me and she gets stimulation from it."

A man named Ron, who works at an auto assembly plant, bellows, "It's nice. It's nice. I think that those girls like standing up in front of men and getting shot. Maybe they don't like it at first, but when they get all wet they've got to like it. They've got to like it."

As each woman finishes her turn on the stage, she goes to a dressing room in the back to dry off and change back into street clothes.

A woman named Rio says, "It didn't feel very good. This was the first time that I ever did it. I didn't know what to expect. Men in a place like this, they see tits all the time. But I didn't know what a bunch of animals they were going to turn into when they got guns in their hands.

"I was a little bit scared. Some of the men put their beer and their wine and their drinks into the guns, and that can hurt your eyes if it hits you there. I guess they're just having fun, but I don't know. Maybe I shouldn't be surprised. What can you expect when you put a gun in a person's hand?"

Brandy, the first woman to be shot at, says, "I thought it was great. I had a good time. I think it turns the men on, and that's fine with me. It's kind of a high for me—it really is. I didn't have any bad feelings at all. I just hope the guys who were shooting at me liked it as much as I did. I'll tell you one thing—I'm married, and when I get home tonight my husband and I are going to have a good time."

A woman named Kimberly says, "It was definitely exciting and unusual. I guess the men are being immature in a way, but hey—if their fantasy is shooting a woman, it doesn't bother me. If they want to play, I'll play too."

A woman named Marty says, "They're all with their buddies, and they want to impress their friends. It's a power game. Most of the women cover their faces when they're up there, but I try to look out into the audience and make eye contact with as many of the men with the guns as I can. A lot of times, they'll turn away. If a woman looks them in the eye, they'll turn away.

"They'd rather not think of a woman staring them right back in the eye. And I know what they're thinking—they look up onstage and they think I'm a bitch, and they want to shoot the bitch. But I'm not a bitch, and I won't be intimidated by them. I'm not a bitch."

A woman named Kelly says, "I don't really think about it when I'm up there. I know that there's a lot of guys out there who want to shoot me because it gives them a good time, and they think it's fun. I don't feel as if I'm being used, but I really don't get any satisfaction out of it, either. When I was a little girl, I wanted to grow up to be an actress. I know now that that's never going to happen. That was just a childhood dream. Being up there onstage being shot at—that may not be acting, but it's entertaining. That's as close as I'll probably ever come."

A woman named Kim, who won the hundred-dollar first prize, says,

"How does it feel? It feels degrading. What do I think is going through the men's minds? Frankly, I don't care what's going through their minds. I don't care about them at all. I see them going crazy and banging their heads on the edge of the stage, but I don't think about what they may be thinking. I would never go out with a guy who shoots at me. They may have fantasies, but I don't care what they are. I just block it all out and think of the money I can win. It's healthier."

Now all of the shooting has ended, and Rick Salas has left the microphone and is relaxing in a back office.

"I used to play Army when I was a kid," Salas says. "I dug it. Then Vietnam came around, and everyone was anti-American, antiwar, anti-Army. Even if you liked war games or war movies or war itself, it wasn't something that other people looked up to.

"Sure, there's a little pent-up anger out in our audience. They like shooting at the girls, because the girls are hot and they're good-looking and it's a female body up there. But I really can't tell if they're shooting at the girl's crotch or, say, they're shooting at Libya or Nicaragua. It all becomes the same thing."

Alan Markovitz, the owner of B.T.'s, comes in and muses about the other side of the question: not why the men shoot the guns, but why the women go onstage and permit it.

"I ask myself that a lot," he says. "I think a lot of it comes from the fact that many of these girls came from broken homes and got very little attention when they were children. I think that one of the things they're doing onstage—apart from competing for money—is finally getting that attention. Granted, it's a strange way to get attention, but it is attention of one kind."

Rick Salas continues: "We provide a place where guys can get loose and no one has to know about it. I'll admit that some of these guys are frustrated and have to let their frustrations out this way. But that's okay. When the guns are in their hands, they're in control, and they have free rein. They don't have to hold anything in.

"But is there anyone out there who would take a real gun in his hand, and who would shoot it at a real woman? I like to think not."

\*   \*   \*

Out in the main part of the bar, the entertainment has gone back to topless dancing. The Uzis have all been stored until next time, and the remaining men in the bar are looking at the dancers up on the stage.

A visitor to B.T.'s, who has observed all this and has been stunned by it, is preparing to go home. As he is walking through the bar, he finds himself standing next to a dancer named Darlene. Darlene has not been shot at tonight; she will not agree to participate in that particular entertainment. Now, though, she is preparing to go back up onstage for the more conventional topless performance.

"What did you think of tonight?" Darlene asks the visitor.

The visitor says that he cannot quite find words for it. The anger he had seen in the room, the naked hostility in the faces of the men who had been firing the Uzis at the women . . . the visitor says that now he must go back and put it all down on paper, and he is not sure exactly how he will be able to do it.

"Think of it as a dream," Darlene says. "That's how I handle it. I see it and I keep telling myself: it's only a dream. . . ."

# Mr. President

"**W**e're going to have spaghetti tonight," said Thomas Lucas on his seventeenth birthday. "My mom makes excellent spaghetti. Especially the sauce. She uses sausage, chicken, mushrooms, peppers—I've only made spaghetti sauce once, but it can't come close to Mom's."

Thomas Lucas was sitting in the wood-paneled living room of his family's home in Salt Rock, West Virginia. He is a big, handsome kid—five feet eleven, 185 pounds—and on top of the television set in the living room was a photograph of him in his red-and-white Barboursville High School football uniform. Last year Thomas was a starting defensive tackle on the team.

But things have changed for Thomas Lucas since last summer. His life will never be the same—and, in at least a minor way, the lives of American high school students will never be the same, either.

Because Thomas Lucas won an election last summer. And he is now the first male to be the national president of Future Homemakers of America.

Thomas Lucas's family lives in the West Virginia hollows. This is Chuck Yeager country, where the men are supposed to be tough, laconic, rugged, and all of the other adjectives that have always added up to a definition of maleness. So it is all the more surprising that the first male president of Future Homemakers of America should come from here.

"In junior high school," Thomas said, "the boys are all required to take home economics as well as shop, and the girls are all required to

**149**

take shop as well as home economics. In high school you don't have to do that, but when I was a freshman I decided that I'd keep taking home economics. And when the teacher announced that there would be a Future Homemakers of America meeting, I went to it.

"I didn't do it for any particular reason. I just did it to meet some kids. I was the only boy there. But it turned out that I liked it."

Approximately 11 percent of the 315,000 members of Future Home-makers of America nationwide are males. But, until very recently, it was unthinkable for a boy to become president of the forty-one-year-old organization.

"A lot of people define homemaking as just sewing and cooking," Thomas said. "But my definition of a homemaker is someone who con-tributes to the well-being of the family. That should be a male as well as a female. You have to understand, there was never a time when I thought that men and women weren't equal. I was born in 1969, and that was at the beginning of the women's movement."

As might be expected, Thomas has taken some teasing from his school-mates about this whole thing. "Yeah, there have been some remarks," he said. "The macho image of a lot of high school guys is the same that it has always been. You know, 'I'm tough.' Always getting in fights to prove their masculinity. All this boastfulness about themselves, and put-ting down other people. They're so locked into that image that they can't associate outside that.

"People couldn't understand that I was a football player and that I was also in FHA. But football and FHA are just two different things that I did. I'm not playing football this year, because of my FHA duties. That's okay with me.

"You hear so much about football being a character builder. If you ask me, football creates animosity between people. I know that it's sup-posed to develop sportsmanship and develop physical well-being and make you feel good about yourself. But all football was for me was going out there and knocking heads with someone every day. Future Home-makers of America is a hundred times more of a character builder than football, and Future Homemakers of America has offered me a hundred times more good things than football ever could."

Thomas is aware that for many boys, the quintessential modern hero is the movie character Rambo. "Look, I saw *Rambo* three times," he said. "I liked the story of it. It was an exciting movie, and very suspenseful. But it's fantasy. What I'm doing is real."

*    *    *

Thomas's stepfather, Larry Brown, came into the living room. Brown is forty-one years old and a dealer account manager with Ford Motor Credit Company. He is a burly, bearded man, and he listened to his son talking about Future Homemakers of America.

"When I was in high school, something like this would never be done," Brown said. "The boys just didn't take home economics. My conception, when I was growing up, was that the wife was the homemaker and the husband was the provider. And there are still a lot of men who would rather have their son be the football captain than the president of FHA.

"But I'm very proud of Thomas, and the more I learn about what he's doing, the more proud I am. Frankly, if anything, we felt at first that he was a little too dedicated to it. We saw Future Homemakers becoming his whole life. But what can we say? He set his sights on becoming national president, and now he is.

"In this day and age, I think it's wrong to want to bring your son up to be macho. I think that what Thomas was just saying about the macho image you get from movies is right. Basically, the macho image is ignorant. The macho guys you see in the movies seem to be playing with about half a deck upstairs.

"What Thomas is doing represents a change for everybody. With more and more women in the work force, men are going to have to adapt, and accept learning skills around the house. They're not going to have any choice."

Thomas cut in. "The real prejudice against what I'm doing doesn't come from kids my own age," he said. "Oh, there's some of that, but I can handle it. But the bad stereotype comes from adults. Not to put down you adults or anything, but teenagers are a little more liberal in their thinking than adults.

"Like at the national convention in Orlando, where I was elected. I had my delegate name tag on, and there was this woman in the lobby of the hotel who was just staying there as a guest—she wasn't a part of the FHA convention. And she looked at me and she looked at my tag, and she said, 'Oh, you're a homemaker, are you?' She kind of snickered. I knew she was making fun."

Thomas's mother, Sue Brown, thirty-eight, walked into the living room for a moment from the kitchen, where she had been preparing dinner.

"I've never believed that a woman should have all the homemaker's chores," she said. "Oh, women do help keep the social aspects of the family going. They send out the greeting cards and buy the presents for Christmas and call people to invite them to things. On things like that, men have to be sort of dragged along. It shouldn't be that way. It's unfair.

"But Thomas—Thomas has done household chores since he was small."

"I mow the yard," Thomas said. "I take out the garbage. I dust. I do the dishes. I make the bed. Mom still does most of the cooking."

"You can be a man and still be like Thomas," his mother said. "Thomas is no sissy. I don't think he's going to be a househusband and just stay home when he gets older. But he's been taught to do his share. And I think his being elected national president proves that it doesn't matter if you're from a hollow in West Virginia. Your mind can go anywhere."

There was a knock at the front door, and Thomas's mother went to answer it. In a few moments a lanky young man walked into the living room. He was Anthony Thompson, a high school buddy of Thomas's, and he had been invited to come over for the birthday dinner.

"Thomas was always a go-getter," Anthony said. "I think it's great that he made it to president."

It didn't seem to occur to Anthony that there was anything particularly unusual about the fact that the group that Thomas had "made it to president" of was the Future Homemakers of America. He seemed simply to admire the accomplishment.

"In junior high school, Thomas and I both ran for student body president, and I won," Anthony said. "But now Thomas has established himself in a far more prestigious position than president of Salt Rock Junior High School."

Anthony said that he had no desire to join FHA. "I guess that I just don't have the interest that Thomas has," he said. "I'm not saying that I think it was a weird thing for him to do. There are a lot of people who would think it would be a feminine move, but I don't think so. I'm sure that there will be some feeling against him in school this year now that he's national president, and that some people will stereotype him. But he can handle it. I know he can.

"People are just brought up in different ways. Take my grandparents. My grandmother waits on my grandfather hand and foot. He wouldn't be able to exist without her. I think all Thomas is saying is that it's about time for boys to learn stuff that has always been thought of as women's stuff."

Anthony said that although he respects what Thomas is doing, he has other goals for himself. "I want to join the Navy," he said.

Thomas said that he had some specific areas on which he wanted to concentrate as national president of FHA. "I want to help develop and expand drug-abuse programs, programs about drinking and driving, programs about teen pregnancies. When people hear about Future Homemakers of America, they tend to think in terms of the cooking and sewing, and think that's it. But cooking and sewing is really only a small part of FHA. Those things are necessary, because everyone should know how to keep their own home going. FHA is really a lot more than that, though.

"I hope to get married and have two or three kids. That's one of the nice things about being one of the few boys in FHA—you really get to meet a lot of girls."

Thomas's mother had gone back into the kitchen, and now she returned to the living room.

"If everyone is ready, dinner is served," she said.

One more person had joined the group—Thomas's original home-ec teacher, who was also his FHA adviser. The group sat down around the table.

"Mr. Future Homemaker, I see you're letting your mother do all the work setting the food on the table," Thomas's stepfather said.

Thomas blushed and shook his head.

"Just kidding," his stepfather said.

A salad was the first course. Thomas's stepfather dripped some dressing on the table.

"Honey, watch," Thomas's mother said.

The home-ec teacher said, "Thomas, should we tell the story about the Jell-O?"

Thomas didn't say anything.

"Should we, Thomas?" she said.

"What story is that?" Thomas's mother said.

"The story about the time that Thomas burned the Jell-O," the home-ec teacher said. "Didn't Thomas ever tell you that story?"

"We don't hear about a lot of the things that Thomas does," his stepfather said, laughing.

"I burned the Jell-O once," Thomas said, not amused.

Out in the living room the radio was still turned on to a country station, and as if by some corny cosmic joke, the song that happened to be playing was the old Johnny Cash number, "A Boy Named Sue." But under the circumstances it seemed terribly out of date and irrelevant—almost like something you would find in a time capsule. The spaghetti was served, and then Thomas's mother brought a cake to the table.

The group began to sing:

*Happy birthday to you,*
*Happy birthday to you,*
*Happy birthday, President Lucas,*
*Happy birthday to you.*

The cake was cut. "You drink coffee?" Thomas's mother said to Thomas's friend Anthony.

"I do," Anthony said.

"I'm gonna tell your daddy," Thomas's mother said.

# Brother

On a recent weekend Brian Hathaway, twenty-six, who works at a car dealership in Philadelphia, was listening to the radio when he heard a singer with a beautiful voice.

"I was really struck by the voice," Hathaway said. "It was . . . special. One of those voices that make you stop what you're doing and pay attention."

The host of the radio show said that the singer was named Freddy Cole, and that Freddy Cole would be performing in Philadelphia that very evening—at a restaurant called Babe's Steakhouse. The host also said that Freddy Cole was the younger brother of Nat "King" Cole.

"That really surprised me," Hathaway said. "I never even knew that Nat 'King' Cole had a younger brother."

Although Hathaway is of a generation that grew up on rock and roll, he is an admirer of another kind of music—the kind of music performed by Frank Sinatra, Tony Bennett, and the late Nat "King" Cole. Nat "King" Cole, of course, is legendary among music lovers; he died of cancer in 1965, only forty-five years old.

Hathaway decided that he would go to Babe's Steakhouse and listen to Freddy Cole sing. Hathaway invited his girlfriend, Pam Wilson, to accompany him; they arrived at Babe's early, to make sure they would get seats.

"There were only fifty or sixty people in the restaurant," Hathaway said. "I'd say the place could seat one hundred and fifty or two hundred."

Hathaway and Pam Wilson had dinner, and sat back to watch Freddy Cole perform. "He was really wonderful," Hathaway said. "His voice was very deep, and it was crisp and expressive. It was the kind of voice that you listen to, and you think: 'This man has experienced life.'

"He sang a lot of songs: 'You Are the Sunshine of My Life,' 'As Time Goes By,' 'On a Clear Day' . . . I wanted the music to go on and on. He was just that good."

It seemed like a perfect night of entertainment. But something happened—something that makes Brian Hathaway feel lousy.

"I had heard on the radio that Freddy Cole had records that would be for sale at the restaurant," Hathaway said. "So I asked the manager of the restaurant where I could get the records. I assumed there was a counter where you could buy them.

"The manager said he would find out. To our complete surprise, Freddy Cole came walking over to our table. He thanked Pam and me for coming to see him. He was holding two albums. He asked us if we would like them autographed, and we said yes, and he signed them.

"He did this for us, and then he told us that the price of the two records was $20. I sensed a combination of warmth and sadness in his voice.

"I paid him, and I was fumbling for something to say. So I said, 'Freddy, I really enjoy your voice and I really enjoy your music. It reminds me of your brother, and I really enjoyed his music. . . .'

"As soon as I said that, he looked away from me. He looked over at his piano. I think he said, 'I appreciate that.' I realized immediately that he had been hearing this for his whole life—hearing people comparing him to his brother.

"I tried to make up for it. I said, 'Even though you remind me of your brother, your voice is beautiful in its own right.' But I knew it was too late. I had already said the words. He went back to join the members of his combo.

"Later on, as we were getting ready to leave, I walked up to him at the piano and told him again how much I had enjoyed his performance. He nodded very pleasantly, and Pam and I walked out.

"The thing is, I feel I insulted the man. I told him how much I enjoyed his music, and then I had to ruin it by saying that it reminded me of his brother. I could almost see it in his eyes. He seemed to be thinking, 'Here it comes again.'

"I just wish I could tell him how bad I feel."

A day or two after I spoke with Hathaway, I decided that I would try to find Freddy Cole and pass the message on. Cole lives in Atlanta; his family there gave me a number where I could reach him in Lake Tahoe, where he was performing.

"The young man doesn't owe me any apology at all," Freddy Cole said. "I'm glad that he came to see me, and I'm glad that he enjoyed the show."

Cole, fifty-seven, said that he, Nat, his other brothers and their sister grew up in Chicago, and that he long ago learned to live with the memory of his famous big brother.

"The records that I sell at my shows are pressed on my own private label," he said. "The label is called 'Dinky.' That's the name Nat gave me when we were both growing up. I guess he called me 'Dinky' because I was smaller than he was. So that's what I call my record label."

He said that he was proud to be Nat Cole's younger brother, and that Brian Hathaway should not feel bad about what he said.

"To the contrary," Freddy Cole said. "Nat was Nat, and I'm Freddy. That's the way it has always been. If that's all I had to worry about, then I wouldn't have very much to worry about at all."

# Dorothy's List

**D**orothy Jean Hanson is a widow whose husband died eight years ago; she prefers to keep her exact age confidential, but is happy to admit that she is "over sixty."

She has a young friend—a woman of twenty-four—who has been having some problems with men.

"She has had steady relationships with four men, but each relationship has ended," Dorothy Hanson said.

The other day her young friend was down in the dumps about the end of the most recent relationship.

"I told her I would sit down and write her a foolproof list of instructions on how to catch a man—and keep him," Dorothy Hanson said.

Which is exactly what she did. "I don't mean it as a joke," Dorothy Hanson said. "If these modern young women will follow the instructions on this list, they will find men and get married."

Her theory is that today's young women make it too easy for men. "These girls aren't getting anywhere," she said. "They don't offer any challenge, so the men don't marry them."

There are dozens of books currently on the market advising women how to attract men who will eventually become their husbands. "My list is definitely better than any book," Dorothy Hanson said. "The books are too long—all those paragraphs. They don't get to the point. I give my secrets in twenty-four quick instructions. And my advice is free."

So, to all the women out there who are looking for husbands . . . here is Dorothy Hanson's "How to Catch a Man."

1. At first meeting be polite and smile sweetly.
2. If *you* like him, stop a while and engage in casual conversation.
3. Definitely show interest in what *he* has to say.
4. Do not overwhelm this delicate creature called "man" with your problems.
5. Never, and I mean *never*, tell him about past boyfriends or financial woes.
6. Always show your independence.
7. Never say "Poor little me," "I have to support myself in this cruel world," etc.
8. Do not hurry to invite him to dinner.
9. Let him take you to dinner at least five times before you invite him to dinner.
10. Do not engage in *sex* after dinner or later in evening. You did make him dinner.
11. Dress fashionably and laugh at *his* jokes and smile a lot.
12. By now this creature called "man" is drooling and panting for your body.
13. About two months have gone by and he is ready to "strike."
14. *He* will suggest getting engaged.
15. Go with him to pick out engagement ring . . . diamonds preferred.
16. Kiss him passionately when he puts ring on your finger.
17. Maybe, very coyly, let him have a little sex, but shyly say he is the first one and tell him to "Be gentle."
18. Do not make sex an everyday occurrence. Go slow.
19. I suggest once a week and then be sure to say it goes against your grain as you were a virgin until now.
20. This poor creature "man" is driven to distraction. He cannot concentrate. He cannot function properly. He cannot eat.
21. When marriage ceremony is over do this:
22. Shower him with kindness and love.
23. He is worth all your affection if you love him.
24. Many happy years.

I asked Dorothy Hanson if she had presented the list to her twenty-four-year-old friend.

"I did," she said.

"And what did your friend say?" I said.

"She kind of laughed," Dorothy Hanson said.

"And how did you respond to that?" I said.

"I said, 'Well, what you're doing isn't working,' " Dorothy Hanson said.

She said that she was a virgin when she got married, and that she had a wonderful life with her late husband.

"You will notice, though, if you look at my list, that I permit the woman to have sex once she has become engaged," Dorothy Hanson said. "I have allowed this in recognition of the fact that times have changed."

She said that she is aware of the fact that many people have already chuckled now that they have read her list of instructions. But she insists that the instructions will work and will lead to many weddings.

"If the girls try it, they'll see I'm right," she said.

I asked Dorothy Hanson what she thinks will happen to a young woman who ignores her rules.

In a sweet voice full of wisdom and concern, she said:

"Then the men will say of that girl, 'She's just another bimbo putting out.' "

# Coin-Operated

The most amazing jukebox story in the country comes out of Pittsburgh.

In that city, Helen Reutzel, fifty-nine, owns and operates what is believed to be the last remaining "live" jukebox service in the world.

It works like this: In a tavern or a restaurant, a customer will drop a quarter into the jukebox. But the record to be played is not actually in the jukebox. When the coin is inserted, a "ding" is heard in the studio of Telephone Music Service—Helen Reutzel's company. Telephone Music Service is connected to the tavern by telephone lines.

The customer in the tavern picks up a telephone on top of the jukebox. Miles away, in her studio, Helen Reutzel picks up a telephone, too. The customer tells her what record he wants to hear. Helen Reutzel finds it in her library of more than one hundred thousand records. She puts the record on a turntable in her studio. It is piped over the telephone lines and is heard in the tavern.

"My father, Bill Purse, started the Telephone Music Service in 1929," Reutzel said. "At one time, our clients included 120 bars and restaurants in the Pittsburgh area. After my father died, I took over the company. Now I have only eight taverns and restaurants who still use the service. But I'm trying to keep it going."

The studio of Telephone Music Service is open between 2 P.M. and 2:30 A.M. daily. Each tavern has a loose-leaf binder with a listing of approximately two thousand songs that can be played. But customers are urged to request any song that they may remember from any year. Reutzel probably has it.

"During the evening, the calls come in nonstop," Reutzel said. As she was explaining this to me, there was the sound of a "ding." Then another "ding." She excused herself and picked up the telephone.

It was a patron of a tavern called Karoline's, who had dropped two quarters into the jukebox and wanted to hear "The Marine Hymn" and "The Hawaiian War Chant." Reutzel found the records, put the first one on, and then returned to our conversation.

"Services like ours were very common all over the United States prior to World War II," she said. "Today, people are used to automatic juke-boxes. Most of the time, when someone goes into one of the eight taverns where we have our jukeboxes, they have to be instructed on how to use the jukebox. They can't believe that they're supposed to talk to someone and request their song."

Although it would seem impossible to keep track of all one hundred thousand records, Reutzel has them all numbered, and can find them in rapid fashion. "Take 'Cowgirl in the Sand' by Neil Young, for example," she said. "That's Number LPY8. 'My Girl' by the Temptations is Number D338. 'El Paso' by Marty Robbins is Number BG221. If I don't know where a record is by heart, I'll just look it up in my card file."

When there are dull moments in the studio—when patrons in the eight taverns aren't calling—Reutzel manages to keep herself busy.

"I run the sweeper, or I clean the records, or I file new songs," she said.

Just then there was another "ding."

Reutzel said into the telephone, "Joe Walsh? He has a new record? What's it called?"

She listened to the answer coming from the customer in the tavern.

"The song is called 'Confessions'?" she said. "I don't have that. How about 'Rocky Mountain Way'? That's by Joe Walsh, too."

Apparently that was a satisfactory compromise, for Reutzel removed 'Rocky Mountain Way' from the rack and piped it over to the tavern.

"People like my service because it's personalized," Reutzel said. "Any-one can drop a coin into an automatic jukebox, but how many people can actually talk to someone far away and order any record they want? One woman, for example, said she wanted to hear 'Summertime.' I told her that we had fifteen records called 'Summertime.' So she started singing it to me. I told her that the song she wanted was called 'In the Summertime.' She said, 'Oh, yeah! That's it!' She said that it used to be her father's favorite song.

"Now tell me . . . could you do that with a regular jukebox?"

# The World's Oldest
# Fuller Brush Man

Just after dinnertime the other evening, Coffman Shenk, ninety-five, the world's oldest Fuller Brush man, returned to his home near Gettysburg, Pennsylvania.

Shenk, who started with the Fuller Brush Company in 1922, had been going door-to-door on his route for five hours. He was wearing a dark blue suit. "Wearing proper clothes is important for any person who deals with the public and wishes to keep up his self-respect," he said.

Shenk's territory is Pennsylvania's Adams County. He will call on customers in the afternoon and early evening, and then spend the hours until bedtime doing his bookkeeping.

"The job is not a great deal different than it was in the Twenties," he said. "One of the differences I do see is that people have more money to buy things. When I started, delivering the products was often a harder task than selling them. Because when I came back to deliver them, a lot of the time people wouldn't have the money to pay for the products. You don't see that so much now. There is more money in circulation."

One problem remains: getting inside the customer's house in the first place. From the very beginning of the Fuller Brush Company's eighty-year history, that was the ultimate challenge.

"I've been here so long that getting in the front door is fairly easy for me now," he said. "My customers know me. You try to keep yourself presentable and polite, and you make sure that you don't do anything in the area that will give yourself a bad reputation."

Still, there are certain tricks that a good Fuller Brush man uses to persuade a person to let him in.

"We have always offered a free gift to the person who opens the door," Shenk said. "Usually it is a small brush. It can be used as a vegetable brush or a little scrub brush. Some people, though, prefer a spatula."

It has been years since the Fuller Brush Company limited its products to brushes. Now the firm offers a variety of household products—too many, in fact, for a salesperson to carry all at one time.

"Right now, we don't carry the sample case that we used to," Shenk said. "You should have seen that case—it was as big as a suitcase. Today we carry a shoulder bag. And I do most of my selling through a small illustrated brochure that I take with me."

One thing hasn't changed—as a Fuller Brush man, even the oldest one in the world, Shenk is responsible not only for taking orders, but also for getting the merchandise to the customers once it is shipped from headquarters. "I mail in my orders every two weeks," he said. "Then, when the products are delivered to my house, I get in my car and take them to the customers."

Every Fuller Brush salesperson has his or her own favorite product. With Coffman Shenk, it is the featherweight carpet sweeper.

"It weighs only three or four pounds," he said. "I recommend it to all my customers. It is very light and easy to use, and it does excellent work. It generates static electricity, and that provides a magnetic pull to the dirt on the carpet.

"I'll operate it myself in the customer's home. I don't have to get down on my hands and knees—the featherweight carpet sweeper has a wooden handle. After I've operated it, I'll show the customer all the dirt that has been picked up. The customers are always impressed by the dirt."

Even though, at ninety-five, Shenk has become about as familiar in a community as a Fuller Brush man can become, he does not always socialize when he visits a customer.

"With some of them, we'll more or less socialize and engage in a general conversation," he said. "But many people are only interested in seeing the products I have to offer. I'll just go into the house and show them what I have, and they'll order, and I'll leave, and that will be that."

Shenk does not work full-time anymore, but he is proud of the orders he brings in. "In a recent two-week period I took $400 in orders," he said. "There have been times when I have done even better than that."

One modern frustration is that many people have gotten out of the habit of buying from door-to-door salespeople. They don't trust the whole idea.

"That's the problem," Shenk said. "You have to make your own way. A lot of people like to do their buying in stores; they just prefer it that way. So you have to work hard at making yourself accepted.

"Every Fuller Brush man more or less creates his own image. If he's honest and dependable and friendly he soon develops a stature in his community. People don't mind letting him in."

Shenk is reluctant to talk about plans for the future. "At ninety-five, it's best not to make plans," he said. "If you start thinking about the years to come, you lose sight of the fact that there might not be any."

Nevertheless, as far as the immediate future is concerned, he will remain a Fuller Brush man.

"I'm not an expert at anything," he said. "I have to work for what I get."

# Nature Boy

Some people I didn't know had treated me in what I considered to be a rather mean fashion. I was wondering what the proper response might be.

Now, if a similar thing happened to you, you might seek the advice of an attorney.

Or you might ask for wisdom from your pastor or priest.

Or you might turn to a family member for solace.

Not me. My first thought was to find Buddy "Nature Boy" Rogers.

Buddy "Nature Boy" Rogers was a blond-haired, muscular, impossibly handsome professional wrestler who came to national prominence during the first days of television. Please do not confuse Buddy "Nature Boy" Rogers with someone like Gorgeous George. Gorgeous George was a joke; Gorgeous George was a silly, primping cartoon of a man, calculated to draw laughs. Buddy Rogers, though . . . Buddy Rogers was just about the studliest guy I had ever seen. You didn't laugh at Buddy Rogers. You gazed in awe.

The only reason that, as a boy, I ever was able to see Buddy Rogers in person was due to an accident of geography. Buddy Rogers was a big national star. He wrestled regularly in the largest arenas in New York and Chicago. But because Columbus, the city of my youth, was approximately halfway between the two metropolises, the major wrestling stars would often stop off for an extra payday.

On Saturday afternoons, a local television program known as "Lex's

**167**

Live Wrestling" was broadcast on Channel 4 in Columbus. The host was Lex Mayers, a heavyset, bespectacled Columbus Chevrolet dealer who, between falls, would proclaim the wonders of his used cars. This all took place at Old Memorial Hall on East Broad Street, and for fifty cents one could be a member of the audience. Which I was, just about every Saturday during my twelfth year on Earth.

And there, right in Old Memorial Hall, was Buddy "Nature Boy" Rogers. He was everything a skinny, shy Midwestern boy longed to be. He was huge and golden-haired and rippling with muscles, and he could flash a sneer that would melt women's hearts and fill men with envy. And the walk! Buddy Rogers moved about with this strut—it was so cool and so cocky that he seemed to be strutting even when he was standing still.

He was often cast as a "bad guy." I remember once, a wrestler named Leon Graham had injured his back during a tag-team match in which Buddy Rogers was involved. Leon Graham was being taken to the hospital on a stretcher. Buddy Rogers offered to help carry the stretcher. The fans cried out in protest. Buddy Rogers raised his hands to the crowd, the picture of innocence. He was allowed to assist with the stretcher. As he and the other stretcher-bearers passed a ten-foot drop, Buddy Rogers raised his knee sharply and suddenly beneath the stretcher, propelling poor Leon Graham down those ten feet to the cement floor. Graham landed hard and did not move. This couldn't have been faked; I saw it with my own eyes. Buddy Rogers sneered and strutted away.

Clearly, in my time of need, Buddy "Nature Boy" Rogers was the man to help me.


Along the streets of a pleasant, quiet neighborhood in Lauderdale-by-the-Sea, Florida, I looked out of the car window for the right address. It was early evening. A few houses up, I saw a man and a woman standing on their front lawn.

"Were my directions okay?" said Buddy "Nature Boy" Rogers.

He and his wife, Debbie, led me into their home. I had not been specific when I had asked him if I could talk to him, and I'm sure he wondered what the exact reason for my visit was. As I followed him inside, I could see that he was limping. And of course, many years had passed since the days of "Lex's Live Wrestling."

Buddy Rogers and I sat at a table on his screened-in back porch. I said that I was in search of vengeance—vengeance of the physical sort. I had thought that perhaps he could help me.

"Bobby, I wish I could," he said. "But I was just in the hospital. I had an artificial hip put in. Then I slipped and fell out in the garage, and I had to go back into the hospital again. Bobby, I'm sixty-seven years old."

We just sat there. Mrs. Rogers brought us each a glass of vodka.

"Do you mind if I stick around for a while anyway?" I said.

Rogers didn't say a word to me. He just flashed me that sneer.


He said that he had retired from wrestling in 1963. I mentioned the name of Hulk Hogan to him, and a look of distaste crossed his face.

"If I was in my prime right now, there'd be no Hulk Hogan," he said. And he was right; Hulk Hogan, for all his success, is really just a pale imitation of Buddy Rogers—a vivid but ultimately unthreatening creature of marketing and clever promotion, the Gorgeous George cartoon fast-forwarded to the present. "I was born too soon," Buddy Rogers said. "I'd inhale them guys today."

Mounted on the wall of the screened-in porch was a plaque bearing the phrase: "Tomorrow is a vision. Yesterday is a memory. But today is a beach!" Rogers, who grew up in Camden, New Jersey, said he is quite content to be living in Florida.

He said again that he would still be capable of physical violence if it hadn't been for the recent hospitalization.

"If he didn't have the hip operation . . ." said Mrs. Rogers.

"I could still do some things, right now," Rogers said. "If I latch onto your head, you're not going anywhere."

I mentioned what I had seen him do to the unfortunate Leon Graham—the knee under the stretcher, and the sickening fall to the hard cement. Had he felt any remorse for that?

Nature Boy shrugged. "That's the chance you take," he said.

"Buddy," I said, "that's not the chance that *you* took. That's the chance that Leon Graham took."

He shrugged again, not very interested.

I asked him if women had pursued him during his days of stardom. He looked over at Mrs. Rogers.

"Go ahead, Buddy," she said. They were married after his retirement from wrestling.

"I'd be lying to you if I said that the women didn't come around," he said. "And the funny thing is, they seemed to be more attracted to me when I was a bad guy than when I was a good guy." Like many wrestlers, Rogers's ring personality shifted from year to year and city to city.

"I don't know why they liked me more when I was a bad guy," he said. "I think it's the nature of a woman. I think it's a challenge for a woman to take a guy like me and think, 'I can straighten him out.' "

And how did he treat those women?

"I'd treat 'em like dirt sometimes," he said. "I'd treat 'em like they were wrestlers. I guess everyone else treated them sweet and nice and gentle. I know it's not a good thing to say, especially in this day and age, but it always seemed that the badder I'd treat them, they'd like it better."

I glanced over at Mrs. Rogers to see if she was showing any disapproval, but she was smiling, almost proudly.

I asked Rogers if he had any videotapes of his old matches.

"I don't think so," he said.

"Buddy, we have that one," his wife said.

"Well, that one," he said.

Mrs. Rogers left the room and came back in with a cassette. "I don't even know how to work the VCR," she said. "Our son, Dave, does, but he's asleep in the other room."

"Let me try it," I said.

We walked into the den, and I slipped the tape into the slot of the machine.

"Is that couch too low for you, Buddy?" Mrs. Rogers said. He had sat down.

"No," Rogers said.

"This chair's higher," Mrs. Rogers said.

"I'm okay," Rogers said.

I hit the "play" button. Suddenly, on the screen, it was June 29, 1960, in Chicago's Comiskey Park, and Buddy Rogers was in the ring preparing to wrestle Pat O'Connor for the heavyweight championship of the world. More than forty-one thousand fans filled the baseball stadium.

The ring announcer's voice: "In this corner . . . weighing two hundred forty-two pounds . . . from Camden, New Jersey . . ."

The next words were drowned out by the boos of the crowd.

In his Florida living room, Buddy Rogers said, "The minute you walk out of the dressing room and toward the ring, they develop a hate for you." His voice was devoid of any particular emotion.

The match began. What was amazing—what I had forgotten—was that there were no extreme close-ups in television coverage of wrestling matches back then. It was from a distance, and all in black and white. Yet even without the camera tricks that are now used to build up athletes' personalities in the eyes of viewers, Rogers dominated the screen. Pat O'Connor somehow became invisible.

"You would have been something in color, and with close-ups," I said.

On the couch, Rogers stared at the screen.

The TV announcer: "Listen to the crowd as Rogers falls full-length on the mat!"

On TV, Rogers picked himself up and walked in circles around the periphery of the ring. Before I could mention it, the voice of the TV announcer said it for me:

"The Buddy Rogers strut!"

"Did you have to practice that?" I said.

"No, it was natural," Rogers said.

"That's the way you walked down the hallways of your high school?" I said.

"I guess it was," he said.


When the tape had run out, with Rogers winning the match, Mr. and Mrs. Rogers asked me if I felt like going out to dinner. I said of course.

I went outside first and waited by the car. Buddy Rogers came out of the house.

"Have you got your cane, Buddy?" his wife said.

"No," he said. It was the first time a cane had been mentioned.

"Should I get it for you?" Mrs. Rogers said.

Rogers paused for a moment and then said, "Forget it."

But she went back into the house and came out with a cane. We drove for about five minutes, and pulled into the parking lot of a shopping strip. We were going to eat at an Italian place called Casa Bella.

Buddy Rogers and his wife entered the restaurant before I did. Walking behind them, I found myself grinning like a kid. Can you imagine a man with a cane strutting? Believe me, it's great.

# Listening to David

I was walking into a radio studio in New York, and the person who was walking out was David Eisenhower. Eisenhower had been on the air to promote his biography of his grandfather, *Eisenhower: At War*. Someone introduced us, and we shook hands, and that was that.

For the next few days, though, I found myself thinking about him. Back in the late Sixties and early Seventies, a lot of young Americans took great pleasure in describing themselves as "freaks." With their long hair and faded jeans and drug use, they proudly proclaimed their distance from the rest of society.

The freaks weren't really freaks, though; there were too many of them. When being a freak becomes conventional, one is no longer a freak. If the truth be told, the person really considered the freak of that era was David Eisenhower. Clean-cut, conservatively dressed, a little gawky, he was the grandson of Dwight D. Eisenhower and the son-in-law of Richard Nixon. David Eisenhower was the one nationally famous young man who stood out from the crowd.

Now, of course, everything has changed, and David Eisenhower is in the mainstream. I was curious about what it had been like for him back then; I tracked him down, and we talked about it.

"I'll admit it, I got curious about all of the experimentation I heard about back then," Eisenhower, thirty-eight, said. "Julie and I didn't cultivate the image we had intentionally. It was just part and parcel of who we were. Were we isolated? Well, in a way. I suppose we felt slightly isolated."

172

Did Eisenhower ever become tempted by his peers in college to try drugs? Marijuana, for example?

"I really don't know," he said. "Deep down in me, I thought that those antics were slightly frightening. They seemed self-destructive to me. I didn't judge people one way or another for using those things. But marijuana, dope. . . . I grew up kind of afraid of drugs.

"It's probably for the same reason that I'm not a gambler. I don't gamble because I know that if I started, I'd never stop. I've gambled two times in my life. Once was at a horse track, and once was at a casino when I was in the Navy. I lost five or ten dollars—the house was ahead of me a little bit. So I told myself, 'Don't mess with this. You'll never stop.' I suppose it was the same with drugs. I knew that if I tried them, I'd get hooked.

"My hair was not all that short in college. Never shoulder-length or that kind of stuff, though. My friends in college told me that the women really went for the extremely long hair on men, but I decided never to do that, either. I saw hippieness on campus, and I had some friends who were hippies. But you have to remember, I grew up in Gettysburg, Pennsylvania. I was raised on Army posts and in Gettysburg. I wasn't exactly a small-town boy, but close enough to it. If my name had been David Thompson instead of David Eisenhower, I still think I would have turned out the way I did. I still wouldn't have joined in all that stuff."

He said he learned something from his experiences in college, and his distance from so many of his contemporaries. "What I realized kind of early on is that there is such a thing as separate worlds. You live in one world, and other people live in other worlds. When I look back on those college days, it seems to me that we were living in fairly dangerous times, and in restrospect I'm glad I took the course that I did.

"I think that there was a tremendous amount of energy that accompanied all the experimentation everyone was doing. I was fascinated by it, just watching it. I sometimes wonder what ended up happening to some of those people, in relation to what ended up happening to me."

His grandfather was buried on David's twenty-first birthday. "A lot of people think of me as the son of Dwight Eisenhower and the son of Richard Nixon," he said. "In fact, I am the son of neither. The sons of famous men are complicated people. The grandsons are one generation removed.

"What my grandfather expected from me was proper decorum and respect. Especially when I was around him and his contemporaries. He realized that you can break somebody, break his spirit, if you lean on him too hard.

"When I was sixteen, my grandfather sold me a 'sixty-two Plymouth Valiant that he had owned. He sold it to me for $50. The one rule I had to obey was that I would never exceed fifty-five miles per hour. I had to promise him that. I would drive my grandfather around Gettysburg, and the whole time I was driving he would keep his eyes on the speedometer, like a hawk. He didn't know if I had proper road judgment. When I was in college I got a speeding ticket, and it made the newspapers, and my family had to keep the newspapers away from my grandfather."

And David's relationship with his father-in-law? What does he call Richard Nixon?

"I call him Mr. Nixon," Eisenhower said. "I've always called him Mr. Nixon. That's just the way it is. It's always been Mr. Nixon. He has never said, 'Call me Dick.'"

# A Piece of Furniture

For months, I have been trying to get hold of a fellow named Eddy G. Nicholson.

I have called him at his office. I have called him at home. He will not speak with me. Eddy G. Nicholson has become an obsession with me.

Here's why:

I read a newspaper article that said that Eddy G. Nicholson had paid $1.1 million for a chair.

The chair—an eighteenth-century mahogany wing chair made in Philadelphia—was sold to Nicholson at Sotheby's international auction house in New York.

There was a photograph of the chair accompanying the newspaper article. The chair looked like any dumpy old chair that you might find in your great-aunt's sitting room. But Eddy G. Nicholson had paid $1.1 million for it, which made it the most expensive piece of furniture ever sold in America.

Eddy G. Nicholson was quoted in the newspaper article: "The chair is absolutely the most gorgeous thing. If you look at it, it floats like a ballerina. I shall put it next to the tea table."

The "tea table" referred to by Nicholson was one for which he had paid $1,045,000 in 1985.

Now . . . I don't understand antiques, but there is no way that an old chair can be worth $1.1 million (never mind a tea table being worth $1,045,000). I kept calling Nicholson—he lives in New Hampshire—because I had one burning question: Did he plan to actually sit on the chair?

**175**

Since he wouldn't take my calls, I got in touch with the Sotheby's auction house, where an employee—requesting anonymity—spoke to me about the $1.1 million chair.

"Yes, Mr. Nicholson will sit in the chair," the Sotheby's man said. "Mr. Nicholson uses everything he buys. He will definitely sit in the chair."

I asked the Sotheby's man if he considered the chair to be worth $1.1 million.

"You have to figure if Mr. Nicholson bid $1.1 million for it, then it was probably worth $1 million to someone else," the Sotheby's man said. "Something is worth the money if someone is willing to pay for it."

I said that it was astonishing to me that someone would actually pay $1.1 million for a chair.

"I am in the antiques world," the Sotheby's man said, "and it's astonishing to me, too."

I made several more attempts to reach Eddy G. Nicholson. I just had to find out if he was sitting in that chair. But I got nowhere.

So I did the next best thing. I called Lita Solis-Cohen, a noted antiques writer, who covered the auction at which Eddy G. Nicholson paid $1.1 million for the chair. Solis-Cohen knows Nicholson, and I thought that she might be able to give me some clue to the man and his purchase.

"That chair had very good lines, very beautiful carvings, and a stance of assurance," Solis-Cohen told me. "The whole chair is almost a gesture of confidence."

Yes, I said, but $1.1 million for a chair?

"A chair is a chair," Solis-Cohen said. "But this is a work of art."

I asked her the question that had been tormenting me: Did she think that Eddy G. Nicholson was actually sitting on the chair?

"Of course," she said. "He's furnishing his house."

He's furnishing his house?

"He's not putting the things he buys in display cases," she said. "This is simply a chair for his house."

I asked—just hypothetically—if Eddy G. Nicholson were to invite some friends over, would he allow them to sit on the chair?

"He would certainly let his friends sit on it," Solis-Cohen said. "Eddy G. Nicholson is the most wonderful man."

I asked if Eddy G. Nicholson was a pretty old guy.

"Oh, no," Solis-Cohen said. "I think he's forty-five."

But really, I said to Solis-Cohen. Let's be frank. $1.1 million for a chair? Did she think it was worth it?

"I think he got a very good price," she said.

But it's the highest price ever paid for a piece of American furniture.

"Oh, then I guess you haven't heard the news," Solis-Cohen said.

Heard the news?

"That price is not the record anymore," she said. "There was another chair sold at Sotheby's last month. It went for $2.75 million."

# Eddy Calling

**W**ell I'll be darned.

No sooner had my last column gone to press—the column about Eddy G. Nicholson, the man who paid $1.1 million for a chair—than who should call me but Eddy G. Nicholson.

If you read the column, you know that I had become obsessed with Eddy G. Nicholson and his $1.1 million chair. I was filled with questions. Would Eddy G. Nicholson actually sit on the chair? Why would anyone pay $1.1 million for a chair? Where would he put the chair?

And then the phone rang. And it was Eddy G. Nicholson.

"I understand you've been trying to get hold of me," he said.

I said that I certainly had. I was consumed by the idea of the $1.1 million chair. I asked him where it was.

You're not going to believe this.

"It's out being reupholstered," Eddy G. Nicholson said.

I thought I was hearing him wrong.

"You paid $1.1 million for a chair and then you sent it out to be reupholstered?" I said.

"Yes," Nicholson said.

"You thought the chair was worth $1.1 million, but you didn't like the upholstery?" I said.

"That's correct," Nicholson said. "The upholstery I did not feel was appropriate."

"What was wrong with it?" I said.

"Well, for one thing, the chair was overstuffed," Nicholson said. "The arms and the seat were overstuffed."

"Did you at least like the fabric?" I said.

"Not really," he said. "I'm having new fabric put on."

This was getting confusing. The man had paid $1.1 million for a chair, and then the first thing he had decided to do was get it redone because he didn't like the looks of it.

"The upholstery is not the important thing," Nicholson said. "What is important is the structural part of the chair—the wood and how it is put together."

He said the reupholstered chair will be delivered to his house in New Hampshire within the next two months.

And then will he sit on it?

"Of course I'll sit on it," he said. "It was made to be sat in."

And if his friends come over, will they be allowed to sit on it?

"You bet," Nicholson said. "I do not put 'Do Not Sit' signs on my chairs."

He said that he would probably place the chair next to his $1,045,000 tea table.

I asked him if it didn't make him nervous to have a $1,045,000 tea table standing in the middle of his living room, where someone could take a false step and trip over it.

"Well, I certainly make sure that people don't put their cocktails down on it," he said. "I run around with little coasters so that doesn't happen."

And he isn't concerned that all of his friends will line up, waiting their turn to sit in the $1.1 million chair?

"Most people don't even know," he said. "I'm sure that if I don't point it out to them, they'll never realize that the chair cost a million dollars."

But doesn't that get to the point of all this? Doesn't he wonder what the average person thinks about a man who would pay $1.1 million for a chair?

"I know that some people probably would think it's crazy," Nicholson said.

And that's okay with him?

"The chair is well worth the price to me," he said. "On the day it arrives, I will mix myself a drink, sit down in the chair, and try to fantasize about who may have sat in it in the centuries before."

# Final Edition

The first newspaper that ever gave me a job was dying. The Columbus *Citizen-Journal*—perennially second in circulation, advertising linage, and news columns to the dominant Columbus *Dispatch*—was going out of business. On a Monday the staff would put out the final edition; it would be delivered to subscribers on Tuesday morning, and that would be that.

I got on a plane and flew to Ohio. I walked into the newsroom and asked if they would mind if I wrote a column for the last paper. They said that would be fine; they seemed a little confused that I would be there, but they said it would be fine.

I was seventeen years old; the year was 1964. I had been hired for the summer as a copyboy at the *Citizen-Journal*. I arrived at the newspaper building and walked into the city room. This was before the days of computer terminals and video-display screens. As I entered the room I was greeted with the sound of a floorful of typewriters banging away; the smell of pastepots that sat atop every desk; the sight of men and women talking into telephones that were cradled between their shoulders and their ears.

At that precise moment, I fell in love. I had not yet spoken to a single person in the room, but I knew for sure that this was what I wanted to do for the rest of my life: work in rooms like this room, with people like these people.

*  *  *

Now, on the last day of the *Citizen-Journal*, I sat on the edge of a desk and looked around the room again. Little had changed. Small things like the design of the tiles on the floor brought a rush of memories to me. I glanced up at the big clock hanging from the ceiling. The first deadline clock I had ever seen.

The city room of the *Citizen-Journal* was the most exciting place I had ever been in my life; to a seventeen-year-old it seemed like the hugest room in the world, vast, a force of nature. Now as I sat there, watching the people ready to pack their things and move out, I realized it was just another city room in the headquarters of another dying newspaper. But somehow the room seemed as close to me as my old bedroom in the house where I grew up. The warmth and good feelings were the same.

Sam Perdue, who started working at the old Columbus *Citizen* in 1951 and who now was sixty-four years old, was wandering around the city room aimlessly. A young reporter asked him what he was doing.

"Just watching it all, like sand into the sea," Perdue said.

Sam had been one of the first people to teach me the basics of looking for good stories. Once, when I had been sitting at my desk doing nothing, Sam had asked me what I was working on. "Nothing," I had replied. "I don't have anything to write."

Sam had stared at me. "Nothing to write?" he had said. He had gestured toward the windows, out toward the streets of Columbus. "There are people out there!" he had said. It was a lesson I never forgot.

Now, on his last day of work, Sam paced around the room. I approached him, and he said, "You know, Bob, I never learned how to sell the sizzle on the steak. I just saw myself as a working stiff. I don't know what I'm going to do now. Maybe I'll try TV. If they want an old guy with white hair."

A reporter named Thomas Holden was sitting at his desk. His phone rang. The caller was a woman from a dental association.

"Do we want to do a story on periodontal disease?" Holden said into the telephone. "Ma'am, in the first place, we just did a story on teeth. And in the second place, our newspaper is going out of business today."

I went back to the photo lab to visit with Dick Garrett and Hank Reichard. Dick had begun work at the old Columbus *Citizen* in 1946, the year before I was born; Hank had come to the paper in 1951.

We talked back and forth, and I realized that I wasn't able to say what I was really thinking: how when I was first allowed to go out on stories with one or the other of them, riding on the passenger side of the front seat while they drove, I thought that was the coolest thing a person could ever do. Cruising around the city, with nothing in mind other than finding stories we could give to our readers the next morning ... I couldn't believe we were getting paid to have that much fun.

Now Hank was developing a picture he had just taken; the picture was of a man named Ronald O'Brien taking the oath of office as city attorney. It would run in the final edition. On the back of the photo, where for his entire career Hank had written "Photo by Hank Reichard," he now took a pencil and wrote "Last photo by Hank Reichard."

Dick Garrett said, "It's funny. I don't even own my cameras. They've always belonged to the company. After I turn them in today, I'm going to have to go out and buy a camera to take pictures of the grandkids."

I walked back out into the city room, to look for a desk where I could write my column. I realized that I didn't know the largest percentage of the staff; most of them were younger reporters who had come to the paper after I had left.

One of them, Julie Hauserman, said, "This morning my alarm radio went off, and the first story on the news was about the *Citizen-Journal* dying. They said it ... and then they went on to the next news item. And it occurred to me: There are other stories. The city goes on. We're not the only story in town. We're just another story."

Someone had a tape player turned on; the Rolling Stones' "Sympathy for the Devil" was playing.

"We need something else," a reporter called out. "How about Bob Seger's 'The Famous Final Scene'?"

Another voice called, "How about the Doors' 'The End'?"

And yet sitting around the periphery of the room were some more of the old-timers, to whom those song titles meant nothing. One of them said, "Looks like I ought to finish this damn story while there's still a newspaper around to put it in."

Bill Keesee, who had been an assistant city editor while I was at the paper, reminded me of the time there was a riot at the Ohio Penitentiary. He recalled that he had been on the golf course when the riot started, and that he had hurried into the office and assigned me to get over to the pen. We exchanged a few sentences about how that story had been covered, but then there didn't seem to be very much else to say.

I found a seat and began writing my column.


As I was writing, a reader of the paper appeared at the city-room reception desk, lugging a case of champagne. "I just want to thank you all for putting out a good newspaper," he said, and was gone.

"You know," said Susan Prentice, another of the younger staff members, who had grown up in Columbus, "this is the only place I ever wanted to work in my life."

I knew what she meant. Of all the nice things that have happened to me during my time as a reporter, none of them would have happened if the *Citizen-Journal* hadn't given me a chance when I was starting out. The first stories I ever had in print were on the pages of the *Citizen-Journal*; the first interviews I ever conducted were conducted on behalf of the *Citizen-Journal*. The first time I had a front-page article I thought I was in heaven.

It can happen to a kid. A kid can walk into a room like this, and it can happen. And it's funny; although I have traveled all over the world in search of stories, part of me is always still sitting in the city room of the *Citizen-Journal*, silently wondering if the editor on the desk will think my story is good enough to warrant a by-line.


At 2:30 P.M., by arrangement, television and radio reporters and outside photographers were allowed into the newsroom for a half hour of interviewing and picture-taking. For the allotted thirty minutes, this brightened up the atmosphere. People talked into TV cameras, and the champagne was popped and poured into paper cups, and staff members took snapshots of each other and exchanged addresses and phone numbers. Someone even threw some confetti.

Then, precisely at 3:00 P.M., the visiting reporters were escorted out of the room by building security guards. The champagne was still in the cups, and the confetti was on the floor, but now it was deadly quiet.

Arlen Pennell, a staff photographer, asked everyone to gather in front of the city desk for a final team photo. He posed everyone, and then walked into the shot himself, clicking his camera with a remote-control switch.

Now it was late afternoon. One by one, people were leaving. They carried boxes and bags. I finished my column and turned it in to the copy desk.

I went into the men's room—the men's room where I had washed out so many pastepots during that first summer as a copyboy. Someone had scrawled on the mirror, with soap, C-J LIVES!

There was nothing for anyone to do. A skeleton crew would be there during the nighttime hours, getting the edition ready to go to press. But for most of the reporters and editors, it was over.

"I just don't want to walk out of here," said Susan Prentice.

Frank Gabrenya, the entertainment writer, stood by the door in his overcoat, not moving. "Getting the coat on was easy," he said.

Reporter Jack Torry said, "I can't stand this. I can't stand this. I know there must be worse things in the world than this, but I can't stand it."

I walked back to my hotel. I had a drink in the bar, and watched some television. I tried to read a book.

Something kept telling me, though, that I ought to go back to the city room. There would be nothing for me to do there; that I knew. But it just seemed that as long as the room was still there, I should be there.

So I walked back—walked back to the newspaper building, and took the elevator up to the mezzanine, and pushed open that same glass door I had first pushed open when I was seventeen. The same words were painted on the glass: CITIZEN-JOURNAL. EDITORIAL DEPARTMENT.

I had been right. Virtually everyone was gone. There were four, maybe six people remaining.

I walked around the city room. Up on the wall was the long piece of cardboard with all the important phone numbers inked on it: Police, Fire Department, Sheriff's Department, Jail, Clerk of Courts, State Highway Patrol, all the local hospitals, FBI, National Weather Service.

I feel so implausibly lucky to be allowed to do the kind of work that I do. Newspapering, at its best, is a kind of prolonged adolescence; when you're on deadline with a good story, you never feel completely grown up. You're a kid again—the adrenaline is flowing and the energy is total, and you're a kid doing the thing that you do best.

I first got that feeling in the city room of the *Citizen-Journal*—the city room where right now the phones weren't ringing and the voices weren't sounding. At about 11:30 copies of the final edition were delivered up from the pressroom. The front page looked good—the top half was a photo of the nighttime skyline of the city, and the headline, superimposed in white, said, GOODBYE, COLUMBUS.

The remaining staff members started to leave. They told me that there was a wake for the newspaper going on up on High Street, at a bar called Mellman's. They said I was welcome to join them.

But I couldn't leave. I couldn't leave. I looked up at that old deadline clock; it said that the time was 11:47 P.M. I thought to myself: Sure, it will happen again to some other kid somewhere. But it will never happen in this room again. Isn't this something, I thought. The paper's dead, and everyone's gone. And I can't leave.

# The Friends of
# Engelbert Humperdinck

$A$t seven o'clock on the morning of the moonlight cruise, Millie Krisor, sixty-nine, awakened in room 373 of Northwest Community Hospital in Arlington Heights, Illinois. Mrs. Krisor, who is co-president of the You Made It Happen In Chicagoland, Enge! fan club, had been hospitalized for pneumonia and leg pains.

She was not feeling at all well. But as she looked around the room, she was determined that the moonlight cruise was not going to leave without her.

At the same moment, Engelbert Humperdinck, forty-nine, slept in his suite at the Ritz-Carlton Hotel in downtown Chicago.

Humperdinck would be presenting a concert that night at the Arie Crown Theater. It had been a number of years since he had had a major hit record. But he had figured out a way to keep assuring himself respectable crowds when he sang.

He encouraged and courted fan clubs around the country—one of which was the You Made It Happen In Chicagoland, Enge! club. Most of the members of the clubs were women in their forties, fifties, and sixties who considered Humperdinck to be—as his publicists phrased it—the King of Romance. The fan club members would purchase every record that Humperdinck released; would buy tickets to every concert that Humperdinck gave; would recruit other people to go to the concerts. They would call radio stations and demand—of often disbelieving disc jockeys—that records by Engelbert Humperdinck be played on the air.

In return for their loyalty, the fans asked only that Humperdinck treat them as living, breathing people—that he socialize with them, talk with them, be their friend. Tonight the moonlight cruise, arranged by the You Made It Happen In Chicagoland, Enge! club, would be leaving from a dock behind the Arie Crown Theater immediately following the concert. Some 210 fans would be on board—as would Humperdinck. The fans had invited him, and he had said yes.

For the outing, a 150-foot-long cruiser had been chartered by the fan club. The ship had three decks, two of them enclosed. A midnight supper would be served on board; there would be an open bar, plus a selection of eight appetizers and salads, three vegetables, three potatoes, four entrées, and a dessert buffet. The ship would navigate Lake Michigan for two hours.

"If I weren't going on the moonlight cruise tonight?" Engelbert Humperdinck said. We were riding in the back seat of his limousine, on the way to the concert.

"If I weren't going on the cruise, I suppose I'd go out after the show, have dinner somewhere, perhaps go to the nicest disco in town and see what happens. But the club has asked me to go on the cruise, so I am going on the cruise."

Humperdinck was wearing a black pinstripe suit and three gold rings. He said that his principal residence was in Los Angeles. "I live in Jayne Mansfield's old house," he said. "The one they used to call the Pink Palace.

"I took a lot of the heart-shaped situations out. The heart-shaped swimming pool is still there. But the heart-shaped bathtub and the heart-shaped fireplace—they were hardly masculine."

The limousine pulled into McCormick Place, the convention-center complex that houses the Arie Crown Theater. A banner across the front of the hall welcomed the National Plastics Exposition and Conference. The limo stopped next to a stage door.

Humperdinck left the car and began to walk through a cavernous backstage area. An usher in a sport coat, holding a clipboard, was standing in the middle of the area. Apparently he had been assigned to keep unauthorized people away from the dressing rooms.

"Excuse me," the usher said, stepping in front of Humperdinck. "Are you the comedian?"

Humperdinck's face turned to ice. He kept walking. When he got to another man in a sport coat, he said, "That person back there—could you remove him, please? He's sort of rude."

In Humperdinck's dressing room was a stuffed toy camel, left for him by members of the You Made It Happen In Chicagoland, Enge! club. Humperdinck picked it up and displayed it. There was a card attached to the camel's neck. The card said: "Chicagoland is Humpy-Land."

"Humpy," Humperdinck explained. "Hump like in camel, and hump like in Humperdinck."


A comedian named Johnny Dark opened the show for Humperdinck. He informed the crowd of some 3,800 that Humperdinck had been named "one of the three sexiest men in the world by a national magazine."

Humperdinck then came out and sang and danced for the audience. The crowd responded most enthusiastically to his rendition of his biggest hit, "(Please) Release Me," which was first played on the radio in January 1967.


Forty-five minutes after the end of the concert, Humperdinck and his companions were lost somewhere in the sprawling McCormick Place complex. The group had set out on foot for the exit leading to the ship, had made several wrong turns, and was now in the middle of a lobby area. No one had any idea how to get to the boat.


On board the ship, docked in the water behind the theater, Millie Krisor was waiting. She had obtained a six-hour pass from the hospital; she wore her hospital identification bracelet on her right wrist.

"I started the You Made It Happen In Chicagoland, Enge! club because my children were grown and married, and there was a void in my life," she said. "Then I saw Engelbert perform, and I thought: My God, I have never seen anyone in my life who appeals to me like that."

*    *    *

Humperdinck and his companions, having finally found their way out of the building, walked down a path to the ship.

The women on board lined the railings. Like Mrs. Krisor, they wore fancy clothes—mostly cocktail dresses, and even a few evening gowns. When they saw Humperdinck, they applauded.

Humperdinck stopped by the side of the ship and looked up at the women, as if surprised to find them there.

"Where are we going?" he called.

"Anywhere," they called back. "Anywhere you want."

Humperdinck walked up a gangway onto the ship and began to circulate. The women mostly stared at him; there was no screaming. Although it was crowded on board, it was almost silent.

Then a band began to play. The song was "Let's Hear It for the Boy." One of the female dancers from Humperdinck's stage show—Chris Soranno, a tall, striking blonde from Las Vegas—went out onto an area that had been cleared of chairs and tables and began an energetic, sexy dance. Around her neck she wore a necklace that featured the words POVERTY SUCKS. Three women from the You Made It Happen In Chicagoland, Enge! club joined her and danced all around her.

The ship pulled out onto Lake Michigan. Glenda Schowalter, forty-three, said, "Just about everything about Engelbert appeals to me. I think he has a fantastic voice, he's great to look at, and he's a nice person. I've never actually met him, but I've been to other club outings, and I'm proud to be one of his fans."

Humperdinck was led to a long head table, where he was served a glass of Rémy Martin cognac. He surveyed the room and said nothing.

"I had heard Engelbert's music, and I had seen him in Vegas," said Evelyn Hernandez, fifty-two. "I was interested in joining a club, and I wanted to find out more about him—where I could see him, and information like that. At a club doing like this, I don't have to talk to him personally—although I have met him once, in Cleveland. But the point of coming to an event like this is not to make personal contact. It's to be a part of the club activity."

Many of the women carried souvenir programs from the concert, which had been sold for five dollars a copy. The center spread of the program was a color shot of Humperdinck wearing a dark-blue bathrobe, his chest and legs exposed, a huge gold cross around his neck, a snifter of cognac in his hand. Some of the women seemed to want to get Humperdinck to autograph the photograph. But the way he was sitting at the head table—staring straight ahead, seemingly almost hypnotized—discouraged them.

Alone at a table far from Humperdinck was Irma Wetherton, sixty-nine. "I love Engelbert," she said. "I shook hands with him tonight as he got onto the boat. He said, 'Hi,' and I have no words to tell you how it made me feel. I live by myself, and Engelbert means just about everything to me. He looks beautiful tonight, but he always looks beautiful. I wish I could take him home with me."

The meal was served. For almost everyone on the ship it was a buffet, but waiters brought platters to Humperdinck at the head table and allowed him to make his selections while seated.

Humperdinck continued to say very little. He just kept looking out at the people. The ship made circles in Lake Michigan.

Debbie Wright, thirty-one, said that she was the vice-president of a splinter club called Eternally Engelbert. "We're a little more subtle," she said.

She said she thought she had figured out why Humperdinck came to events like this one:

"He seems to truly realize that his life has been granted to him by us."

Perhaps that was what was going through Humperdinck's mind as he looked at the women who were looking at him. There was still not much noise in the room. The women simply sat at their tables and stared at Humperdinck.

He had become slightly more animated as the cruise progressed. A woman named Judy Way, forty-two, was wearing a low-cut gown; Humperdinck had taken a black pen and signed his name across the left side of her chest.

And now he picked up a microphone and moved it to his mouth. First he sang the opening bars to one of his songs, "Portofino." The women applauded.

Then he turned to the woman in the seat next to him. This was Millie Krisor, still wearing her hospital bracelet.

"Millie," Humperdinck said into the microphone.

He began to sing a song, apparently composing the words as he went along. The song was directed at Mrs. Krisor; verse by verse it became increasingly bawdy and lascivious. Humperdinck sang, "You're going to be in your hospital bed in a couple of hours . . ."; he sang, "We're going to take your panties off. . . ." Humperdinck gazed into Mrs. Krisor's eyes as he sang. She blushed. There was laughter in the room, although several of the women began to look slightly puzzled.

The boat headed for shore. It rocked into place in the dock behind the theater. The women moved slowly toward the gangway. It was 1:30 A.M.

The women did not attempt to say good-bye to Humperdinck. They just filed off the ship and walked toward the parking garage.

Humperdinck, too, walked off the ship. Surrounded by members of his traveling party, he went quickly to his limousine and slipped inside.

He sat in the back seat, wearing tinted aviator-style glasses. Some of the women passed the car, bending down as they did to peer inside and get one last look at him.

The chauffeur started the engine and pulled away.

The limousine passed a group of the women trying to hail a cab. They called Humperdinck's name.

"I always sleep with a light on in my room," Humperdinck said. "It started when I was a kid. I can't fall asleep unless there's a light on."

# Growing Up Is Hard to Do

The news had broken that Ann Landers was leaving her home newspaper of thirty-one years, the Chicago *Sun-Times*, to join the paper for which I work, the Chicago *Tribune*. A letter was hand-delivered to my desk; the letter was from the president of the *Tribune*, Charles Brumback, and it said that there was going to be a reception to welcome Landers to the paper that very afternoon, at 2:30 P.M. I was invited.

So when the proper hour arrived, I rode the elevator to the twentieth floor of Tribune Tower and joined a roomful of people. Virtually all of the men were dressed in suits and ties, and the women in nice dresses. I had not worn a sport coat to work that day—I almost never do—so I was at the reception wearing corduroy slacks, a shirt, and a loosened tie.

Ann Landers entered the room and made a short speech, and then champagne was served. My colleague Mike Royko was about twenty feet away from me. I raised my hand to gesture hello. Royko called out, "Why don't you put a jacket on and grow up?"

He may have been joking (he may very well not have been joking). And he may not have known it, but he was touching on something that had been bouncing around my mind in the weeks prior to the Ann Landers reception. The fact is, my fortieth birthday was fast approaching, and I still did not feel grown-up. I had been vaguely aware of this all through my thirties, but now it seemed to me that a forty-year-old should definitely be a grown-up, and yet I clearly did not qualify. Even if, as Royko suggested, I had put on a jacket, I still would not have felt like a grown-up at the party. But how old are you supposed to be before you become a grown-up in your own head?

I got a chance to ponder this some more in the days following the Landers reception when, out of the blue, I received a letter from Jeff O'Hara.

Jeff O'Hara was a guy I went to high school with. He was a quiet sort—we were in physics class together. In 1985, when my graduating class had its twenty-year reunion, there was a mini-yearbook handed out that detailed where everyone was living and what they were doing.

Some members of the class, though, were "among the missing." No one had been able to locate them. The assumption was that they had sort of dropped off the face of the earth; life had not treated them well, and no one had any idea of how to find them.

Jeff O'Hara was among the missing in the reunion mini-yearbook. I remember thinking: Gee, isn't it surprising that a nice fellow like Jeff O'Hara would end up as a derelict or something. Jeff O'Hara—couldn't be found.

So when Jeff O'Hara's letter arrived, I was interested to look at the stationery and to note that he had not, indeed, been consigned to some urban skid row. Jeff O'Hara, his letterhead informed me, is president of Red Lobster U.S.A.

I knew I had to talk to him. Here was a guy my own age, and he was president of Red Lobster. How do you do that? How do you be a president of a huge corporation? How do you decide that you're grown-up enough for such a job?

I called him at his company's headquarters in Orlando, Florida. We joked about the fact that the reunion committee had been unable to locate him. I told him that the real reason I was calling was that I was having these thoughts about being a grown-up. Could you be approaching your fortieth birthday and still feel like a kid?

"There are days that I wonder about that, too," Jeff said.

He said those words, yes, but still, he was president of Red Lobster. "Can I ask you something, Jeff?" I said.

"Sure," he said.

"How many people work for you?" I said.

"Thirty-four thousand," he said.

There it was, right there. Jeff O'Hara has thirty-four thousand men and women working for him. I sit in front of a computer screen and write little stories.

He said that there are 387 Red Lobster restaurants in the United States, and that the company does almost $1 billion in annual sales. But then, in the next breath, he said, "I remember high school like yesterday. I still can't believe that I have kids."

"What do you wear to work every day?" I said.

"A suit," he said.

"Never even a sport coat and slacks?" I said.

"No, it's always a suit," he said.

"How many suits do you own?" I said.

He laughed. "You're serious?" he said.

"Yes," I said. "I have to know."

"Ten suits," he said. "Maybe twelve suits."

I asked what he was going to be doing that afternoon.

"I have to make a speech to President Reagan's Committee on Employment of the Handicapped," he said.

"Did you write the speech?" I said.

"No," Jeff said. "I have someone who writes my speeches. I fine-tune them."

I asked Jeff if Red Lobster's public relations department could send me a picture of him. I had to see what he looked like now.

The photo arrived the next day via an overnight delivery service. Jeff O'Hara definitely looks like the president of a major corporation. And boy, does he wear a suit well.


So I kept thinking about Jeff O'Hara and his grown-up job, and then it occurred to me that I knew someone who had a job even more grown-up than president of Red Lobster U.S.A.

When I was a beginning reporter for the Chicago *Sun-Times*, there was another twenty-two-year-old rookie on the staff. His name was Doug Woodlock. We would chase around the city hustling for by-lines, and we would eat lunch together almost every day. We thought we were two hotshots. Greene and Woodlock, kid reporters, knocking on journalism's door.

Except that now Greene is still writing stories and hustling for by-lines, and Woodlock? He is federal judge Douglas P. Woodlock, assigned to the U.S. District Court in Boston.

Now . . . how can you look in the mirror in the morning and deal with the fact that a federal judge is looking back at you? I called Doug, and he gave me a quick accounting of his career path: Georgetown Law School, law clerk for federal judge Frank Murray in Boston, attorney with Goodwin, Procter & Hoar in Boston, assistant U.S. attorney in Boston specializing in prosecuting political corruption and organized crime, back to Goodwin, Procter & Hoar, and then the nomination to the federal bench.

"When I was starting out as a reporter, I used to go chasing people's stories," Doug said. "The difference now is that people bring their stories to me."

I asked how he could sit up there on the bench and make decisions that affect the courses of people's lives.

"If not me, then who?" he said. "It's institutional. When you start hearing your first cases, there is a period of time when you wonder if the people in the courtroom will think there's an imposter on the bench. But then you figure it out: someone's got to play the role. So I do."

I asked him how he found out that he was being named a federal judge. He said that he had been hearing rumors about it for months. Then, on the day of the Boston Marathon, he was alone in his law office.

"The phone rang, and I picked it up myself," he said. "A voice said, 'This is the White House calling. Can you hold?' I said that I could. A few moments later, another voice said, 'Mr. Woodlock, this is Ronald Reagan. I've got a piece of paper on my desk that I've just signed, and I think you might be interested in it. It's your nomination to be a U.S. district judge for the district of Massachusetts.' I said, 'Thank you very much, Mr. President. This is an honor to my family and my friends. I hope I'll justify your faith in me.' And the President said, 'I'm sure you will. Congratulations.' And in a twinkling he was gone."

I thought back to all of our hurried lunches after the first-edition deadlines in 1969 Chicago. I thought of him now, sitting in his courtroom. And as soon as I got that mental picture, I had to ask him.

"Where do you get your robes?" I said.

"Actually, I had a hell of a time," he said. "I didn't know who to ask. So I asked another judge named Dave Nelson. I asked him where he got his robes. He said that he used to get them from the Cardinal's tailor, but the Cardinal had died, and then his tailor had died. So I just phoned a men's store—Paul Carr, it's called—and asked them. I'd bought suits and shirts there before. I told them that I took a size forty suit, and they said they'd take care of everything. And one day I went and I picked up my robes."

"How could you tell if the robes fit?" I said.

"Well," Doug said, "they weren't too small. I could tell that. They go down to my kneecaps—actually a little below the knee."

"What do you do?" I said. "Slip the robe over your head?"

"No, there's a zipper in front," he said.

"Is it at all weird for you to hear people calling you Judge Woodlock?" I said.

"That's a strange transition," he said. "At first I would feel funny when the court officers would say 'Your Honor.' I'd look over my shoulder to see who they were speaking to. But it's like everything else. You get used to it."

I asked him if he ever thought about what might have happened had he remained a newspaperman.

"I think I would have worn myself down, like shoe leather, working the streets," he said. "There is a problem for journalists, I think. There comes a point when a journalist says to himself, 'All I've ever done is observe. Can I *do*?' And that breeds either an inferiority complex, or it breeds cynicism. At first the cynicism is just a style you affect, but then you internalize it. You really do become that cynical. You are no longer able to be moved, or to laugh as much, or to care about events. Once you've gone to five hundred fires and seen five hundred tragedies, a shell builds around you. I didn't want that to happen to me."

I asked him if that couldn't happen to judges, too.

"I'm sure it can," he said. "I imagine that once you've been on the bench and done twenty years of sentencing, maybe you don't take it so seriously."

I hadn't even thought about that aspect of his job. I knew he was a judge, and yet I hadn't considered the fact that he sent people away to prison.

"The first long sentence I gave was eight years," he said. "The crime was bank robbery. I'll admit it to you: I lost sleep before passing sentence, and I lost sleep afterward. It's a terribly intimidating responsibility to fulfill."

\*    \*    \*

Both Jeff O'Hara and Doug Woodlock wrote to me after our conversations. The letters were friendly in tone, but underneath the words I got the feeling that they had been considering what we had spoken about. Three of us, each about to turn forty, each having taken different paths.

When I had called Judge Woodlock in his chambers and he had come to the phone, I had immediately and involuntarily said, "Hey, Dougie." It's the way I had always greeted him when we were beginning reporters together. Now I suppose that seldom happens to him.

Mike Royko at the Ann Landers reception: "Why don't you put a jacket on and grow up?" It's funny how a throwaway sentence can start you thinking. . . .

# Tip of the Cap

$\mathbf{H}$ow many of us can claim to have changed anything really cool in the world—much less something as cool as the baseball caps that Major League players wear? John Nash Ott can. He is seventy-eight years old, he lives in Sarasota, Fla., and his story . . . well, read on.

John Nash Ott is a retired banker who heads up something called the Light Research Foundation. He has all these theories about the nature of light and how light affects human health and behavior. He tried to explain all of this to me, but frankly I got a headache trying to under-stand. Maybe I need more light.

Anyway . . . according to John Nash Ott, he received a visit in the early 1970s from a man named Rex Bowen, who was a scout for the Cincinnati Reds. The two of them began discussing the nature of light, and Rex Bowen brought up the subject of baseball caps. He explained that traditionally the undersides of the visors on the caps worn by Major League players were green.

John Nash Ott said this was all wrong. He said that if the underside of a visor on a baseball cap was green, it could harm the performance of the baseball player.

"The color can cause malillumination," Ott explained to me. "Do you know what malnutrition means? It's when things are lacking in your diet—things you should have. Malillumination is the same thing, but with light."

Apparently John Nash Ott persuaded Rex Bowen, the Cincinnati scout, that the Reds would do much better if the undersides of their cap visors were gray. Apparently Rex Bowen persuaded the Reds' front office to give it a try. According to legend, when the Reds started wearing baseball caps with gray undersides on the visors, batting averages improved, running speed improved, mental alertness improved, and they won the pennant.

"It's really very simple," John Nash Ott said to me. "The light is reflected off the underside of the visor. There are neurochemical reactions that channel through the retinas of the eyes. This connects with the master glands. The pineal and the pituitary glands help control the entire endocrine system, which in turn controls the basic body chemistry."

And all this happens differently if the underside of the visor is gray instead of green?

"Of course," John Nash Ott said.

I said that there was something I didn't understand. (Actually, there were many things I didn't understand, but I just chose this one.)

"How is light supposed to reflect off the *underside* of a baseball cap visor?" I asked. "Doesn't light come from above?"

"Oh, there's a lot of light reflected from the underside of the visor," John Nash Ott said. "There's the natural reflection of light bouncing off the ground. If a batter holds his head up, or if a fielder looks up to catch a fly ball, the light will reflect off the underside of the visor."

The upshot of all this is that, according to published reports, other baseball teams began to follow the Reds—and now the majority of teams in the National League, plus several in the American League, insist upon gray undersides in player cap visors.

Even though I had read about this, it seemed pretty unlikely. So I checked with the company that manufactures caps for twenty-three of the twenty-six Major League baseball teams: the New Era Cap Company, in Derby, New York. I spoke with the firm's vice-president, Valerie Koch.

"It's true," she said. "It's a very strange deal, but it's true. The teams think it helps to have gray on the undersides of the visors instead of green. They must believe it works. The Astros changed to it last year, Kansas City has it, Pittsburgh has had it for a while. . . . We're seeing more and more of it."

And it all started with John Nash Ott. I asked him if he felt a surge of pride every time he watched a baseball game on television and saw the gray underside of a player's cap visor.

"I never watch baseball games on television," he said.

Well, then, I said, how about baseball games he's attended in person?

"I can't remember ever having been to a baseball game," he said. "I was never a great baseball fan, and I'm not a great baseball fan today."

Surely, though, it must be a thrill to know that all those Major League players feel he is helping to improve their skills.

"I've never heard from a single baseball player," he said. "They're probably unaware of the fact that the color on the undersides of their visors has even changed."

But certainly there are days when he gazes at a baseball cap in the privacy of his own home, and thinks about what he has accomplished.

"I don't own a baseball cap," he said. "They showed me one once, but no one ever sent me one."

Wouldn't he like one?

"Now that you mention it, that might be nice," he said. "I think I ought to look into getting one. I don't play baseball, so I don't really need one. But it might be fun to wear it around the house."

# Good Golly

There are some things even I won't do.

Mrs. Bobbie Novak, of Wheaton, Illinois, is a woman who wants very much to make her little daughter happy. The daughter, Becky, is six years old, and will be turning seven in August. The family plans a nice ice-cream-and-cake birthday party in the backyard for all of Becky's playmates.

There's a slight problem, though. There is one person Becky has invited to her party, and that person has not responded.

"Becky really wants Little Richard to come to the party," Mrs. Novak said.

I thought I was hearing things.

"Becky sent a letter to Little Richard, and she checks the mailbox every day to see if he can come to her birthday," Mrs. Novak said. "But there's never a letter."

Little Richard, for the two or three of you who don't already know it, is the wild-eyed rock-and-roll star who hit it big in the Fifties and who has seemed to get stranger and stranger over the years. I deal with a lot of weird people as part of my job, but there is no way I am going to try to get Little Richard to come to Becky Novak's seventh birthday party.

"You don't really want Little Richard at the party, do you?" I said to Mrs. Novak.

"It's not me," she said. "It's Becky."

Wheaton is a conservative, well-to-do suburb—sort of like the neighborhood in "Leave It To Beaver," but with more money. How does a six-year-old girl in Wheaton fall in love with Little Richard?

"My husband bought a 'Little Richard's Greatest Hits' tape last year," Mrs. Novak said. "Becky became addicted to it. She makes us crazy with the tape. It's the first thing she plays in the morning when she's getting dressed. We hear 'Good Golly Miss Molly' and 'Tutti Frutti' blasting all over the house."

I asked Mrs. Novak if she was a Little Richard fan. "I saw him back in the Fifties when he appeared on television," she said. "I remember that skinny mustache and that wild hair and cape. I never imagined I would have a daughter who would become infatuated with him. But she really wants him at the birthday party, and I thought perhaps you knew him."

"We've only met once," I said. Which is true. I was supposed to be on a television show in Washington a few years back, and the makeup people worked out of a trailer. I entered the trailer to wait my turn. The man who was in the chair finished getting made up, and turned toward me. Little Richard, with this odd gleam in his eye and a really disturbing grin. I shook his hand quickly, said "Pleased to meet you, Mr. Penniman," and got right out of there.

"So if you know him, maybe you could get him to come to Becky's party," Mrs. Novak said.

"I'm not going near this thing," I said.

I did agree to speak with young Becky herself. "He's my best singer and I love him," Becky said.

"Becky," I said, "don't you like Michael Jackson?"

"No way," she said.

"What about Madonna?" I said.

"No," she said.

She said her favorite Little Richard song is "Long Tall Sally," but that she also is very impressed with "Slippin' and Slidin' " and "Jenny, Jenny, Jenny."

"I'm not asking him to sing at my birthday party," Becky said. "I just want him to be there as a guest."

Her father, Dan Novak, who owns a Baskin-Robbins store, concurred. "All Becky wants is for him to sit at the picnic tables in the backyard with her other friends."

"I don't believe this," I said. Mrs. Novak was talking again; she said that Becky carries a tape player with her all the time, constantly listening to Little Richard at top volume. "On Sundays we go to St. John the Baptist Church," Mrs. Novak said. "Becky wears her nice little Sunday dress. But the whole way to church she sits in the car playing Little Richard songs."

I said it to Mrs. Novak one more time: I will not try to get Little Richard to come to Becky's seventh birthday party.

"Well, who else are we going to get for the party?" Mrs. Novak said.

"Who *else* are you going to get?" I said. "How about a magician?"

"Becky really wants Little Richard to be there," Mrs. Novak said.

"Awfully nice speaking with you," I said.

# Herman Gollob's Bar Mitzvah

On the morning of his bar mitzvah, Herman Gollob awakened at 4:30 A.M. He was understandably nervous, and he knew that he would be unable to fall asleep again. So he went into the bathroom and began to shave.

He started to spread a thick lather of Noxzema lime-scented foam over his face. In the mirror, he could see that the overnight stubble of his beard was coming in grayer than ever. Then—as he had done virtually every morning for the past forty-four years—he took his razor and began on the left side of his face, directly beneath the sideburn.

The hours seemed to drag. Finally, at 9:00, Gollob climbed behind the wheel of his Plymouth Horizon and drove the short distance to his temple—Congregation Shomrei Emunah in Montclair, New Jersey. He felt like making the drive alone. His wife and his children would follow later. Gollob, fifty-eight, wanted to think about the upcoming ceremony in solitude.

"I guess you never realize what you're suppressing all along," Gollob explained one evening not long after his bar mitzvah was over. "I guess you don't even let yourself think about it."

Born in Waco, Texas, in 1930, Gollob moved with his parents to Houston when he was three. "My father had very little to do with the Jewish community," Gollob said, more than a trace of the Southwest still

204

in his voice. "He did not believe in organized religion. Our family did not belong to a temple. But Dad was always proud of being a Jew. He always said never to run from a fight, and never to deny your Jewishness." Gollob's father was a lawyer, and on the wall of his office he displayed a framed quotation: DO JUSTLY, LOVE MERCY, AND WALK HUMBLY WITH THY GOD.

Herman, who had no brothers or sisters, grew up never attending synagogue, and when he was of college age he enrolled at Texas A&M. He graduated in 1951 with a degree in English, then served in Korea as a lieutenant with the Air Force. After the war he went to California, seeking a career in some aspect of show business.

"My dad always thought that some of the great western movies were modeled after biblical stories," Gollob said. "When I went to Hollywood, my dad said to me, 'If you ever run into George Stevens, ask him if he had biblical images in mind when he directed *Shane*.' I never did meet George Stevens, but I was at a party with Alan Ladd one night. I said, 'Mr. Ladd, did George Stevens have the Bible in mind when he was directing *Shane*?' And Ladd said, 'I haven't got the faintest idea, kid. What are you drinking?' "

Gollob eventually moved East and went into the book-publishing industry. He is currently senior vice-president and editor in chief of Doubleday. In that executive position he had the authority to give himself two days off on the Thursday and Friday before his bar mitzvah.


"Several years ago, some good friends of ours invited us to their son's bar mitzvah," Gollob said. "As hard as it is to believe, I had never been to a bar mitzvah. The experience of seeing the ceremony . . . it was a feeling of awe. The beauty and the pageantry of the ceremony overwhelmed me. I got the shivers."

Traditionally, Jewish boys are bar mitzvahed when they reach the age of thirteen—the phrase that is often spoken is, "Today I am a man." Gollob, in his mid-fifties, felt a yearning that startled him. Unbeknownst to his wife, Barbara, he sent away for some mail-order tapes.

"The tapes were in Hebrew—one of them was Richard Tucker chanting the sabbath melodies," Gollob said. "I got some books too. Every Saturday morning in the den of our house, I began to observe the sabbath by myself. I was sort of struggling, trying to learn the Hebrew.

Barbara thought it was truly odd. It seemed very strange to her. Too solitary."

So, for the first time, the Gollobs joined a temple. Soon after, Herman Gollob decided that it was time for him to be bar mitzvahed.

"This is a man of tremendous skill and willpower," said Rabbi Joshua Chasan of Congregation Shomrei Emunah. "I knew that once he set his mind to doing this, he would follow it through to its completion."

It was Rabbi Chasan who guided Gollob through his bar mitzvah training. The rabbi was accustomed to training children for the ceremony. But Gollob, his new pupil, was sixteen years older than Rabbi Chasan. Nevertheless, for an entire year Gollob would go to the temple and study with the rabbi. In addition, Gollob would practice on his own, two and a half hours a day, seven days a week.

"I would ride the bus from New Jersey to my office in Manhattan very early," he said. "I would play my Hebrew tapes and listen to them through headphones. I'd be at my office by seven. No one else was around. I'd close my door and chant. One morning one of the secretaries arrived a little before her usual time. She knocked on the door and said, 'Are you singing?' "

On business trips, Gollob would take his tapes, as well as photocopies of the religious service. "I'd sit in my hotel room and just do it," he said. "In years past, I'd probably be downstairs hanging around the bar. Now I was up there chanting away."

He was getting better and better. But as the date of his bar mitzvah grew nearer, he found himself filled with anxiety.

"I suppose it was the fear of failure and humiliation," he said. "On the day of your bar mitzvah, you're up there for three and a half hours."

Never mind that he had risen to the heights of his chosen field; never mind that he had presided over literally hundreds of business presentations. "That didn't matter," he said. "This was completely different. I was like a little boy. I would wake up in the middle of the night in a panic."

Rabbi Chasan felt that Gollob had nothing to worry about. "As we worked together, I could hear the power in his singing," the rabbi said.

"It was so rich, it was so textured and so warm . . . I found myself wondering, 'How did this man come up with such an intuitive understanding of this music and this language and this ceremony?' I believe there is a way that we are connected with our past and with our heritage—a way that is not immediately understandable, but that is undeniable."

For many thirteen-year-old Jewish boys, the bar mitzvah is one part religious ceremony, one part social occasion. They invite their friends and schoolmates; their parents invite their own friends. Often there are parties in the evening, with dancing and dinner.

"I wasn't going to do that," Gollob said. "I didn't invite anyone, although I let a couple of guys from work know about it. I sort of told them that they were welcome to come if they wanted." His bar mitzvah, in accordance with tradition, would be part of the regular Saturday services at the temple.

On the Thursday and Friday before the ceremony—the two days off he had taken from his job—he went to the synagogue and practiced in the sanctuary. "Several times during the rehearsals, I found myself crying," he said.

He wondered why he was feeling such deep emotion. From his lifetime knowledge of literature, he remembered some lines from the poet William Butler Yeats: "How but in custom and ceremony / Are innocence and beauty born?" Yeats had used the phrase "a radical innocence." That, Gollob thought, was what he was trying to find—an innocence so strong and so pure as to be almost radical.

But if that was what he was trying to find, what was he trying to escape?

Another literary passage came to mind—this one from Herman Melville in the novel *Moby Dick*. The words were from a soliloquy by Captain Ahab as he sat alone in his cabin, gazing out the stern windows, observing the excruciating beauty of the sunset upon the sea:

"This lovely light, it lights not me; all loveliness is anguish to me, since I can ne'er enjoy. Gifted with the high perception, I lack the low enjoying power; damned, most subtly and most malignantly! damned in the midst of Paradise!"

Gollob rehearsed and he wept and he rehearsed some more, and at 10:30 on Friday night he went to sleep.

\*    \*    \*

There were between seventy and eighty people in the temple on Saturday morning.

"I put on the prayer shawl and the skullcap," Gollob said. "As soon as I started, I knew it was going to be all right."

For three hours, he made his way through the ancient ceremony. Near the front of the congregation he could see his wife, his twenty-six-year-old daughter, Emily, and his twenty-four-year-old son, Jared. Both children had been living away from home, but had returned for their father's bar mitzvah.

"My son seemed to be riveted by what was going on," Gollob said. "The intensity with which he was looking at me was quite remarkable. My wife and daughter? I suppose you could call it pride. At least that's what it looked like to me."

When it was over, Gollob felt exuberant. He and his family stood in a receiving line with the rabbi and accepted the congratulations of the congregation. Back home he and his wife and children watched old family movies. Then, exhausted, he went upstairs and took a nap.


"A lot of people, jokingly, have asked me if the whole point of all this was to be able to say, 'Today I am a man.' "

Gollob was reflecting on what the experience had genuinely signified to him.

"That's not it, of course," he said. "What does that mean, really? What does that mean—to 'be a man'?

"Does it mean that you are ready to go out into the community and earn a living? I did that a long time ago. Does it mean reaching maturity? Some people never achieve that.

"No, it wasn't a matter of being more mature, or being more substantial, or being more pious. I think it was a lot simpler than that.

"In my life, I had touched all the bases except one. I had had a good career, a good marriage, good children, a good home. I had had all the fun and met all the responsibilities. Touched every one of those bases. Or so I told myself.

"But there was one little piece missing. One little piece I never filled in. You can cover it up and cover it up and cover it up. But that piece is still not there, no matter how hard you try to cover it up.

"This was a long time coming. This was something I felt I had shirked. I didn't even realize I felt that way. But I did. I must have. Somewhere inside me there was the feeling that I had an obligation, and that I had never fulfilled the obligation.

"And now I have. Or at least I've started."

# "Could You Direct Me to the Terror?"

Miami—We were off in search of America's terrifying future.

"I think it's about eight more blocks up the street," said my friend, who was driving the car and who lives in Miami.

"Let me check," I said.

I was carrying a newspaper clipping—a clipping I had brought down with me from the North. The clipping documented as graphic an example of the fear of crime in south Florida as I had ever read.

According to the clipping, people in the Miami–Ft. Lauderdale area have become so alarmed about crime that they have begun blocking off their streets—blocking off the streets with big metal barrels. The theory was that if criminals couldn't get into a neighborhood, then they couldn't rob the residents of that neighborhood.

This was something new—public streets being closed off to the public. "People are afraid," a police official was quoted as saying, approving the barricades. The clipping said that in one relatively affluent area, eighteen barricades were already in place, with another one hundred planned. That was the area we were looking for. The terrifying future of America—barricades on public streets.

"Excuse me," my friend shouted out the car window while honking her horn. This startled me, until I saw that she was talking to a police officer. We were on Biscayne Boulevard, and a squad car was next to us, and my friend was asking precise directions to the neighborhood in question.

"I'm not sure drug-crazed criminals would ask a cop how to get to the neighborhood," I said.

"I just want to be sure," my friend said.

We turned onto a side street. We drove. And drove. And drove.

"I don't see any barricades," I said.

"I know," my friend said. "Maybe we're going in the wrong direction."

"Well, just keep driving," I said.

Which she did. Nightfall had come, but the neighborhood seemed exceedingly peaceful. Holiday lights were out. A slight breeze was blowing. If there was any abject terror, it was hard to detect.

"I think that might be a barricade over there," my friend said.

But it was only a brown picket fence, in front of a neat, two-story house, like something out of Huck Finn.

"Head back the other way," I said.

"There!" my friend said.

"Where?" I said.

Her headlights were focused on two garbage cans.

"That's not a barricade," I said. "The people have taken out their trash."

"I was just trying to help you find your story," my friend said.

Two joggers came running down the street, out for an evening run.

"Should we ask them where the barricades are?" my friend said.

"That really doesn't seem fair," I said. "You figure if a criminal has to ask, then the barricades aren't really doing their job."

"Well, this doesn't make sense," my friend said.

I had to admit, she was right. We had been driving for fifteen minutes. This was a small neighborhood. We had passed some houses three times. Yet we had failed to see a single barricade.

"Could the story have been wrong?" my friend said.

"Come on," I said. Not only had the newspaper clipping featured a picture of barricades at the end of one street, but also a report on the barricades had appeared on a network news broadcast, and a third story had been sent out over a major wire service.

"Well, I really feel guilty," my friend said.

"Why should you feel guilty?" I said.

"Because," she said. "I feel like I'm disappointing you."

I knew what she meant. I wanted to see the south Florida of fear and gang warfare and drug lords and machine-gun fire. We had followed the map and asked the cops. And here we were—not a barricade in sight. This could have been a suburb of Omaha.

"Don't feel guilty," I said. "Maybe they take the barricades down at night."

She looked over from behind the wheel.

"Okay, okay, you're right," I said. "It wouldn't make any sense to keep the criminals out during the daytime and then let them in at night."

"If you're not all that hungry, we can keep looking," my friend said.

We had to be the most suspicious vehicle in the area. We were stopping at every corner, peering at expensive homes—and not only had we not found any barricades, but no one had said a word to us.

"I don't know," I said. "We've been here thirty minutes. Let's give it another ten."

"Could we have taken a wrong turn?" my friend said.

"Maybe," I said.

"Look!" she said.

"That's not a barricade," I said. "It's just a dead end."

"I'm willing to keep looking," she said.

"Then let's do it," I said. I was determined to find the blood-curdling terror of south Florida if it took us all night.

"Should I go left or right here?" my friend said.

"Try left," I said.

# "Ahoy, Shipmates"

**D**an Sullivan, sixty-five, a marketing and advertising consultant, was doing his grocery shopping at Walt's Food Store in South Holland, Illinois. He paid for the items and received his change. He stuffed the bills in one pocket and the silver in another.

When he got home he unpacked the items, and then pulled the change from his pockets. He noticed that there was some writing around the edges of the back side of one of the dollar bills.

He examined the bill. In blue ink was written:

"Ahoy Shipmates Only—1942 to 46—U.S. Coast Guard—W252— LST16—E. Puskaric." And then there was listed a street address in Lyons, Illinois.

"I couldn't figure out what this was all about," Dan Sullivan said. "I'd never seen anything like that before. My imagination ran wild."

Hey, what are we here for?

E. Puskaric, it turns out, is Edward Puskaric, sixty-two, a maintenance welder for Reynolds Metals Company in McCook, Illinois.

"Yes, I wrote that on the dollar bill," Puskaric told me. "I'm trying to find my shipmates from World War II."

I asked him to translate the notations on the dollar bill for me.

"Well," he said, " 'Ahoy Shipmates Only' is to limit the people who respond. I only want to hear from the men who were actually my shipmates. '1942 to 46—U.S. Coast Guard' refers to the years I was in the service. 'W252' was the first ship I served on. It was a buoy tender, and we were stationed in the area of Pearl Harbor. 'LST16' was the second ship I served on. It was a landing ship for tanks, and we were stationed in the South Pacific."

I asked him how he possibly expected to find his shipmates by leaving a message on a single dollar bill.

He laughed. "Are you kidding?" he said. "I've been doing this for ten years."

He said it began when "I was sitting around one night, thinking about how much I'd like to see some of the men I served with. How much I'd like the chance to get together with them again.

"Thursday is pay day at my job. So that Thursday, I got my check, and I cashed it after work at Lyons Federal Trust and Savings Bank, like I always do. I made sure that they gave me ten singles among the change. And then I went home and I wrote that message on the outside margin of the ten bills. And I went out and spent them during the course of the next week.

"My theory was that money circulates. You never know where it's going to end up. You never know who's going to see it.

"For ten years, I've kept up my routine. I'll get my paycheck, cash it at Lyons Federal, get ten singles and go home. I'll have something to eat. Then, around 7 P.M., I'll sit down at the wooden table we have in our kitchen, and I'll take a blue pen and I'll write the message ten times. Then I'll spend the money."

So Puskaric has been doing this for ten years?

"That's right."

Ten one-dollar bills a week?

"That's right."

That comes out to about $500 a year.

"I guess that's right."

So, in the ten years, Puskaric has put out more than $5,000 worth of singles with his message on them.

"I never thought about it that way, but I guess you're right."

I asked him if he had located any of his shipmates.

"No, I haven't," he said. "Over the years I have received fifty or sixty letters, from about twenty states. New Jersey, Idaho, California, Florida . . . I told you, money really gets around.

"When the envelopes arrive, I always know that they're in response to my dollar bills. That's because they're addressed to 'E. Puskaric.' Anyone who knows me would address a letter to Edward Puskaric. The only place I put 'E. Puskaric' is on the dollar bills.

"I always get excited, thinking it's from one of my shipmates. But the letters are always just from curious people who want to know what I'm trying to do. So I write them back and explain what I'm trying to do."

I asked Puskaric if he didn't think there was a simpler way to arrange a reunion with his shipmates.

"Well, I subscribe to the American Legion magazine," he said. "In every issue they have a section that announces reunions. But I don't know . . . I'm not much of an organizer. I'd rather do it this way. I know it seems a little haphazard, but it's the way I like to do it."

He said he was only seventeen when he went into the Coast Guard. "My parents signed for me," he said. "I was the youngest man on the ship. We had a pretty nice bunch of guys. It helped me grow up fast. It gave me a lot of responsibility for that age.

"So I'm still hoping that one of my shipmates will see one of the dollar bills. I wonder what they're all doing now. I imagine that quite a few of them have passed away. Some of them were in their thirties back then. They were a lot older than I was. You get a little melancholy."

# Some Like It Hot

Some two thousand miles from her home, Arlene Lorre, thirty-two, peered into a bathroom mirror. Lorre, an actress who lives in Los Angeles, was in a large hotel in the Midwest. On the floor of the bathroom was a Toshiba cassette player. Frank Sinatra was singing "You Make Me Feel So Young."

Lorre pulled her hair back from her face and pinned it in place. She picked up a calendar. For each month there was a picture of Marilyn Monroe. Lorre studied a photograph of Monroe that apparently was taken in the 1950s. In the photograph, Monroe, wearing a shiny black dress covered by a white fur coat, was walking past a uniformed police-man.

"I'm always trying to get this eyebrow effect," Lorre said. She examined the photograph of Monroe, then went to work on her own eyebrows.

By now, Sinatra was singing "You're Getting To Be a Habit with Me."

Lorre handed me the calendar. "Go through all the pictures of Marilyn," she said. "Cover up the rest of her face. You'll see—she may be smiling, but in every picture the eyes are always sad."

Lorre changed the tape. Now Los Lobos were singing "River of Fools." Lorre was bouncing in her chair. She slipped a nylon wig cap over her own hair, then placed a platinum-blond wig over the cap. She left the room, and when she came back she was wearing a white crepe strapless gown.

She examined herself in the mirror. For the forty-five minutes it had taken her to get ready, she had been talking in a normal voice. But now, seemingly out of nowhere, she said in a squeaky, breathy burst, "Eeek, a mouse!" It was pure Monroe.

She brushed on bright-red lipstick, and then added some gloss to that. "It's not Marilyn unless it's wet," she said.

She took one last look at herself. She switched the tape player off.

"All right," she said. "Ready to rock."


By some estimates there are about one hundred women in the United States who make at least part of their livings by impersonating Marilyn Monroe. Arlene Lorre would love to work full-time as a legitimate stage and screen actress. But to make money until the break she hopes will come, she is Marilyn approximately fifty times a year. She portrays Monroe at conventions, at store openings, at private parties, at retirement dinners. It brings her between $8,000 and $9,000 annually.

Roger Richman, a Beverly Hills agent who represents the estate of Marilyn Monroe, has seen Lorre work and pronounces her "extraordinary." I tell him that it sounds as if he likes her. "Not at all," he says. "I despise her. I don't license her."

For her part, Lorre says that she does not wish to pay Richman a licensing fee. "Why should I?" she says. "I get enough work without him."


Lorre walked from her room to the elevator. A man wearing a convention tag was waiting for the car to arrive.

"Gosh, look," she said, full of wonder. Her voice had turned totally into Monroe's. "A businessman."

The man blushed and looked away.

The elevator door opened. The whole way downstairs, everyone in the crowded car stared at Lorre. She was wearing elbow-length, cream-colored gloves, imitation-pearl cluster earrings, and a rhinestone necklace. She didn't seem at all bothered by the attention.

In the lobby bar, a group of French executives from a washing-machine company based in Paris was gathered around a low table. Lorre approached them, heard them conversing in their native language, and breathed, "How do you say *champagne* in French?"

As if on cue, four of the Frenchmen pulled cameras from their jacket pockets. One by one, they stood next to Lorre. She wrapped her arms around them as the flashbulbs went off.

"Tootaloo," she said, and walked away.

We climbed a short flight of stairs and entered a function room where there was a cocktail party going on for an association of ophthalmologists. She stopped in front of a man and said, "Hi, I'm Marilyn. What's your name?"

"Charles Bouska," the man replied in a somewhat tentative voice.

"Hi, Chuck," she chirped.

We left the room and entered the hotel's bar-restaurant. As soon as the piano player caught sight of Lorre, he began to play "Diamonds Are a Girl's Best Friend."

John Philbin, a retired union official, was at a table with his wife, Gwen. Lorre sat down in an empty chair across from them.

Philbin, after a momentary loss for words, said, "What's your purpose in life?"

"To be wonderful," Lorre said in Monroe's voice. "What's yours?"

We left the restaurant. In the hallway was a psychologist named Rich Simon, who was at the hotel for a national convention of family therapists.

"You remind me of someone," he said.

"Thank you ever so," Lorre said.

"You're talking to *Doctor* Simon, by the way," he said.

"I'm crazy for doctors," Lorre said.

We walked on. A man named Bob Ravich stopped in his tracks when he saw Lorre. Noting her bare shoulders, he said, "Aren't you cold?"

Lorre did a little dip and hunched her shoulders together. "I'm boiling," she said.

"There's a group of us having dinner in the next room," Ravich said. "I'd like to extend an invitation for you to join us."

"Thank you for extending yourself," Lorre said breathily, and walked into a waiting elevator.


Back in her room, Lorre removed her Marilyn wig, hung the crepe gown in a closet, and scrubbed the makeup and lipstick from her face. She changed into jeans, a T-shirt, and a black baseball cap.

"Obviously, I'd prefer to do legitimate acting full-time," she said. She was back in her own voice. "If people see me doing this character too much, it tends to limit me. But a person has to support herself.

"The way I look at it, at least it's performing. At least it's making people laugh. When I do it, I have the self-esteem of being an entertainer. What's the alternative? Waiting tables?"

She said that she had studied Marilyn Monroe movies and records— "There are some albums of Marilyn songs"—and that she is constantly working on the voice. "There's the high-pitched, more breathy voice," she said. "Then there's the low, mysterious voice. And then there's the squeak."

I asked her why she thought there was such a continuing demand for the Monroe image.

"Can you think of another star with the same effect?" Lorre said. "Just Santa Claus. Everybody loves Santa Claus, and everybody loves Marilyn. She's a lot like Christmas, I think."

I told her that I had been observing the reactions of the people she had approached. A lot of them, I said, behaved as if they were in the presence not of a Marilyn Monroe imitator but of Marilyn Monroe herself.

"Yeah, I know," she said. "They suspend their disbelief. Some people go so off-balance that they can't remember their names. They spill things, they drop things on themselves. That's true, by the way, about not remembering their names. It happens all the time. I'll come up and say, 'Hi, I'm Marilyn. What's your name?' And they won't know."

I asked her if many men came on to her when she was in her Marilyn getup.

"Actually, most men get very shy," she said. "Human beings are timid. They're real timid. And Marilyn is really alive. Whatever she's doing, she's at the top of that emotion. If she's happy, she's delirious. If she's in love, she's drunk from it. In general, most people don't like to display the peak of their emotions in public.

"Late in the evenings, when people have been drinking, some men hand me their hotel-room keys. But then they yank the keys right back, to let me know they're kidding. There will always be one man, though, who gets hooked like a dog every night. He'll follow me around, and he'll want my undivided attention. What he really wants, I guess, is Marilyn Monroe. Who knows? Maybe he wants me. Maybe he wants Marilyn. These guys don't know what the hell they want.

"When I'm Marilyn, I feel like all my raw femininity can be at the surface. Acting, as a business, requires you to be really aggressive. But when I'm Marilyn, I see how much men love the idea of the blonde who is helpless and confused. Men will always be like that. Even in this day and age. You'd be surprised. 'Oh, a curvy blonde. Someone to take care of. Or someone to play with.' "

I asked if she thought successful actors and actresses would look down on what she was doing.

"If you're really an actor, I don't think so," she said. "Maybe someone who's made it a little higher than me would look down. But if Meryl Streep were to see me, I think she'd appreciate me as a technician. She'd appreciate me as someone who was trying to be a character actor and was trying to do her best at it. I think she'd give me a good review.

"To be truthful, though, there are times I feel looked down on, and I feel embarrassed. Like I'm a prop instead of an actor. If I'm in a great big group of look-alikes, for example. If there's a Clark Gable and a Dolly Parton and a Mae West and a Humphrey Bogart and a Charlie Chaplin. I'll be there, and I'll think, 'God, this is a recycling center. This is not what I had in mind when I was studying acting.' "

She said that her life is filled with ironies. "Actors are always hungry," she said. "But a lot of times, when I'm doing a banquet, it is made clear to me that I am not supposed to eat any of the food. So I'll work the room, and everybody will be eating and drinking, and I'll be starved. And then the evening will end, and they'll give me a check, and I'll go out to the parking lot and I'll realize that I don't have the cash to get my car out. It'll be nine dollars or fifteen dollars, and I won't have the cash. And I'll think, 'Thirty minutes ago I was Marilyn Monroe.'

"Mostly, though, I spend a lot of time thinking about Marilyn herself. She would have turned sixty-one this year. I see the reaction people have to me, and I wonder if she had any idea of what kind of impact this image of hers had made. I wonder if, before she died, she thought, 'Yeah, I was a sensation, but what's going to happen all these years later? . . .' "

The next morning I spoke with Arlene Lorre again.

"I went to breakfast about 8:00," she said. "I was wearing workout pants and a T-shirt and that baseball cap and no shoes, just socks. My hair was hanging down in my face.

"And do you know who was having breakfast? Those French guys—the guys from the washing-machine company. The ones who were having their pictures taken with me last night.

"They were all dressed very nicely, and they looked over at me when I walked in the room, and I could tell that they had no idea who I was. They saw the way I was dressed, and I could imagine them thinking, 'You scum,' or 'Who is that sorry creature?'

"I just laughed inside. I do that a lot."

# Cap'n Stan, the Music Man

It had been a hectic day. I was in another city, and I had been scheduled to catch an American Airlines flight in the late afternoon. But I got a phone call—I had to leave earlier. I was to hurry to the airport and get on a Pan Am flight.

I made it there just in time. I settled into my seat—and within a few moments I noticed that I was in a better mood than I generally am on airplanes. In fact, I was even smiling.

I couldn't put my finger on why this was. And then I noticed.

Instead of the bland elevator music that most airlines pipe through the cabin while passengers are boarding, there was a Dolly Parton tape playing. Dolly was singing "In My Tennessee Mountain Home," and then she was singing "Traveling Man" ("Well, the traveling man was a two-time lover, stole my heart then he stole my mother. . . .").

I called a flight attendant over. "Does Pan Am always play Dolly Parton music while the passengers are boarding?" I said.

She smiled. "No," she said. "This is the first officer's tape. He brings tapes with him on every flight, and he puts them in the tape machine. Today it's Dolly."

Now . . . this struck me as unusual. The major airlines are conservative, bland institutions. They like to do everything according to the rule books. I once interviewed the man who provides "boarding music" for most of the big airlines. He is John Doremus, president of John Doremus Inc., and he told me that the whole point was that the passengers weren't even supposed to notice the music while they were getting onto the plane. The Doremus music was designed to be innocuous and unmemorable; it was supposed to subliminally soothe the passengers to their seats.

And yet here on Pan Am was Dolly Parton, and I loved it. I went into the cockpit to seek out the first officer.

He was Stan Huie, thirty-eight, and he has been with Pan Am for eight years. Before that he was an Air Force pilot.

"As far as I know, I'm the only pilot who brings his own tapes," Huie said. "I favor country music. There's something in country music that lifts your emotions. A lot of passengers on airplanes are either dragging from business or are not at ease flying. I think my tapes help cheer them up."

Huie did admit that not all Pan Am flight attendants appreciate his tapes.

"Some of the flight attendants tell me that it's inappropriate or unprofessional to play my tapes," he said. "In those cases, I let the flight attendants rule. The back end of the airplane is theirs. We drive the airplane; the flight attendants are in charge of everything behind the cockpit."

If the flight attendants don't like his tapes, however, they have to remove them themselves. "I get on the airplane and put the tapes in," he said. "If they object, they have to take them out."

Huie said that he varies the tapes he brings with him on trips. "There's one Irish folk music tape I like to play," he said. "And I have a James Taylor tape that I really like."

He said that if he had his choice, the tapes would play much louder than they do: "I like to hear the words." Having said that, he added that he would never play any heavy-metal rock music or other types of music that might offend passengers.

When he boards flights on other airlines, Huie said, he is not averse to listening to the elevator music that is featured: "It's better than nothing. It's better than listening to motors and generators and all the extraneous sounds of the airplane environment."

But, he said, passengers will occasionally stick their heads into the cockpit and thank him for his tapes. "They'll learn about me the same way you did," Huie said. "They'll comment to the flight attendants about the music, and the flight attendants will tell them that it's me."

He has one minor problem: "I tend to lose tapes a lot. I'll leave an airplane at the end of a flight, and I'll leave the tape on board. I have a fairly high attrition rate."

I told him that I knew what was going to happen: I was going to write a column about him, and some unsmiling Pan Am executive was going to read it and was going to order Huie never to play his tapes again.

"That's okay," Huie said. "Go ahead and write it. I think that this is a symbol that Pan Am gives more personalized service. Our airplanes aren't cattle cars.

"If I get orders not to play the tapes anymore, then I'll stop playing the tapes. But most people seem to enjoy them, so I hope that doesn't happen."

I asked him if he considered himself to be a maverick.

"A maverick?" Huie said. "No, I'm not a maverick. I'm just a guy who likes good music."

# Overtime

In today's success-oriented world, it is not uncommon to find workaholics in the executive suites of America's leading corporations.

But I believe I have done it—I believe I have found the most extreme workaholic in the United States.

He is Robert Hyland, vice-president and general manager of KMOX radio in St. Louis. KMOX is one of the nation's oldest and most successful commercial radio stations, and Hyland, who is in his sixties, has been the top man there for years.

Here is his work schedule:

Hyland arrives in his office at 2:30 each morning. That's right—two-and-a-half hours after midnight. He doesn't go home until 5 P.M.

I had heard rumors about this, but I frankly didn't believe them. It sounded impossible. I sought Hyland out, though, and he confirmed that it is true.

"I need all the time at work that I can get," he said. "I'm involved in a lot of civic affairs in addition to the radio station—I'm on the board of a hospital, of a college, of the St. Louis Zoo. So for twenty years I've been keeping this schedule. As a matter of fact, I used to report to work at 1:30 A.M. But last year I had a cancer operation, so I pushed it back to 2:30."

I was hearing him say these things, but I couldn't comprehend it. He kept going.

"I've never required much sleep all of my life," Hyland said. "I'm not one of those people who need sleep to be refreshed. I'll go to bed between 9 P.M. and 10 P.M., and I'll wake up at 1:30 A.M. I have an alarm clock, but I never set it. I wake up automatically. I shower and shave, and I'm at the office by 2:30."

There is no one else in the KMOX executive offices at that time, of course. "It's a good time to get a lot of work done," Hyland said. "The phone isn't ringing, and there are no distractions. I have a pile of paperwork on my desk, and I go through it. Then, around 9 A.M. [after Hyland has been at work for six and a half hours], the other people show up, and we have staff meetings."

And then he continues to work until 5 P.M. He doesn't do this once in a while; he does it every night and every day. He even does it on Saturdays. "But I'll go home a few hours earlier on the sixth day," he said.

I was silent. I didn't know how to respond to all this.

"I think what you're thinking is that you're talking to a nut," Hyland said. "But if that's what you're thinking, you're wrong. I just don't think that most people have the commitment to their jobs that I do."

I said that I just didn't understand it. He is the top guy in his company. He can delegate all the authority he wants. So what is he doing reporting to work at 2:30 A.M.?

"No one tells me I have to do it," he said. "I do it of my own volition. I'm a hands-on manager. In this competitive business world today, if you're not a hands-on manager, you're gone."

I got a little psychological with him. Is he consumed with fear that, if he didn't continue keeping these ridiculous hours, everything he had built up would fall apart?

"Not at all," he said. "I just sincerely love what I do."

But couldn't he just wake up at 1:30 A.M. and do the paperwork at home?

"That's not my style," he said. "I like to put on a suit and come to the office."

His wife of twenty years, Pat, sleeps through the night. "She never wakes up when I get up to go to work," Hyland said. "She never complains. She has to have breakfast by herself, but a lot of wives do that."

And how does Hyland feel at 4 A.M., the legendary "dark night of the soul"? Is he lonely in his office? Does it seem that he is living in some kind of bizarre vacuum?

"I don't even pay attention to what time it is," he said. "I'm working too hard. The only time I'm aware of the hour is when my secretary,

Norma Wallner, arrives. That's when the rest of the company starts its day."

I said that at least Hyland must have witnessed some beautiful sunrises.

"My office overlooks the Gateway Arch," he said. "Sometimes the sunrises are beautiful. Sometimes they're blah. Most of the time I don't even notice."

# In Good Faith

**Y**ou don't have to be an expert in the field of international relations to know that a certain tension is building between American people and Japanese people. The Japanese economy has been doing so well (often at the expense of American companies), and Japanese business concerns have been buying up so much property in the United States, that the potential exists for a new and unfortunate era of negative feelings between citizens of the two countries.

So perhaps it's not a bad idea to tell this story.


Tadatoyo Yamamoto, forty-four, works as a vice-president for the Japanese subsidiary of an American company—the Eaton Corporation, whose world headquarters is in Cleveland. Yamamoto is based in Tokyo, but he visits the United States from time to time.

On one visit, a trip to Chicago was on his schedule. He arrived at O'Hare International Airport and rode a bus downtown, where he had reservations at the Drake hotel. As he stood in line waiting to check in, he put his briefcase on the floor.

As the line moved forward, he reached down for his briefcase. It was gone.

Inside the briefcase were approximately 129,000 yen in cash (the equivalent of more than $900); Yamamoto's passport; all of his credit cards; his visa allowing him to travel in the United States; his return ticket to Japan; and photos of his family. Understandably, he panicked when he realized the briefcase was gone.

He reported this to the Drake hotel's security department. Security officers tried to find the briefcase, but had no luck. They were diligent—not only did they check thoroughly around the hotel and make arrangements for Yamamoto to talk with the police department, but they contacted the airport bus company and the airline on which Yamamoto had arrived, on the off chance that he mistakenly thought he had brought the briefcase into the hotel while actually leaving it elsewhere. But in the end Yamamoto reluctantly concluded that someone had stolen it while he was preoccupied in the check-in line. With assistance from his company and the Japanese consulate in Chicago, Yamamoto was able to get back to Tokyo—disappointed, disillusioned, and newly uneasy about the United States.

Three weeks later, Yamamoto received an envelope in Tokyo. It had been mailed from Chicago. It contained his credit cards, his airline tickets, and other personal items. The return address on the envelope said that it had been mailed by a "Mr. Joseph Loveras" in Chicago. There was no letter enclosed.

Not long after that, Yamamoto received another envelope, sent via express delivery from the United States. Inside this envelope were money orders for more than $900. This envelope, too, was from a "Mr. Joseph Loveras" in Chicago. And this time there was a handwritten letter, on plain paper, enclosed:

> Dear Mr. Tadatoyo Yamamoto—
> I'm sorry to hear of your missing property. I hope this money order and the items . . . will restore your faith in the people of Chicago. This is being sent in the fastest way, so you can receive it in 2 days.

The letter was signed "Mr. Joseph J. Loveras."

Yamamoto was totally confused. What had happened to his briefcase? Who was this Joseph Loveras?
Yamamoto wrote a letter to Loveras:

Dear Mr. Loveras—

I received the international postal money orders which you sent. Thank you very much . . . I thank you for your generosity and am very keen to know who you are. Are you connected with the Police Dept. or a philanthropist?

Not exactly, it turns out.


I went to Tokyo and spoke with Tadatoyo Yamamoto. He filled me in on what had happened.

"I was so upset when my briefcase disappeared," he said. "My trust in the American people, who have always been so friendly to me, was damaged. I had some sleepless nights in America before returning to Tokyo."

When he received the letters from Joseph Loveras, Yamamoto was "completely puzzled. How was I to interpret this? Could this be the man who had stolen my briefcase? But if he was, why would he send the money and the tickets back? If he wasn't the man who had stolen my briefcase, how did he get my possessions? And how did he get my home address?"

The next time Yamamoto traveled to the United States, he called Loveras on the telephone. Loveras was no police officer, and he was no wealthy philanthropist. Loveras was a sixty-seven-year-old disabled veteran who lived in one room in a transient hotel, and who had been out of work for years.

"He explained to me that he was walking through a parking lot, looking in trash cans," Yamamoto said. "He said he found a beat-up briefcase. For some reason the money and the airline tickets were in a part of the briefcase that the thieves had not looked into. I still don't know why.

"Mr. Loveras told me that he took the briefcase back to his room. My name and address were on the tag on the outside. The briefcase was too battered to send back to Japan—he said that it was in such bad shape as to be virtually useless. But he mailed my tickets and my business papers. Then he went to the bank and spent his own money to change the yen into money orders. And he spent his own money to send it to me by express delivery, so I would get it quickly.

"I was thinking that the money—nearly $1,000—must seem so huge to him. But he told me that he is a very religious man, and that he could not keep money that was not his. He said his conscience would not allow it."

Yamamoto was staying at the Drake hotel again, and invited Loveras for lunch. "He seemed uncomfortable at the invitation," Yamamoto said. "I got the impression he would not feel at home in such a fancy place. So we met at a cafeteria. We talked for more than an hour. I tried to give him a financial reward. He hesitated to take it, but finally he did. I don't think I have ever met such a pure person."

Back in the United States, I got in touch with Joseph Loveras. We met for breakfast at a McDonald's restaurant.

Loveras was quite shy; he is hard of hearing, and I had to speak loudly so that he could understand me over the music and the other noise in the place.

"I found Mr. Yamamoto's briefcase while I was salvaging through the . . . well, I don't call them garbage cans. I call them public cans," Loveras said.

He said that when he opened the briefcase and found the money and the airline tickets, his first thought was, "This isn't mine." He concluded that someone must have stolen the briefcase, had somehow missed the compartment where the valuable materials were stored, and had tossed it in the trash. Loveras went back to his room in the transient hotel, got an envelope, went to the post office, and mailed the tickets and the personal papers to Yamamoto in Tokyo. Then he inquired about how to send the money to Japan; he knew it would be unwise just to put the cash in the mail. One morning he walked to the First National Bank of Chicago, a distance of several miles.

"I had never even been inside the bank before," Loveras said. "I didn't know how to get a money order. But the people at the bank helped me."

The money orders cost $41—which he paid himself and did not take out of Yamamoto's funds. Then he spent another $31 for the express delivery of the money orders to Japan—again, out of his own pocket. Joseph Loveras has a total income of $493 a month. Of that, $227 comes from the Veterans Administration; $266 comes from social security. His rent for his single room is $265 a month.

"I don't eat out in restaurants," he said. "Mostly I eat spaghetti in my room. I boil it. It costs less to boil the spaghetti than to buy it in cans."

He said that he was born in New York State, and that his mother was killed in an automobile accident when he was a young child. "I don't remember her," he said. "One of the first things I do remember was being in a crib in St. Agatha's orphanage in Nanuet, New York." He said he has a sister, but has not seen her since he was a teenager. He was placed in five foster homes, he said, and then at the age of twenty joined the Army. After World War II, he said, he came home to "nothing much." He had some troubled times. He was married, but that ended; he said that he has a son who should be thirty-eight years old by now, but that he had lost track of the boy.

Some of his acquaintances, he said, told him he was stupid to send the money to the businessman in Japan. "I don't think I was stupid, though," Loveras said. "The money belongs to that man, not to me."

When I asked about Yamamoto's invitation to meet for a meal at the Drake, Loveras said, "I would feel out of place at somewhere that nice." And then he said, "I don't own a suit."

I asked him if he made a practice of salvaging through the garbage cans to look for additional spending money. He said that wasn't it. He said he looked for aluminum cans, which he then turned in for half a cent apiece—which he gave to the Christian Children's Fund.

"Do you know that you can support a needy child for seventy cents a day?" he said.


Tadatoyo Yamamoto made another trip to the United States, and went to the transient hotel where Joseph Loveras lives. Loveras was out ("I spend most of my days just walking," he had told me), so Yamamoto left him a note.

On this visit Yamamoto was staying at a hotel out in the suburbs, and Loveras phoned him that night. "We spoke for about twenty minutes," Yamamoto said. "I told him that I want to visit with him every time I am in the United States.

"And I asked him again why he would go to all the trouble to return everything to me. He told me that if he had not done it, it would have made him feel bad for the rest of his life."


Joseph Loveras said he had heard that some people are saying that the Americans and the Japanese might be starting to harbor ill will toward each other because of international economic conditions. Loveras said that he didn't understand all the details of this; he said that he wasn't very well versed in such global matters.

"I really feel I have found a friend in Mr. Yamamoto," Loveras said. "He's married and he has two children. What a fine gentleman."

# "Best Wishes to You . . ."

$S$he was going through her footlocker. She does that sometimes; so many of her childhood memories are stored in her footlocker—she has taken it with her every time she has moved around the country, and it serves as a constant reminder of who she used to be. Her name is Colleen Todd; she is thirty-three, a senior writer with the J. Walter Thompson advertising agency, and when she wants to remember herself as a young girl, the footlocker is where she looks.

So there she was, going through the footlocker again. The things were all there—her first corsage, her high school yearbook. And buried among it all was the letter from George Harrison's mother.

She picked it up and opened the envelope. She had almost forgotten about it. . . .

In 1964, when the Beatles' music first came to the United States, Colleen was twelve years old. Like many young people in 1964, she slept, breathed and lived the Beatles. And like many girls, she was in love with all four of the Beatles. She was very fickle. One week she would be in love with Paul, one week she would be in love with Ringo; it changed.

During her George Harrison period she knew that she was really, truly, deeply in love. George was the quiet Beatle. Although he seemed much, much older than she was, the fact is that in 1964 George Harrison was only twenty-one years old.

Colleen bought all of the Beatles' records and watched all of the Beatles' appearances on television. She didn't want to be just like all of the other girls, though; she wanted to have a special relationship with her Beatle.

Somewhere—she either read it in a magazine or heard it on the radio—she came across the home address of George Harrison's mother, in Liverpool, England. She immediately sat down and wrote Mrs. Harrison a long letter. She told Mrs. Harrison how popular the Beatles were in America, and how much she thought of George.

Soon after, Colleen received an envelope postmarked from Liverpool, England. It was hand-addressed to her.

She opened it up. It began:

Dear Colleen—

Thanks for your letter. I had a letter from Sydney, Australia, and this young lady said that George was her favorite there. . . .

So I'm happy to know that George is really popular there. Yes! We did go to the London and Liverpool premiere [presumably of the movie *A Hard Day's Night*]. Very enjoyable. Beatles were right alongside of us and Princess Margaret. I danced with most of the men from the film in the Dorchester Hotel afterward, and met and spoke to Her Royal Highness.

Best wishes to you—
Louise Harrison

Included with the letter was a postcard, on the back of which Mrs. Harrison had taped a snippet of cloth from the lining of one of George's coats.

When she received the letter, Colleen could hardly believe it. George Harrison's mother had actually read her letter, and had written to her. The first thing she thought of was that she had to call her best friend, Sara Turner, and tell her. Sara Turner had moved out of town, but Colleen got permission to call her anyway—making a long-distance call was a big deal in 1964.

She took the letter to school. She showed it to people, but she would not let them touch it. Later that day some boys teased her—they told her that they had the letter. She ran back to her locker to make sure it was still safe inside, which it was. In the girls' restroom, she took out the card with the piece of George's coat taped to it, and let the other girls look.

It was so long ago. Now, as a thirty-three-year-old woman, Colleen held the old letter in her hands and read it again. She wondered if a twelve-year-old girl today would think to write to her favorite star's mother, just to say how much she admired her son?

She doubted it; the world has changed, and young girls are more sophisticated, and now a young fan of a rock star probably would try to get to the rock star himself—not write to his mother in another country. And the idea of security is now so important; the mother of a rock star undoubtedly would be cautious about writing to some fan who had somehow managed to obtain her address.

Colleen Todd reread the letter and thought about a lot of things. She didn't even know if Louise Harrison was still alive. She thought about the Beatles, and about growing up, and about time going by. She felt like doing something, and suddenly she realized what it was. She felt like calling Sara Turner to tell her about the letter.

# Hy and Louie

On their first day of college in 1968, Marsha Lockwood and Michael Cramer met. They were both freshmen at the University of Massachusetts, in Amherst. They liked each other immediately. They learned that they came from neighboring Massachusetts towns; Marsha was from Worcester, Michael was from Shrewsbury. They were only three weeks apart in age. They both had played instruments in their high school marching bands (Marsha had played the flute, Michael had played the clarinet). Their families had friends in common.

They began to date. They started to fall in love. And they discovered something.

They both had grandfathers who worked in the same office building in Worcester. Marsha's grandfather, Hyman Brodsky, was an accountant. Michael's grandfather, Louis Cramer, was an insurance man. The two grandfathers were both in their seventies.

The two grandfathers' offices were in the Slater Building, a famous office building in downtown Worcester. They were the two oldest tenants in the Slater Building. When they had been young boys, they had gone to Hebrew school together in Worcester. They had been good friends all during their childhoods. As young adults, they had worked in neighboring offices in the Slater Building.

Then, in the 1920s, they had a feud. It was over a business matter. Hyman Brodsky and Louis Cramer were furious with each other. They stopped speaking to each other entirely.

They did not speak a word for fifty years. When they would be in the elevator of the Slater Building with other businesspeople, they would

**237**

talk to the others but not to one another. They would not even look at each other. If they happened to find themselves with just the two of them in the elevator, the two boyhood friends would ride upstairs in total silence. Fifty years of this.

Meanwhile, the romance of Marsha Lockwood and Michael Cramer was growing more and more serious. They graduated from college and took jobs in the Worcester area. And, in 1974, they became engaged to be married.

Hyman Brodsky and Louis Cramer were riding upstairs in the Slater Building elevator. One of them—no one remembers which one it was —said casually:

"Well, it looks like the kids are going to get married."

And the other said:

"Yes, it looks that way."

The silence of fifty years had been broken.

In July of 1975, the month before the wedding, Marsha Lockwood's mother had an engagement party for Marsha. The two grandfathers were invited. It was the first time they had been at a social occasion together in fifty years.

"That was the start," Marsha recalls now. "They were sitting next to each other all through the party. I eavesdropped. They were talking about their days in Hebrew school back when they were boys. They were talking about how the rabbi was very strict, and how they had both been afraid of him. Now, the events they were talking about had happened when they were ten years old. Now they were seventy-seven. But it was as if no time had passed at all."

There were a number of prewedding parties for Marsha and Michael, and the two grandfathers attended every one of them. They became fast friends once again; they were inseparable. They were "Hy and Louie"; anytime anyone looked around, Hy and Louie were talking away with each other.

"Their friendship seemed to grow immediately," Marsha recalls. "I think it was a case of them realizing that there was no one else around with the same memories they had. They just had each other. And although no one ever said it out loud, it became pretty clear that they had both forgotten what that original terrible argument had even been about. They both knew it had been a business argument, but neither one of them remembered the details."

Marsha and Michael were married; Hy and Louie remained the best of friends. They even looked alike; each was about five foot nine, each wore glasses, each was slightly overweight, each had a full head of gray hair. When they rode the elevator in the Slater Building, they talked away.

Marsha kept thinking that she and her new husband had changed history in a way. Not prominent, worldwide history; but by meeting and falling in love, they had changed the personal histories of their two grandfathers—Hy and Louie—and somehow that seemed very important to her.

Hyman Brodsky and Louis Cramer died within a year of each other. Hy died on August 18, 1983; Louie died on August 17, 1984.

When Marsha remembers the two old men, she envisions that first time they were together again, at the engagement party given by her mother.

"One of them was sitting on a chair," she says. "The other was sitting on a piano bench. They were bending so close to each other that I think they were actually physically touching. They were having this very animated conversation. If you hadn't known about them, you would have thought that they were in the midst of some long conversation that had gone on for fifty years. It was as if they had never stopped talking. When I think about Hy and Louie, that's the picture I see."

# Championship Game

Ted and Todd Kliman just had their annual championship one-on-one basketball game. Ted is the father; he is fifty-six years old. Todd is the son; he is nineteen.

The Klimans live in Greenbelt, Maryland. Ever since Todd was a small boy, the father and the son have been playing one-on-one. They make an event of the yearly championship game. It is just the two of them out on the basketball court, but the championship game means something.

"It sort of brings us together," said the son. "It feels good just to be out there on the basketball court with my dad. We see each other out on the court, and we talk while we're playing, and the whole feeling is sort of like 'This is my father.' 'This is my son.'"

The two Klimans have a hard time putting into words just what it is about the one-on-one championship games that mean so much to them. Part of it has to do with the basic fine feeling of doing something physical together. Part of it has to do with the idea that another entire year has gone by, and here they are playing the championship game again.

"We make a big deal out of it," said the father. "The loser has to buy the winner a meal at a restaurant of his choice. We're quite serious when we're playing—we're both really trying to win. Playing the basketball game is just a great way of relating to my son."

Usually there is no one there to watch the championship game—it's just the father and son out on the court, each trying to win the game. There's no scoreboard and no play-by-play announcer. But somehow the annual playing of the game has become more important to the father and the son than all of the Super Bowls and World Series combined.

"A lot of my friends, I don't think they're as close to their fathers as I am to mine," said the son. "I think it's too bad that you don't see this kind of thing that often."

The father agrees. "There's something nice about one-on-one basketball," he said. "You get very close. It's not like playing tennis, where you're yards apart. In one-on-one basketball there's a lot of body contact—you're physically close together. Sometimes during the game things get tense, and we get miffed at each other. But I don't think we ever lose sight of the reason we're there."

Both the father and the son are constantly aware of one undeniable fact: The father, at fifty-six, is no longer a young man, and the son, at nineteen, is in his physical prime.

"I remember when he was eight years old," said the father. "He had trouble even getting the ball up to the hoop. I would help him, and I would always let him win. But things change. He started to get bigger and better, and I got older. The balance changed. He started to win. I started to have trouble keeping up."

The son is a little uncomfortable about this development. Yes, he has the strength and the stamina. But in a way he wishes the years would not pass so quickly.

"I guess I am a little worried about my dad's physical shape," said the son. "There are times when I think I should take it easy on him. But I don't; he would be able to tell, and he would resent it if I let up on him. He plays very hard and gives a good effort every time."

There is one thing that is usually unspoken between them: The idea that one day this will have to end. Neither is sure how many more years it will be appropriate for the father to get out on a basketball court and give all his energy to the one-on-one championship game.

"It will be pretty disappointing when it happens," said the son. "When we have to stop, there will be the loss of a connection. A lot of the good feelings about being father and son will be gone."

"I know that someday I will not be able to go out there and play," the father said. "I won't say that I dread the thought of that day—but I sure don't look forward to it. We run hard, we fight for rebounds, we block shots . . . no, I don't look forward to the day when that ends."

For the record, the son defeated the father in this year's championship game, 48–42. When you talk to them, though, you get the sense that the final score really doesn't mean very much. What means something to them is what they feel when they're out there together on the basketball court.

"I'm very proud of my father," said the son. "It's so good that we're able to do this together. The sensation I get when I'm out there on the court with him is a feeling of happiness, more than anything else. I'll tell you this—If I ever have a son, I know that we're going to play our own championship game every year."

"When I'm out there on the court with my son, I think to myself what a fine young man he has turned out to be," said the father. "We play the game, and of course I see him as an opponent. But what am I really seeing? What am I really feeling? I'm seeing my son. And I'm feeling this tremendous amount of love. I just love my son so much."

# The Case of the
# Kidnapped Couple

<hr>

You may think it's a piece of cake, traveling the American Beat. You don't run into the cases we do.

The call came from Allan Hertle, seventy-one, of Glenview, Illinois. Hertle and his wife, Anne, also seventy-one, had been on a trip to the East Coast and were driving back through Pennsylvania, on their way home.

"I was on Highway 202, just outside West Chester," Hertle said. "I passed a police car that was parked on the median strip. As I passed it I noticed that there was a civilian in the back seat.

"The next thing I knew, the police car was following me. He had his siren and his light on. I figured I was speeding, but then I realized I hadn't been going that fast. I pulled over.

"This pleasant-looking fellow in a police uniform walked up to my car. The first thing he said was, 'You weren't doing anything wrong.'

"I looked back at his cruiser. The other fellow was still in the back seat.

"The policeman introduced himself as Chief something. He said he was with some sort of West Chester association. I don't recall the name of the group. He said that once a year they like to take some out-of-state people on a tour of the community—drive them around the countryside, buy them lunch, show them the historical spots, give them a big dinner, and then put them up in a motel for the night. He said that in the morning he would put us on the highway and send us on our way."

And what did you think of this, Mr. Hertle?

"I was pretty suspicious. How did he pick us? I was just afraid that there was something else to it. I didn't want to go with him. It sounded like one of those pigeon-drop con games you hear about.

"I told him that my wife and I had to be going. We got out of there in a big hurry. We talked about it, and we thought that maybe there was something else to it. Maybe they were trying to sell us on a retirement community or something. Maybe they were looking for senior citizens to pull over to take advantage of.

"I just keep wondering: How many people does this happen to? Who was that guy in the back seat? And what's the real story behind it?"


We called the West Chester, Pennsylvania, Police Department. Corporal Gary Cummins listened to the story.

"We don't stop anybody like that," he said. "Pull people over and tell them that we want to give them a tour and buy them lunch and take them to dinner and rent them a motel room? That's crazy."

We told him what Allan Hertle had said about the police car with the civilian in the back seat.

"Now, that's troubling," Corporal Cummins said. "We have had several instances around here where people have been approached or stopped by what appeared to be a police car. Someone in a dark-blue uniform gets out of the car. There is a person waiting in the car. The person in the dark-blue uniform asks the driver to get out of his car. So far, no driver has. They smell something funny and they stay behind the wheel and they drive away. It's a good thing, too. Those cars aren't ours."

Corporal Cummins said that the West Chester police don't even patrol Highway 202. "That would be either the West Goshen Township police, or the Pennsylvania state police."

Corporal Cummins had a question:

"You say that the police officer identified himself as the chief?"

That's right, we said.

"Was this chief a white guy?" Corporal Cummins said.

Yes, we said. He was white. Why?

"Because our chief is black, and he's been in the hospital for the last month," Corporal Cummins said.

\*    \*    \*

We called the West Goshen Township police. A civilian dispatcher answered the phone.

"Pulling people over and buying them lunch and driving them around and giving them a big dinner and putting them up in a motel?" he said. "That sounds wacky. Hey, I wish someone would pull me over and do that."

Next on our list was the Pennsylvania state police. Their station nearest to West Chester is in Embreeville.

"This makes no sense," said Sergeant Richard Zenk. "First of all, we don't have any kind of an organization that would do something like that. I have never heard of anything remotely similar to that. We don't lend our name to projects of that kind."

We asked Sergeant Zenk if he had any possible explanation for the story.

"I don't know what to tell you," he said. "I have never heard of a police officer stopping someone on the road and then offering him a tour of the area. You hear about a lot of things on this job, but what you're talking about is a new one on me."

By this time it was late at night. We were going to call Allan Hertle in Glenview, Illinois, and tell him that his case was still a mystery. No one had the answer.

But we decided to wait until morning and make one more call.

In the morning we called back the West Goshen Township police, where the civilian dispatcher had expressed no knowledge of the situation. This time we asked to speak to the chief.

Chief Michael Dunn, fifty-two, came onto the line.

"What can I do for you?" he said.

We said that we knew it was going to sound nuts, but that we had heard a story that took place in his area of the country. We ran through the whole tale about Allan Hertle and his wife and the police chief who had pulled them over. We felt a little sheepish even repeating the saga once more.

When we finished, Chief Dunn said: "Yeah, I was the one who pulled them over."

You were?

"Sure," Chief Dunn said. "I do this every year. I do it in cooperation with the Exchange Club of West Chester. It's part of 'Boost Pennsylvania Week.' "

The chief said that the Exchange Club was sort of like the Rotary or the Kiwanis. "One day each year, we try to find a couple from out of state and make them the guests of the Exchange Club for the day. What we do on that day is look for out-of-state license plates. Then I'll pull the couple over. The first thing I tell them is that they're not in trouble with the law. I invite them to spend the day with the Exchange Club and then to be guests of honor at the Exchange Club's dinner meeting that night."

And was there a civilian in the back seat of the police car?

"That was Steve Douglas," Chief Dunn said. "He's the president of the Exchange Club. He rides with me, and as soon as I get a couple, he takes over."

We asked if it was hard to get a couple to go along with the whole deal.

"If you're asking whether we have to stop a number of cars—yes, we do," Chief Dunn said. "A lot of people tell us that they appreciate the offer, but that they have to be on their way. This year we eventually got a couple with Massachusetts plates on their car, but they were actually from California. They went with the Exchange Club all day, attended the banquet, and spent the night."

We asked Chief Dunn if he didn't see anything at all odd about this.

"No," he said. "It's been going on for years. We have a slogan in this state now: 'You've got a friend in Pennsylvania.' We're just trying to be friendly."


Our next call was to Tom Chambers, the mayor of West Chester.

"Oh, yeah," he said. "The captured couple program."

He said that it was a tradition in the West Chester area. "It's totally legitimate, or I wouldn't be involved in it," he said. "We use the West

Goshen police to help us, because they have jurisdiction over Highway 202.

"Chief Dunn will ask them, 'Can you stay over?' And if they can, they get a whole day-long tour of the area. It's a goodwill thing. This year we got about 120 people at the evening banquet. All the Exchange Club members bring their wives.

"The thing that's really nice about this is that it's just one couple we pick. It would have an entirely different flavor if we stopped couples all day long and invited them all. But the way it has always worked is that Chief Dunn gets one couple, and then he turns the couple over and he stops looking."

We asked Mayor Chambers what exactly went on at the evening banquet.

"I'm at the banquet, and our local representative to the state legislature is at the banquet," he said. "We award the couple with a plate. Everyone has a lot of fun with it. It's a totally positive thing. There's nothing else to it but to get people to go back to their homes and say what a nice place our part of Pennsylvania is."

And Mayor Chambers sees nothing out of the ordinary about this?

"Maybe someday you'll get captured and have a nice dinner when you're in this area," he said. "Then you can decide for yourself."

We weren't finished yet. We called Steve Douglas, the president of the Exchange Club.

"Generally we try to find a couple with no children," he said. "We have learned in the past that if a couple has children, they probably won't want to take the time to join us."

And did he have any qualms about using the police department to stop the people on the highway?

"Think about it," Douglas said. "You can't have private citizens stopping people on the road. In this day and age, you just aren't going to be able to wave people over if you're a private citizen.

"As it is, I don't even get out of the police car until the couple has agreed to be a part of our program. Chief Dunn and I are a little worried that if the couple sees two people approaching their car, it might spook them."

We asked what exactly happened to this year's couple.

"We put them in a car and showed them interesting sights and tourist places around Chester County," he said. "We took them to Longwood Gardens, and then bought them lunch at the Longwood Inn. They really enjoyed that. And then, at the end of the day, we took them to our dinner meeting at the Italian Social Club in West Chester. We had video-taped most of the day's activities, and we gave them the tape.

"Every year, by the time the couple gets to the evening meeting, they can't believe what has happened to them. They sit there at the banquet, and it's like they're in a dream. This year we put them up at Porter's Bed and Breakfast for the night, and they were back on the road first thing in the morning.

"I want to stress that this is totally voluntary on the couple's part. We never hold anyone against their will."


There was one more call to make.

"What, you got kidnapped?" said Hannah Gardner, the editor of the *Daily Local News*, which serves the West Chester area.

No, we said, but we had been looking into the matter.

"I'm aware that the Exchange Club does that," she said. "There is a rumor that one year they saw an out-of-state license plate and the people they stopped turned out to be a priest and his girlfriend. Needless to say, the Exchange Club didn't kidnap them."

We said that most of the people we had talked to before Chief Dunn had never heard of this whole thing.

"We used to cover it in the paper," she said. "We don't cover it any-more. I'm not much on these men's clubs anyway. So I guess a lot of people don't know about it anymore, because we don't write about it."

Did she have any particular feelings about any of this?

"Well, I guess it may have made sense back in the days when there wasn't as much traffic coming through here. It was sort of like, 'See the area. Here we are.'

"But now, the idea of pulling people off the highway . . . I don't know, what can I tell you? They do things like that around here."


So we had our answer. We got back in touch with Allan Hertle in Glen-view, Illinois, and explained to him why he and his wife had been pulled off the road in Pennsylvania.

He listened to the whole story in silence.
Then he said:
"Are you kidding me?"
We assured him that we weren't.
He paused for a few seconds.
"I don't care," he said. "I'm still glad I didn't do it."


We had a glass of grape juice and an animal cookie. Sometimes the American Beat can be hell.

# Racket Man

It's in the back of my closet; it has moved every time I have moved. It went to college with me and has been with me ever since. For a while it was the most important possession in my life.

Its strings are broken now. They're faded, too; you can hardly see the blue stripes in the Victor Imperial gut. When I wrap my hand around the grip, though, it immediately becomes my best friend again. There was a time when I thought that it and I could do anything together. We couldn't; I wasn't as good as I thought I was, and the failings were all mine. It, though—it was the greatest. It was the greatest piece of sporting equipment ever built.

It was the Jack Kramer Autograph tennis racket, made out of wood and manufactured by the Wilson Sporting Goods Company. Hold on a second. I have to stop typing and pick it up again. God, it was beautiful.

The Jack Kramer Autograph was introduced in 1949, and between that year and 1981—when the racket was eliminated from Wilson's line because of the ascension of metal and graphite rackets—ten million were sold. The peak year was 1965, when six hundred thousand Kramers were purchased.

That's what we called them—Kramers. They may have been produced by Wilson, but to anyone who owned one, the racket was a Kramer. Owning a Kramer was a sign that you had arrived as a tennis player. Any number of rackets might have served you well during your days and months as a beginner, but when you got good you had to have a Kramer.

The surprising thing, in light of the racket's success, is that Jack Kramer retired as a tennis player at the end of the 1953 season. As an amateur he had won virtually every tournament you could win. At the age of eighteen, in 1939, he was the youngest player ever to represent the United States in a Davis Cup Challenge Round. He turned pro in 1947 and was the world's professional champion in 1948, 1949, 1951, and 1953. So for most of the years of the phenomenal popularity of the Kramer racket, Jack Kramer wasn't even an active player. It didn't matter. The Kramer took on a mystique of its own.

In the Fifties, Sixties, and early Seventies, you could go to any junior tournament in the country, and it would seem as if 75 or 80 percent of the kids were playing with Kramers. Tennis rackets weren't as expensive back then—the original 1949 Kramer sold for $13.50 unstrung—but price had little to do with it. When you stepped onto the court with your Kramer in your hand, there was no doubt that you were equipped with the best.

"What kind of racket did I grow up with?" said Jack Kramer. He is sixty-six now, and lives in a suburb of Los Angeles.

"In the 1930s, Ellsworth Vines had an autograph racket, and Don Budge had an autograph racket. I used a Don Budge all through my amateur career. In my kidlike dreams, Budge was the leading individual in tennis.

"So when Wilson told me in 1948 that they wanted to put out a racket with my name on it, I was very excited. They gave me one model to try out, and I said, 'This racket is too goddamn stiff. Loosen it up.' They ended up putting seven pieces of lamination in the head of the racket.

"Yeah, it was a good tennis racket. It was still stiff enough that you could hit the hell out of the ball and keep it in. But if you played a steady, controlled game, it was good for that, too."

There were players more famous than Kramer in the years after he retired—Pancho Gonzales comes to mind—but somehow it was the Kramer racket that became the one people had to have.

"In those days, people felt about their tennis rackets like they felt about their cars," Kramer said. "If you owned a Buick, the next car you bought would be a Buick. Same with the Kramer rackets. People kept buying them over and over again.

"The Australians back then—Lew Hoad and Ken Rosewall and all the rest of them—played with Slazengers or Dunlops. But if you were an American kid, or if you were an American country club player, you used a Kramer.

"I have to admit, it was a great disappointment to me when Wilson decided to stop manufacturing the wooden Kramers. To me, wood is still a great racket to play with. But in the early Eighties, no one wanted to play with wood anymore. Everything was graphite or steel. So they told me there would be no more Kramers."


And for six years that was the case. But now Wilson, which manufactures approximately thirty different kinds of tennis rackets, has added a new one to its line. It is a graphite composite racket, and it is called the Wilson Jack Kramer Staff. It doesn't look anything like the old wooden Kramer—but Jack Kramer's name is on a tennis racket again.

Wilson knows it is taking a gamble—most of the new generation of young players have never heard of Jack Kramer—but the company believes that the graphite Kramer will quickly become its number-one seller.

"Jack Kramer is like an old friend to anyone who learned to play tennis with a wooden Kramer," said Kathy Button, a Wilson official. "Jack was the most important factor in Wilson's rise to preeminence in the manufacture of sporting goods. Now we're turning to him again."

One major reason, Button said, is that the current crop of tennis players, some of whom revel in their "bad boy" reputations, don't present the image that Wilson wants to market. "There is something about Jack Kramer, even though he has been retired as a player for thirty-four years, that will lend Wilson more than any of the current stars could possibly offer.

"Jack wasn't the type to fling his racket over the net or to scream at umpires. He represents an era of graciousness in tennis that people miss. In your mind, you picture him in white flannels, leaping over the net at the end of the match to congratulate his opponent."

Having said that, Button affirmed that there was no way that Wilson could bring back the Kramer wooden racket. It had to be graphite.

"I play tennis five or six times a week," Button said. "I see virtually no wooden rackets. No one wants to play with a small wood racket anymore.

"I wasn't with Wilson in 1981, when the decision was made to drop the wooden Kramers, but I imagine that Jack was pretty sad. I think he thought that the company was crazy.

"It was a sound business decision, though. No one was buying them. I can't even tell you how badly we did in sales. We felt it was the end of an era."

In the intervening six years, though, the Wilson company discovered something interesting. People never throw away their tennis rackets. They may not use them any longer, but there is something about a tennis racket that defies the idea of discarding it.

"In closets and basements all over this country, people have the rackets they grew up with," Button said. "And it seems at least 50 percent of those rackets are the wooden Kramers.

"Last year, when we test marketed the first graphite Kramers, we were a little apprehensive. We didn't have to be. We manufactured four thousand of them, and they sold out to dealers in two days. Our current problem is to make enough."


Jack Kramer doesn't hide the fact that having his name on a racket again thrills him.

"It's been a big lift for me," he said. "It peps me up tremendously."

I asked him if he remembered a phrase from the heyday of the wooden Kramers: "*M or W*?"

Kramer laughed. "Do I remember?" he said. "You heard that on every tennis court in America." On the bottom of the grip of every wooden Kramer, there was the red *W* from the Wilson logo. At the beginning of a match, a player would spin his racket with its head on the surface of the court. The opponent would call out *M* or *W*. The racket would land with either the *W* facing up or the *W* facing down—in which case it looked like an *M*. This would determine who served first. The new graphite Kramer, it should be noted, has the red *W* prominently displayed on the bottom of the grip, ready for a fresh generation of *M* or *W*.

Kramer is willing to sing the praises of the new graphite rackets, but when pressed he will tell you that he still has plenty of the wooden Kramer Autographs.

"When they closed them all out, I said that I wanted to buy some," he said. "They said they'd sell them to me for eight dollars a racket, unstrung. They were all in a storehouse down in Tennessee. I bought three hundred of them. I'm down to about 175 now. I've given a lot away. Some people say that they just can't play tennis without a wooden Kramer, so when I hear that, I just give them one. The 175 that I have left are stacked in the garage and in the back bedroom."

Surprisingly—even amazingly—Kramer does not have a tennis court at his house. "My wife Gloria and I picked out the property many years ago, and it's built on a hill," he said. "We just never had it landscaped so that it would accommodate a tennis court. Which was fine with me. I didn't want to have a lot of people hanging around.

"I play very seldom now. I had a hip problem, and I had surgery for it, and I'm told that playing too much tennis will wear my hip out. Once in a while I'll play with my kids or my doctor or my lawyer. Anything that comes down the middle, I'll hit it like Lendl. But on the tougher shots, I miss ones that I used to be able to hit in my sleep.

"It's okay, though. When you get to be my age, you don't get that feeling of rage in your system when you're behind. You don't get disgusted with yourself. You don't care if you lose—it's just exercise. I try like hell to win, but if I don't win, I just walk off the court and have a beer. Thirty-five years ago, if I lost a match, you couldn't talk to me."

There is a certain irony to Kramer's life, and he is not unwilling to point it out.

"For a while there, I was supposedly the best player on earth," he said. "I think that, through my victories, I earned my proper spot among the best players who ever played the game.

"But the racket became more important in my life than the victories. As the years went by, I began to realize that people knew the racket more than they knew me. They didn't know that Kramer was a Wimbledon champion, a Davis Cup player, a pro—they knew the goddamn racket.

"I go into a tennis club these days, and the young players don't know me from shit. A thirteen-year-old doesn't know me as a person unless someone explains it to him. To that kid, I'm just a racket. Oh, once in a while a kid will say, 'I was talking to my coach, and he said that you were the best serve-and-volley player there ever was.' But that's the exception. To most of them, I'm a racket. I don't complain. That's life."

*  *  *

In his contract with Wilson, Kramer has an intriguing clause.

"Wilson has the right to make a deal with my estate after I'm dead," he says. "The idea is, they could continue to manufacture Kramer rackets even though I would no longer be alive.

"I don't know why I love that so much, but I do. I accept the fact that I'm sixty-six years old, and that everything memorable I ever did on a tennis court was years ago.

"But to have people playing with Kramers after I'm gone—what a thrill to think of that. It would be my last association with the game. I'll be gone, but the racket will be alive."

# In the Mood

$S$o here's Gary Coggin, a salesman. He works for a corporation called International Group Inc.—IGI for short. IGI has a number of subsidiaries. One of the subsidiaries is called Petroleum Specialties— Petroleum Specialties is Gary Coggin's bread and butter. He does most of his work for Petroleum Specialties.

There's another IGI subsidiary called Djinnii Industries, with headquarters in Dayton, Ohio, and Gary Coggin and some of the other Petroleum Specialties guys are sent down there to take a tour of the plant. The point is that Gary Coggin and his colleagues may be doing some selling for Djinnii as well as for Petroleum Specialties.

Djinnii Industries is in the microencapsulation game. You may not know what microencapsulation is, but you have encountered it. You know those "scratch 'n' sniff" strips that are sometimes featured in advertisements in magazines? That's microencapsulation—the fragrance is microencapsulated, and when you scratch the strip, the fragrance is released. Actually, according to Gary Coggin, "scratch 'n' sniff" is sort of an outmoded term. "Now we talk about 'snap 'n' burst'," Coggin said. "You know—when you snap the perfume advertisement open, and you smell the perfume. You don't scratch and sniff anymore. You snap and burst."

Anyway . . . there are companies that specialize in this kind of thing, and Djinnii Industries is one of them, so here are Gary Coggin and his salesmen pals touring the plant, and suddenly Gary Coggin spots all these bags stored up on a high shelf, and it looks as if the bags are filled with gold.

"Big bags," Gary Coggin said. "Big, clear bags. Like garbage bags. Only it looks like there's gold in them."

So Gary Coggin asks the guy from Djinnii Industries—the guy who's giving the tour of the plant—if there is really gold in the bags.

And the Djinnii Industries guy says, "No. Those are just the mood rings."

And everything stops. The whole tour of the plant stops.

It turns out that in addition to being involved in the scratch 'n' sniff game, which was to evolve into the snap 'n' burst game, Djinnii Industries was once involved in the mood ring game.

"I couldn't believe it," Gary Coggin recalled. "I didn't know when the last time was that I thought about mood rings."

To be absolutely accurate, upon reflection Gary Coggin did recall when it was. Back in the mid-Seventies he was teaching high school history in Pittsburgh, and all of the kids came to class wearing mood rings. Mood rings were the craze that year; the idea was that the "stone" in the ring changed colors according to variations in the wearer's mood. Level-headed observers said that the colors really changed according to variations in the temperature—either the room temperature or the wearer's body temperature or a combination of the two.

"Mood rings," Gary Coggin said. "I'm looking at bags of mood rings."

More than five thousand mood rings, as a matter of fact. "At Christmastime they're great for stocking-stuffers," said Monte Magill, technical service manager at Djinnii Industries. "We give them to people who come in. Sometimes we give them out by the handfuls. I mean, we can't sell 'em."

Gary Coggin and the other sales guys ask their guide to pull down a bag of mood rings, and the guide does, and Gary Coggin and his buddies start slipping the mood rings onto their fingers.

"I must have had ten or twelve of the things on my hands," Gary Coggin said. "Everybody was wearing them. We had this one meeting later on . . . and I'll be honest, I don't remember a single thing that was discussed. I just remember everybody looking silly and fooling with their mood rings."

Gary Coggin decided that he'd like to take some mood rings home to give to his eight-year-old daughter and some of her neighborhood friends. "The guy at Djinnii said take as many as I want," Coggin said. "He said that he could remember exactly when the mood ring craze ended. He said that the warehouse couldn't keep them in stock, and that the company produced more—and then that right before Christmas that year, the orders stopped. Dead in the water. No one wanted mood rings anymore."

Interestingly, although Gary Coggin remembers that he was teaching high school the year that mood rings were popular, and although the Djinnii executive remembers that the orders stopped coming in right before Christmas of that year, neither man can remember the precise year it was.

"I just know it was the Seventies," Gary Coggin said.

Which makes sense. If the Seventies was the decade that gets no respect, then perhaps the mood ring is the perfect symbol of that decade. Not only were the Seventies not the Fifties or the Sixties—decades that are endlessly idealized—but the mood ring wasn't the Hula-Hoop. In fact, it wasn't even the most famous gimmick-product-craze of the Seventies. The pet rock was.

Now that Gary Coggin is home from the Djinnii factory, he envisions that stash of mood rings that he spotted up on the shelf and he finds himself thinking: "Did that really happen?"

Kind of like the Seventies themselves.

# A Chill in the Sun

**D**AYTONA BEACH, FLORIDA—It's safe to say that if most of America were to watch MTV's coverage of college Spring Break, most of America would walk away from their TV sets stunned and disoriented. Spring Break today is not the International Kiwanis Convention, and MTV does little to disguise this fact.

But most of America does not watch MTV. MTV's target audience is viewers between the ages of eighteen and twenty-four, and they don't seem to be offended by what they see. If anything, they wish they were in Daytona to see it in person.

It's also safe to say that most of MTV's young viewing audience does not understand the economics behind what appears to be an endless succession of "best body on the beach" contests and similar cultural endeavors. When the young viewers see dancers in the sand climb on top of a car and shake their fists triumphantly in the air, the viewers probably consider this to be an act of rebellion—of "youth gone wild," in the words of one song. What the viewers don't realize is that it is no coincidence the car is a Volkswagen—Volkswagen U.S.A. reportedly paid MTV close to $1 million to have that car on the beach within range of MTV's cameras during this year's Spring Break, and to air Volkswagen commercials during MTV's Daytona coverage.

So when a singer named Kevin Paige, during an MTV concert on the beach, defiantly snarled the words "I can do anything I want, you can't stop me," the whooping collegians on the sand in front of him, and the viewers at home, most likely did not stop to consider the irony of his antiestablishment posture in light of the fact that the sponsors of MTV's

Spring Break coverage included such mainstream corporations as An-heuser-Busch, Coca-Cola, Mars candy, Levi's, and Honda.

Some of the televised events, as calculatedly shocking as they are, show a certain sharply demented sense of humor. There is an MTV game show, for example, called "Remote Control"—a sort of "Jeopardy" for a generation whose major cultural reference point is television. At Spring Break, the "Remote Control" categories are not displayed on a game board; they are displayed on loincloths worn by "Hawaiian Tropic Girls"—models employed by a suntan-lotion company. One game cat-egory was called "Babes and Assassins."

And so MTV's Colin Quinn, reading a "Babes and Assassins" question to the panel, asked: "She's the no-talent actress who married Burt Reyn-olds, and he's the no-talent actor who offed Abe Lincoln. Name 'em both!" (The college woman being asked the question quickly said, "Loni Anderson and . . . uh . . . uh . . . uh. . . ." Loni Anderson she knew. John Wilkes Booth eluded her.)

Then there was MTV's "hot-dog eating contest," the culmination of which consisted of college women having their hands tied behind their backs, then having hot dogs smeared with condiments jammed down their throats by college men while rock music played and other collegians cheered. Hot dog after hot dog was shoved into the women's mouths, and while the symbolism of this seemed to be lost on no one, the fact that it was being telecast live into 50 million homes via satellite seemed to be taken for granted. The use of the communications satellite might have raised the philosophical question: John Glenn risked his life in space for this?

To me, though, the most troubling moment during MTV's Spring Break telecast—at first surprising, then disturbing, then almost para-lyzing in its implications—had nothing to do with jokes about presiden-tial assassinations or with crude sexual innuendo.

The moment came when a young comedian was performing before the Spring Break crowd and the MTV cameras. The comedian made a reference to a widely broadcast television commercial—you may have seen it—that features an elderly woman who has become incapacitated during a fall in her home. The commercial is for a service designed to summon emergency assistance for elderly people; in the commercial, the woman cries out: "I've fallen and I can't get up."

On stage, the comedian—wearing a baseball cap and jeans—mock-ingly called out: "I've fallen . . . and I can't get up." He knew that the collegiate audience, raised on TV, would be familiar with the commercial.

They roared in recognition. The comedian used the phrase again, his voice a whining taunt: "I've fallen . . . and I can't get up."

The collegians in the audience were woofing and raising their fists and doubling over with laughter. Their voices echoed the ridicule and derision in the voice of the comedian, and they chanted along with him: "I've fallen . . . and I can't get up."

It was Spring Break, and they were in college, and growing old and helpless seemed to be a thought so distant as to be not even worth considering. The college students and the comedian chanted in unison: "I've fallen . . . and I can't get up." Laughing all the while. Laughing so hard.

# Thirty Seconds

It's funny how a man can live his whole life—a life filled with heroism and downfalls, fatherhood and courage and pain and introspection—and no one notices. No one outside the man's family and his small group of friends.

It's funny what television can do. Take the same man. Film a TV commercial that is brilliantly conceived and executed, and the man becomes known and revered in every corner of the nation. He is the same person; nothing at all about him has changed. Nothing except the most important thing of all: he has been televised.

Novelists can write one hundred thousand words, two hundred thousand words, and not cause a ripple. For Bill Demby, it took only fifty-seven words, written by someone else and spoken by an announcer during a thirty-second television commercial, to totally revise his life.

Here are the words:

"When Bill Demby was in Vietnam, he dreamed of coming home and playing a little basketball. A dream that all but died when he lost both legs to a Vietcong rocket. But then researchers discovered that a Du Pont plastic could make truly lifelike artificial limbs. Now Bill's back, and some say he hasn't lost a step."

There was a tag line promoting Du Pont. The fifty-seven words about Bill Demby and the Du Pont tag line weren't what was so significant, of course. What was significant was the film footage of Demby—his artificial legs visible to the camera—competing in a game of playground basketball with able-bodied men. It began airing in the fall of 1987, and it became one of those commercials that people think about and talk to their friends about. It won a Clio award from the advertising industry; Demby was featured on the ABC program "20/20." He went from being completely anonymous to truly famous in a matter of weeks.

When I caught up with him he was heading for a small college in the Midwest to make an address to the students. The basketball arena had been reserved for the event because an overflow crowd was expected.

"I walked into a McDonald's the other day to get something to eat," Bill Demby said. "This guy said hello to me and I said hi back. I thought he was just a friendly guy. But then he said, 'I liked the commercial.' "

Demby, now thirty-eight, was driving a truck on a road outside Quang Tri, Vietnam, on March 26, 1971, when a Vietcong rocket hit the vehicle. A twenty-year-old Army private at the time, he lost both legs below the knee. He spent the next year in Walter Reed hospital in Washington, and then tried to put his life back together.

Nothing very spectacular happened. He had problems with alcohol and drugs. A promising athlete before going to Vietnam, Demby—with the help of artificial legs—began trying to play sports again. He was in Nashville in 1987 at a basketball tournament sponsored by the U.S. Amputee Athletic Association when he was invited to audition for a Du Pont commercial. Du Pont had manufactured some of the materials used in certain prostheses, and had sent representatives of its advertising agency to the amputee tournament.

"I was very wary about doing it," Demby said. "I knew that on television, they can go into the cutting room and put things together any way they want. As far as the world was concerned at that point, Bill Demby didn't exist. As an amputee, usually I kept to myself."

Demby and four other disabled men wearing prostheses played basketball with personnel from the BBD&O ad agency looking on, and all five men submitted to informal interviews. Before long, Demby was told that he had been selected from the five to be the star of the Du Pont spot.

He was far from thrilled. "Actually, I called them up and said I was not interested in doing the commercial," Demby said.

I asked him why that was. For the first time in our conversation, he seemed to hesitate, as if a little embarrassed. Finally he said:

"I don't like to take my pants off in front of people." Meaning he doesn't like people to look at his artificial legs. Any people, much less millions upon millions of television viewers.

But in the end he decided to say yes. The commercial was shot on a basketball court in New York City, on Columbus Avenue between Seventy-sixth and Seventy-seventh streets, in late August 1987. "They told us that we were just supposed to play basketball, and that they'd film it," Demby said. "The other guys weren't actors—they were just players from the neighborhood. Players without physical disabilities.

"We played basketball from 7:00 in the morning until 6:30 at night. I got very tired. They had rented a room for me at the Warwick Hotel, and when the filming was over I just went to my room, took a shower, and fell asleep with the television set on. When I woke up the next morning the TV was still going. I didn't think much about what had happened. I just thought I had played some pickup basketball and they had filmed it, and now I would go back to my regular life. I went home that day. I felt that nothing had changed."

The advertising agency put the commercial together quickly. Demby and his family, who live near Washington, D.C., received a telephone call advising them to watch the CBS "Sunday Morning" broadcast on September 13, 1987. That was the day the commercial first aired.

"My wife and daughter and I sat in front of the TV set," Demby said. "The commercial came on. The wonderful feeling . . . there are no words to describe it."


The first time Demby realized that something unusual was up came within a few weeks. "I was walking down the street in Washington, and this real huge guy started staring right into my eyes. I was kind of scared. He said, 'It's you. It's you.' I didn't know what he was talking about. I thought that maybe he was going to rob me or something. I said, 'No, no.' And then the guy said, 'You're the one in the commercial. It's the best one I've ever seen.' "

Since that moment, Demby has become used to the public recognition. Sometimes he doesn't much like it. "On occasion it still surprises me when people look at me," he said. "It shouldn't, but it does. Once in a while when someone will ask me about the commercial, I'll find myself saying, 'No, that was my twin brother.' "

There are other times, though. . . .

"A man came up to me—a man who had been having a lot of troubles. He explained the details of his troubles. He told me he had given up on everything. He said that seeing me in the commercial had turned him around. He thanked me for changing his life. Me.

"I walked away so that he wouldn't see me cry."

Soon everything was happening for Demby. He went to a New York Knicks basketball game—he had never even been inside Madison Square Garden before—and the crowd gave him a long standing ovation. Moses Malone and Patrick Ewing shook his hand.

He began to be invited to speak before large groups, such as the college audience he was on his way to address when I joined him. The "20/20" segment was filmed. The irony, of course, was that he was the same man he had been for the almost twenty years after he had returned from Vietnam. But because of those thirty seconds on the Du Pont commercial (a sixty-second version also ran), for the first time in his life people were treating him as if he were special.

"It was very hard to get used to," Demby said. He was interviewed by newspapers and magazines; suddenly people saw him as a symbol of bravery and hope. He knew that if the commercial had not been broadcast, the same people would stare right through him as though he were invisible. Now they adored him.

Not everything made him feel great. "For a long time, I had been hesitant to tell people that I had lost my legs in Vietnam," he said. "I'd always wear long pants, even when I was playing sports. But now everyone knows what my legs look like.

"And my past problem with alcohol and PCP . . . that was my private problem, and now it's out. My daughter was eight years old, and she didn't know about it. She probably never would have, if the commercial hadn't been filmed and people hadn't started talking about me. She was very hurt by it. I tried to explain. I told her, 'It was just a bad part in Daddy's life. He was weak.'"

There is one aspect of the commercial that Demby virtually never volunteers to talk about. The standard line is that the film crew just shot the pickup basketball game and edited the footage down. The most emotional moment in the commercial comes when Demby is knocked to the ground, hard, by an opposing player. On his back, he stares up. Then he gets to his feet. It is one of those magical television instants— a second or two of film that gives the audience goose bumps and stays with them for a long time.

"That didn't happen during the game," Demby said. "We had been playing all day, and finally the director, Rick Levine, called me aside. He said he needed something else. He asked me if I would mind if he had one of the players knock me down."

It must have been quite a question. Imagine saying to a man with artificial legs: "Listen, we know you've been playing basketball for hours, but would it be okay if we had you jump in the air and then we pushed you to the concrete so that you land on your back? We'll only need to do it a few times."

Demby thought about it and said yes. He figured that Levine must know what he was doing. It paid off; without that sequence—especially the expression in Demby's eyes after he hits the ground—the commercial would lose its strongest surge of visceral humanity and power. Still, though: imagine asking the question.


Now, with all that has happened to Demby, you have to remind yourself that there were four other finalists for the starring role in the commercial, and that if BBD&O had selected any one of those four, today no one would know who Bill Demby is. Demby said that he has not heard from or seen the other four since auditioning. He got the thirty seconds; they didn't.

He does his best to keep it in perspective. There are days now when he feels it would be impossible to be any more famous and respected. "But I know that just as fast as this has come, it can leave. It could turn out to be a very temporary thing.

"I have a tendency to think we're all sort of crazy. The idea that thirty seconds could completely change a man's life." He tries not to lose sight of the fact that with or without the commercial, he would still be Bill Demby.

He is finally accepting the idea that strangers will approach him and tell him how much they admire him. "That's just society, though," he said. "That's just people reacting to what they've seen on their television screen.

"I keep having this thought. One of these days the commercial is going to stop running. They all do.

"And not long after that, someone is going to say to someone else, 'Hey, do you remember that guy—the amputee who played basketball in that commercial?'

"And the other guy will hesitate for a second and then say, 'Yeah, I think so. What was his name?' "

# A Father's Words

The letter was handwritten on lined paper, and before I was two paragraphs into it I realized that it was asking for something I just could not do. If you do this for someone one time, then people are going to ask you to do the same thing for them every day of the year.

Somehow, though, I couldn't forget it, and I couldn't throw it away. The letter was about the terrible problems someone was having in his effort to get a job. Employment interview after employment interview, rejection letter after rejection letter . . . it's something that more than a few people have gone through in their lives.

The difference was that the person who was writing to me was not the job-seeker; the person writing was the job-seeker's sixty-nine-year-old father.

"My son is thirty-three years old," the father informed me. The son, according to his dad, has a regular college degree and two masters degrees, including a masters in business administration from one of the nation's most prestigious universities. The father listed a number of academic honors his son had earned. "He has sent out well over four hundred resumes," his father wrote. "He has had approximately fifty interviews over the last year." The son, the father wrote, cannot seem to get hired at any position appropriate for someone with his education. "He has applied through ads in your newspaper, inquired with his university's alumni club, placement bureau, job recruiters, all to no avail. As a matter of fact his feelings are so low that he feels life is not worth living."

There is enough tragedy in this world that the thirty-three-year-old job-seeker's plight undoubtedly ranks nowhere near the top of situations that truly make one's life "not worth living." And all I knew about the man was what his father had put down on paper; I had no independent knowledge of his background or his skills and drawbacks.

Maybe that was what prevented me from throwing the letter away. Not the thought of the job-seeker, but of his dad. For some reason, I felt I had to speak with the father.

"He got good grades all through grammar school and high school, he has always worked to improve himself . . ." he began.

As gently as I could, I told the father that I could not issue a plea for a job for his son. I said that I was just struck by the fact that the dad was being so passionate in going to bat for his boy.

"He has never gotten out and joined some of these groups that other lads have," the father said. "His personality is not that of a backslapper; he is not a person to display a tremendous sense of humor. He's more of a good listener. He will listen to a conversation and he will offer his opinion if he feels it is a valuable opinion. He'll do that."

I asked if people who knew his son had made any suggestions about what he might be doing wrong in job-interview situations.

"Well, one day my son said to me, 'Maybe I'm not coming across to people in the best way I might be,' " his father said. "So we asked some friends, and they said that perhaps my son should get rid of his plastic eyeglasses."

His plastic eyeglasses?

"Yes," the father said. "His glasses were made of thick plastic all around, and we were told that they were the kind of glasses that a schoolboy might wear. They didn't give a businesslike enough impression. So we watched television, and we looked at the kinds of glasses that the news analysts wear, and the frames were thinner. My son bought new glasses like those, and they do make him look better."

The son, the father said, has attended meetings of his university's alumni, but has come home and said, "I'm so out of place. The others are all talking about their jobs and families. What do I have to talk about?" The worst night, the father said, was when the son was particularly hopeful about a job interview he had had, and then the rejection letter arrived. "I have never seen a man of thirty-three cry," the father said. "All I could say to him was, 'Somewhere along the line, there's someone who will see your talents and will have the compassion and the willingness to give you a chance.' "

The father said that sometimes he tried to find hope in the wording of his son's rejection letters: "A number of the letters even said, 'We'll keep your resume on file.' So that's a glimmer."

I didn't know exactly what to say. So I asked the father why he was going to all this trouble. His answer was the most understandable one of all:

"Because he's the only child I have."

There was a silence, and then I said I still wasn't sure what I could do.

And I'm not; I'm not sure. But to the son who is reading this—and you know who you are—I can say one thing with certainty:

Things might not be going so well, and you might believe that your life and your luck will never turn around. There are a lot of jobs in this world, though, and a lot of people who take their jobs for granted. You have something that some people don't have, and that no one should ever take for granted—you have a father who truly loves you. On your darkest nights, never forget that. It's something that no one can ever deny you, and no one can ever take away.

# Easy Does It

Marilyn is forty and married for the second time. Vicki is thirty-seven and married for the second time. Vicki's daughter, seventeen, is a high school senior. We are in Vicki's car, heading for a movie theater in a suburb of a midwestern city. The movie being featured tonight is *The Big Easy*, starring Dennis Quaid. Marilyn and Vicki have each seen the movie nineteen times. Vicki's daughter has seen the movie fifteen times, usually in the company of her mother and Marilyn.

*The Big Easy* has appeared in four theaters within driving distance of the neighborhood in which Marilyn and Vicki live. Now it is in its last week in the area. Tickets at this theater, the end of the line, go for $1.50. Because Marilyn and Vicki both work, they have to see *The Big Easy* either on weekends or at night. Tonight their husbands will cook dinner for themselves.

"We go so we can squirm when we see Dennis," Marilyn tells me. She is in the back seat with Vicki's daughter. I am in the front seat. Vicki is driving.

"When I see Dennis with his shirt off, I just want to rub his belly," Marilyn says.

"I just like to look at his belly," Vicki's daughter says.

"Come on, Vicki," Marilyn says. "We're going to be late."


We park in the lot of the shopping strip that contains the theater. We pay for our tickets. Vicki leads us to the front of the auditorium. Vicki sits on the left. Marilyn sits next to her. I sit next to Marilyn. Vicki's daughter sits next to me.

The movie begins. Dennis Quaid, portraying a New Orleans police detective, turns toward the camera and smiles. Marilyn and Vicki let out soft moans. I look over and see that they are holding hands. Vicki's daughter pulls her legs up under herself.

Three days later I meet Marilyn and Vicki in a restaurant, and try to figure this out.

"*Longing* is the word," Marilyn says. "You look at Dennis, and you know that he knows what makes women happy. And you know that it makes him happy that they're happy. It's as if Dennis is saying: 'Relax, take it easy, don't be embarrassed. Let me take care of everything.' "

I say it seems sort of puzzling that Marilyn, a forty-year-old woman who is on her second marriage, would be drawn to a man who knows how to "take care of everything." It would seem that she would be experienced enough not to require that.

"Sex is an experience no matter how often you have it," she says. "Each time with a new person, you're a little on edge. With Dennis, you know you could relax. His message is, 'I don't care if you don't know what you're doing. I want you anyway.' "

Vicki says, "From the first time that Dennis grins, I'm very happy. He turns around and grins, and you know that he's going to please you for the next couple of hours."

Both women say they have never felt this way or acted this way before—not for a movie star, not for a singer, not for anyone.

"It mesmerizes me," Marilyn says. "I can't get enough of it. It's an addiction. Once I was in my flannel nightgown, and I knew I just had to go see it again. So I went to the movie theater in my flannel nightgown."

On one of the first nineteen occasions that she saw *The Big Easy*, Marilyn took her husband. "He said, 'Now, no moaning,' " she says. "He said he didn't want me to embarrass him. I didn't squeeze his hand during the movie. I felt he would be invading my territory a little bit."

Vicki says, "I've never been turned on like this." When I ask her if her husband is jealous, she says, "I don't think he's jealous so much as perturbed that I'm acting immature."

I ask if either woman's husband has asked that they stop going to see *The Big Easy*. After all—nineteen times?

"Who would be married to a guy who would tell me I could or could not do something?" Marilyn says.

I ask how much of this is fantasy and how much is real.

"I know I'll never meet Dennis Quaid," Marilyn says. "But I do get aroused. When I see him in the movie, I want to have sex."

"I look at him and I squirm," Vicki says.

I point out that, in telling me how they feel when they see *The Big Easy*, they have used that word several times—*squirm*.

"Wriggle," Marilyn says.

"Pain and ecstasy are just about the same," Vicki says.

"Writhe," Marilyn says.

"This one theater where we saw the movie—I liked that one the best," Vicki says. "The theater had those seats that rock back and forth. I would put my feet up on the seat in front of me, and I would look at Dennis, and I would move my legs back and forth."

I say that it seems unusual that the women could see the movie so many times without becoming bored.

"But you notice something new every time," Marilyn says.

I ask her to give me an example.

"Well, in the first love scene with Ellen Barkin?" she says. "It took me a couple of times to notice that Dennis was hard."

"You didn't notice that right away?" Vicki says. "I noticed that the first time."

"I was looking at his chest," Marilyn says.

"I wasn't," Vicki says.

I ask about Vicki's daughter. After all, she is only seventeen.

"So?" Vicki says.

I ask her what she thinks her daughter is experiencing when she sees the movie.

"I know what she's experiencing," Vicki says. "She gets as aroused as I do. We've talked about it."

And that's okay with Vicki?

"Just because she's seventeen doesn't mean she's not grown-up," Vicki says. "We're all women."

And it doesn't bother her, to have her daughter sitting right next to her, being sexually aroused by a movie star?

"Why would it?" Vicki says.

I say I don't know—it just seems to me that it would make some mothers uncomfortable.

"I find that sad and inhibited," Vicki says.

Marilyn says that she has a sixteen-year-old daughter, and that they went to see *The Big Easy* together once. But her daughter did not share her reaction to Dennis Quaid.

I ask her how she feels about that.

"I don't know," she says. "I guess it would be nice if my daughter and I liked the same kind of men."


The next day I phone Vicki's daughter.

"My mom went and saw *The Big Easy*, and she told me I had to see it immediately," she says. "She told me the guy was really, really sexy. The first time I saw it, I thought it was a good movie, but I didn't know why she was getting all worked up.

"I went back to see it again, though . . . and the second time I got as worked up as my mom did. I was thinking about him so much."

She says that her mother and Marilyn invite her to accompany them every time they go to the movie.

"It's like I'm melting," she says. "In a lot of scenes, there's a certain angle of his face, and his eyes light up. They turn colors. What I like the most in that first love scene with Ellen Barkin is the way Dennis is devouring her and breaking down her resistance."

I ask her if she doesn't think it's a little unorthodox—a mother and her teenage daughter sitting together and reacting that way to a man.

"My mom has never been June Cleaver," she says.

I ask her if she thinks her father is jealous of her mother's feelings for Dennis Quaid.

"I think he's a little jealous," she says. "He knows her thoughts are elsewhere."


Before I try to talk to her father about that, I call Marilyn's husband, who is an attorney.

"She's never done anything like this before," he says to me. "To be honest, I do have my moments of jealousy. But if this is what Marilyn is interested in, there's not much I can say. I've never had to deal with it before."

I ask him if he feels threatened.

"I find myself feeling a little competitive," he says. "It annoys me a little. I certainly feel that this fellow is getting an enormous amount of Marilyn's attention. And that's attention I'm not getting. I'm happy that the movie is leaving town, but I don't know what's going to happen when the video comes out."

I ask him if he ever considered asking her not to go to the movie so often.

"I don't feel I would be justified in putting that restraint on her," he says. "I've never felt in our relationship that I've had the right to say, 'No, you can't do this.'

"I did put my foot down once, though. She had a picture of Dennis Quaid, and she put it on the dresser in our bedroom. I told her that I'd prefer that she took it to work with her and hung it up in her office. I thought that having the picture in our bedroom would be a little too intrusive in our lives."

I call Vicki's husband, a business executive, with the intention of asking him the same kinds of questions about his wife and daughter. But he immediately makes it clear that he is not interested in discussing the matter.

"I would not have anticipated this," he says. "I'm just wondering how long it's going to go on."

A postscript: After having these conversations, I tell this story to several people in the entertainment business in Los Angeles. One afternoon my phone rings, and it is Dennis Quaid.

I repeat for him, in detail, the experience of going to the movie with Marilyn, Vicki, and Vicki's daughter. I reconstruct for him what they have said to me, and what Marilyn's and Vicki's husbands have said.

For a moment Quaid is silent.

Then he says, "You're joking."

I assure him I am not.

He laughs, but the laugh is not entirely comfortable. He tries a joke:

"Let's see, nineteen times, multiplied by six dollars a ticket. . . ." But it is clear that he is perplexed.

"Look, tell them that I think it's great that they would like a film of mine so much that they would see it so many times," he says. "Hey, I've only seen the movie twice."

Then he turns serious. "I remember meeting Marlon Brando, who was my idol, and totally blowing it," he says. "I had looked up to him so much, and then on the set of *The Missouri Breaks* I got the chance to meet him, and I became totally tongue-tied—I don't think I managed to say three words. I walked away thoroughly embarrassed, and after that I never had an idol again. Because idols will always disappoint you.

"I guess what I'm trying to say is that I'm happy they like the movie, but it doesn't mean that they know me or I know them."

We talk for a few more minutes. He asks me more questions about all of this. Then he falls silent again.

"It's funny, isn't it?" he says. "It's sweet. Isn't it?"

# Moving On

$\mathbf{H}$er husband's flight was due in at O'Hare, so she drove out to the airport to pick him up. Her husband is a Midwest district manager for a clothing manufacturing company with headquarters in the South; he had been down at headquarters for a series of meetings.

As she stood in the gate area at O'Hare she was feeling great. For the first time in her life, she could truly say that her life was perfect. She and her husband were both thirty-one; they had two daughters, age six and age two. They lived in a beautiful house in a lovely suburb north of Chicago. This school year the older girl would be beginning the first grade, and for the second year in a row the mother would have a position with the PTA.

She and her husband had good friends; it seemed that every time she went shopping in her suburb, she found herself waving to people she knew. The summer had been perfect; she and the girls were always going to the pool or to the park for a picnic. In an era when many people are fearful, she had no fears in her life. Good schools, good neighbors, good friends . . . perfect.

Her husband's flight arrived. They drove home and had dinner; they put the children to bed. Then they went to bed themselves. They made love.

Afterwards, her husband said that they had to talk.

"I've got an absolutely fantastic opportunity," he said.

She waited.

He said that during his business trip, the president of his company had made him an offer. The company wanted him to move south, and to work at company headquarters as vice-president for sales of the entire division. It was a chance that most men dream of, he said.

And if he said yes to his bosses, the family would have to move to the medium-sized southern town that was company headquarters.

Her husband spoke of how good it would be for his career—he would be on the fastest of fast tracks, he would be one of the company's true golden boys. She listened. She said they would talk about it in the morning.

When he had drifted off to sleep she quietly got out of bed and walked to the living room. She sat by the front window and looked out at the neighborhood she loved. She began to cry. She sat looking out the window all night.

It was one of the oldest stories in the world: The wife and children have to move to keep up with the husband's career. So much had changed in our society; so many assumptions had been revised and updated. But here she was, being asked to follow her husband to a town she knew nothing about, and the story felt as if it was being played out for the first time. She loved her life in her neighborhood and her suburb; she would have been willing to live that way forever.

And now she knew that she would be moving.

The events of the next few weeks were rapid. She and her husband flew down to the southern town; its nicer neighborhoods were acceptable, but they weren't what she wanted. She had called her school's principal and had written down a legal-pad-sized page full of questions to ask the principal in the neighborhood down south. The answers she got down there—on everything from per capita expenditures on pupils to the newness of the textbooks in the classes—left her apprehensive. Nothing was more important to her six-year-old than art and music; she felt that she would be cheating her little girl by taking her out of her present school and taking her south to the new one.

Her husband had said that no final decision would be made until they had thoroughly talked things over. But she knew that was not true; her husband was set on taking the job, and she feared that if she stood in his way there would be a time—maybe next year, maybe years later—when his resentments would boil over.

So their house was put on the market. Two months earlier she had put up kitchen wallpaper that she had saved for out of her household expenses. Now strangers were walking through the house, inspecting that wallpaper to see if it fit their tastes. It all felt like a terrible dream to her, but in four short days the house was sold; now all that remained was for her and her family to move out.

Her six-year-old said that she was scared; she said that she wouldn't know anyone in the new school. So the mother said that things would be all right; she said that she wouldn't know anyone in the new town, either, and they would get through it together. Already she was thinking: My husband will be in good shape from the first day. He already knows people at company headquarters; he will walk in and have friends.

The money? Her husband will be making 20 percent more than he is making now. And he will be on good terms with the company—if he had said no to the offer and insisted on staying in the Midwest, things would have been far less cozy with his bosses. Try as she might, the questions kept coming into her mind: Is the money worth it? Is the title worth it? Our lives are perfect right now—is anything worth changing that?

An old, old story that never seems old when it happens to you. She thinks about it now even as she works around the house. She is trying to get things packed. Moving day is in three weeks.

# Something Good

It must have been about a year ago that I was flipping through the mail and found a letter from Carole King.

I wasn't sure if it was *that* Carole King; the envelope bore a California postmark, but then a lot of people live in California, and Carole King isn't all that uncommon a name, although the "e" at the end of Carole was a little unusual.

I called the phone number that this Carole King person had enclosed, and got a machine. When she returned the call I was out. This went back and forth a few times; we never did connect, so I never was quite sure whether Carole King the letter-writer was also Carole King the songwriter.

If her name means anything to you—and chances are it does—the first thing to come to your mind is probably *Tapestry*.

*Tapestry* was an album that Carole King released in 1971. Within two years it sold 10 million copies. Ten million. *Tapestry*, whether you liked the music on it or or not, transcended the record business; *Tapestry* literally became like a piece of furniture, in the sense that you could walk into someone's house or apartment and be pretty sure there would be a copy of *Tapestry* lying around. It was almost a required purchase. If you close your eyes right now, you can probably see the cover.

In those couple of years when 10 million people were buying *Tapestry* and listening to Carole King's voice, we were made aware through the press that Carole King's career had started at least a decade before that. A Brooklyn girl, she had written many hit songs for other people when she was barely out of her teens. *Tapestry* removed the songwriter's anonymity and made her famous as a singer.

A couple of weeks ago Carole King called. The Carole King who had written the letter the year before was, indeed, that Carole King; now she was touring with a band, and she was in the Chicago area. She wanted to know if I'd like to have dinner and come along with her to her show at the Poplar Creek outdoor theater.

It turned out I couldn't; I was headed out of town, and by the time I returned she would be gone. We had a very pleasant phone conversation, and I was still thinking of her as the *Tapestry* woman, and then, just to check things out, I hunted down my copy of something called *The Rolling Stone Illustrated History of Rock & Roll*.

That's just what it sounds like—it's a reference book. I looked up Carole King, and a lot of her early songs—the pre-*Tapestry* songs, the songs other people had recorded—were listed.

I was astonished. This woman wrote the soundtrack to some of the happiest times of my life.

Knowing that she had written some old hits was one thing; seeing the specific list of songs was another. Working in collaboration with various other songwriters, she created the special, personal history that still echoes in so many of our heads.

Some of her songs are very, very famous, and probably mean a great deal to some of you: "Will You Still Love Me Tomorrow," originally recorded by the Shirelles; "Up on the Roof," by the Drifters; "Crying in the Rain," by the Everly Brothers.

The songs that leapt out at me, though, were not as celebrated as those. Still, they came along at a time in my life when I was precisely ready for them—it was almost as if I needed them to express what it was I was feeling.

There was a song called "Hey Girl," sung by Freddy Scott; "One Fine Day," sung by the Chiffons; "I Can't Stay Mad at You," sung by Skeeter Davis. Okay, maybe we're not talking about Cole Porter here. Doesn't matter. We're all born when we're born, and Cole Porter wasn't around when a lot of us were first falling in love.

One particular song . . . it was called "I'm Into Something Good," and it became a hit when it was recorded by the British group Herman's Hermits. Before that, though, "I'm Into Something Good" was recorded by a female singer whose name I cannot remember. I can hear the voice, though. And I can feel what I was feeling then. I would wake up, and the words would come out of the radio—"... something tells me I'm into something good"—and it was true. Something very good was just about to happen to me, was already happening, really, and it was almost as if Carole King had read my mind and was affirming that fact. Something tells me I'm into something good.

How does a girl come out of Brooklyn and do that? How does a girl come out of Brooklyn and get inside your head like that? And how does she know how to write songs as varied as "Pleasant Valley Sunday," which the Monkees recorded, and "A Natural Woman," which Aretha Franklin recorded?

Guess I won't get to ask her. By the time I figured out it was Carole King who was inside my head during all those wonderful times, Carole King had left town.

Maybe that's just as well, though. Whatever we might have had to say to each other, she already said to me a long time ago.

But then, she knows that.

# A Day for Cornelius

With some stories it seems impossible that there could ever be a happy ending. Still, you come as close as you can.

The murder of four-year-old Lattie McGee in Chicago by his mother and her boyfriend was almost incomprehensible in its cruelty. The details of the months of torture inflicted on that child are beyond explanation; the fact that Lattie's killers are serving life sentences will not erase the memory of what was done.

With all the public interest in Lattie, the story of his brother, Cornelius Abraham, got kind of lost. Cornelius was six during the summer that Lattie was tortured and killed; the same things that were done to Lattie—the beatings, the starvation, the burning with an iron, the nights of being hung in a locked and darkened closet—were done to Cornelius, too. Somehow he survived. He watched his brother slowly being killed and was unable to stop the killers. Cornelius's testimony in court helped convict them.

Cornelius has just turned nine. He is a thin, extremely quiet boy; he lives with relatives, and the two great loves of his life are reading and basketball.

On a recent Sunday afternoon, Jim Bigoness and I took Cornelius to the Chicago Stadium. Bigoness is the assistant state's attorney who prosecuted Lattie McGee's killers.

Cornelius has the wide, all-seeing eyes of a frightened doe. It's not hard to figure out why. Those eyes have seen things that no human should ever have to see. On this particular day, he seemed almost unable to believe that he was really in the Stadium. To every Chicago youngster who follows basketball, the Stadium is a shrine. Think of where Cornelius once was, locked up and tormented and hurt. And now he was in the Stadium, about to see his first Bulls game.

He said nothing. He just looked around.

Bigoness and I said that we had somewhere else in the building we had to go; we asked Cornelius to come with us.

We walked down a stairway. Cornelius stood between us. Then a door opened and a man came out. Cornelius looked up, and his eyes filled with a combination of wonder and awe and total disbelief.

Cornelius tried to say something; his mouth was moving, but no words would come out. He tried to speak and then the man helped him out by speaking first.

"Hi, Cornelius," the man said. "I'm Michael Jordan."

Jordan knelt down and spoke quietly with Cornelius. He made some jokes and told some stories about basketball; he didn't rush. You have to understand—for a long time the only adults Cornelius had any contact with were adults who wanted to hurt and humiliate him. And now Michael Jordan was saying, "Are you going to cheer for us today? We're going to need it."

Jordan went back into the locker room to finish dressing for the game. Bigoness and I walked Cornelius back upstairs to the court. There was one more surprise waiting.

Cornelius was given a red shirt of the kind worn by the Bulls' ballboys. He retrieved balls for the players while they warmed up.

Then, as the game was about to begin, he was led to Michael Jordan's seat on the Bulls' bench. That's where he was going to sit—right next to Jordan's seat. During the minutes of the game when Jordan was out and resting, Cornelius would be sitting with him; when Jordan was on the court, Cornelius would be saving his seat for him.

I try not to be a vengeful person. But I hope I can be forgiven for thinking: The two people who killed Lattie McGee and tortured Cornelius were in prison on this afternoon. I hoped they understood that they are going to spend every day for the rest of their lives in prison. They are going to die in those stinking cells.

Nothing can bring Lattie back, and nothing can undo what was done to Cornelius. But the killers were in prison, and Cornelius was in the Stadium, sitting on the wooden surface of the court right next to Michael Jordan's chair. At one point late in the game Jordan took a pass and sailed into the air and slammed home a basket. And there, just a few feet away, was Cornelius Abraham, laughing out loud with joy.

# It's About Your Heart

Sometimes your life takes you in directions you never quite anticipated. Sometimes you find yourself looking for answers to questions that might have been better left unraised.

I went on tour to promote a book called *Be True To Your School: A Diary of 1964*. The book, based on a journal I kept during the year I turned seventeen, proved to be of interest to talk-show hosts and newspaper interviewers. Before long, I had my routine down pat.

I would tell the story of Lindy Lemmon, my first real love; I would tell the story of ABCDJ (Allen, Bob, Chuck, Dan, and Jack), five best friends; and always I would tell the story of the older married woman. The interviewers couldn't get enough of that story.

In the book I called her Bev, although that was not her real name. She had been the chaperone for a group of high school girls who had rented a summer cottage near Gem Beach in northern Ohio; she was twenty-seven, and her husband was back in the little town where they all lived. The mothers of the girls had hired her to look after them at Gem Beach.

It was the end of August, just before the first days of our senior year. Allen and Jack and I were staying at a motel called the Holmes, in Sandusky. We met the high school girls and spent time at their Gem Beach cottage. Allen and Jack developed crushes on a couple of the girls. All I could think about was Bev. I was not a sophisticated or advanced seventeen-year-old. But we would all go to the beach together, and I would look at Bev, tan in her brown bikini, and I would think that she was the most beautiful woman I had ever seen.

\*    \*    \*

From *Be True to Your School*, the entry dated August 28, 1964:

Allen had a date with Paula again tonight, so Bev and Jack and I stayed in the motel room and watched a Cleveland Browns exhibition football game on TV. Jack was sitting on the floor in front of the TV, and Bev was sitting on the double bed, and I was sitting on the cot.

We kept talking as the game was being played, and at one point the talk got to kissing. I said something really stupid about being a good kisser.

"Talker," Bev said, and Jack laughed.

I didn't know how to respond, so I said, "Just you wait."

Bev turned and looked right into my eyes. "I've been waiting all week," she said.

And I knew she wasn't kidding. She looked at me and said those words, and I knew she wasn't kidding.

Jack didn't catch any of this; he was still intently watching the football game. I just sat back on the cot and wondered what to do.

About a half an hour later, Allen came back from his date with Paula. He said, "Does anyone want to get a pizza?"

Jack said, "I do."

I said, "I don't."

Bev said, "I don't."

So Jack and Allen were walking out the door. I was still on the cot. Bev said, "Either move over or get off, Greene. I want to take a nap."

I was lying there like a dead man. My arms were straight down by my sides. I wasn't moving; I was hardly breathing. Bev sat down on the cot. Allen and Jack laughed at me, and then they got in Allen's car and drove away.

Bev lay down next to me. She draped one of her arms over me. A few minutes went by, and then we started hugging each other and rubbing each other. I thought I was going to go crazy.

As easy as it had been to talk to Bev all week, now I couldn't think of a thing to say. I kept trying to say something, but nothing would come out.

Finally Bev said, "What are you thinking about?"

I thought my chest was going to explode, it was thumping so hard. Bev put her hand on my shirt and said, "It's about your heart." We started kissing. I just couldn't believe it; I was kissing Bev. . . .

I saw her once more in the autumn of 1964, and then once in the summer of 1965. When I went off to college in September 1965, I wrote to her and she wrote back, but when I sent her another letter it went unanswered. The years passed; several times, on a whim, I called directory assistance in her town, but her husband's name was no longer listed.

She marked a turning point in my life: Allen and Jack were both better looking than I was, but she had chosen me. The moral questions—why would a twenty-seven-year-old married woman want to be with a seventeen-year-old high school boy, and why would that high school boy, who had been taught right from wrong by loving and conscientious parents, so eagerly go along with it—should have bothered me, but they never did. On August 28, 1964, I gained a feeling of self-confidence that I had never known before.

I thought about her from time to time. Once, when she was on my mind, I got on the phone and tried to find out if the Holmes Motel still existed. It turned out that the building still stood, but that the name had been changed to the Vacation Inn. I even thought about going there to see what the room looked like.

And then, twenty-three years later, *Be True to Your School* was published, and I was on the road pushing it, and that night with Bev turned into a talk-show anecdote. I told it so many times that it began to take on the tone of fiction, or folklore. I managed to keep the animation in my voice for each new interviewer. But with repetition, the story, which had once seemed so private, became exactly that—a story.

Late one afternoon, I was sitting in my room at the Fairmont Hotel in Dallas, doing a phone interview with a radio station, and a beep kept interrupting the conversation. It was annoying; someone was trying to get through.

When the interview ended, my red message light was on. The hotel operator said that my secretary, Julie Herbick, had phoned from Chicago. I dialed my office number.

"She called," Julie said.

"Who called?" I said.

"The twenty-seven-year-old married woman," Julie said. "She asked me what name you had given her in the book, and I said 'Bev.' "

I had to catch a flight to Houston. At the Dallas airport, I tried the phone number, but no one answered.

As soon as I landed in Houston I went to a bank of pay phones and tried again. This time she was there.

"This is Bob Greene," I said.

"Well," she said.

"Did you call me?" I said.

"I sure did," she said. "I just went out and bought the book."

All around me, business people were rushing past. This was too confusing.

"Can I call you when I get to my hotel?" I said.

"Sure," she said. "It'll give me a chance to read about myself."

So there I was, on a hot spring night in Texas, lying on my bed and talking to her. She said that she had been divorced, then married again, and was now divorced for a second time. She had a different last name, but still lived in the same town.

"There was a review of your book in our local paper," she said. "There were two pictures with it. One of them was of you now. The other was of you when you were seventeen. I looked at the picture of the seventeen-year-old, and I thought, 'That looks familiar.'

"So I read the review. And about halfway down it said something like, 'During his seventeenth year, Greene fell in and out of love several times—mostly with girls from his high school, but once with a twenty-seven-year-old married woman up at Lake Erie.'

"And I said to myself, 'Holy shit, that's me.' "

She said that when she had bought the book, she had said to the salesclerk, "I know the person who wrote this." While I had been riding in a cab from the Houston airport to my hotel, she had read the August entries in the diary over and over again.

"What do you think?" I said.

"It's very odd," she said. "To think that I could have an effect on a person that would last his whole lifetime."

"Did my account of what happened match your memory of it?" I said.

"Look," she said, "I don't want to hurt your feelings, but what happened that night was obviously much more important to you than it was to me. I know that what happened happened the way you said it did. But I am no longer that person. I've lived through a lot of stuff since that happened. Reading about it was like what seeing yourself in a movie must be like. You know it's you, but at the same time it's not you."

I asked her if she planned on telling any of her friends that she was the woman in the book.

"Actually, I told a couple of them right after I read the review," she said. "Now I have to decide whether to show them the book itself. I guess I will. In fact, I'm sure I will."

"What do you think they'll think of you?" I said.

"That's what I'm trying to explain to you," she said. "It doesn't feel like it's really me. I was just looking to see if I have a picture of myself from 1964. I can't find one anywhere. It's like that person doesn't exist.

"But what do I hope my friends think when they read it? I guess I hope that they think kindly of this lady."

We talked for a long time. After about thirty minutes, I asked her the question I had always wanted to ask. It was the same one I had wondered back then: Why me?

"You're still seventeen, aren't you?" she said. "I can't believe you still wonder about that.

"All I can tell you is that I honestly don't know how I felt then. It was twenty-three years ago. But I've always thought that we do what we're supposed to do at the time. You and I were supposed to meet, and I guess that was supposed to happen. I've always done what I wanted to do, not what people think I should. I think that, on that vacation, the girls I was chaperoning wanted me to be like a straitlaced, frumpy housewife scrubbing the floors. They wanted me to be like their mothers. And as you know, that wasn't me."

I asked her whether, in reading the book, she had found herself liking the seventeen-year-old boy who had kept the diary.

She laughed. "I already liked him," she said. "You were a nice, sweet, confused kid. You were real quiet.

"I don't think I was as beautiful as you thought I was, though," she said.

\*      \*      \*

And now we come to the question—the question that might have been better left unraised.

As I lay back on the bed in that Houston hotel room, talking to her over all the miles, my vision was of her on the beach in 1964. Contrary to what she had just said, in my mind she was that beautiful twenty-seven-year-old woman, full of mystery and promise. She was wearing that brown bikini and the sun was beating down and, in my mind, that was who I was talking to on the phone.

But the reality of it was that I was a forty-year-old man, and she was a fifty-year-old woman.

She said: "Do you think it would be a good idea for us to get together?"

That's what I'm thinking about right now. It would just be for old times' sake; it would just be to continue the conversation.

But do you step on the memories? Is it better to leave it like a dream sequence, in which you're forever seventeen and she's forever twenty-seven, and the beginning of senior year is just a week or two away?

"I'll leave it up to you," she said. "If you want us to see each other, we will. If you don't, we won't."

I sit here and wonder.

# Four Words

If anyone has ever said anything cruel to you—something that has stuck with you for a long time; if anyone has ever said anything very kind to you—something that has stuck with you for a long time. . . .

Well, be assured that you're feeling emotions that have nothing to do with national boundaries.

In the city of Fujisawa, Japan, which is near Yokohama, lives a woman named Atsuko Saeki. She is twenty-six years old; she is single and lives with her parents. She has a job as a sales clerk at the Yurindo Bookstore in her town.

When she was a teenager, she dreamed of coming to the United States. Most of what she knew about American life she had read in textbooks. "I had a picture of the daddy sitting in the living room," she said, "and of the mommy baking chocolate chip cookies, and of a big dog lying by the couch. In my mind, the teenage girl goes to the movies on the weekends with her boyfriend. . . ."

She arranged to attend a college in the United States—Lassen College, in Susanville, California. When she arrived in the United States, though, it was not the dream world she had imagined. She couldn't blame anyone; it was no one's fault, and certainly not the college's fault. She considered herself naive to have pictured American life in such storybook terms.

"People were struggling with their own problems," she said. "People had family troubles, and money worries, and often they seemed very tense. I felt very alone."

At college, one of the classes that was hardest for her was physical education.

"We played volleyball," she said. "The class was held in an indoors gymnasium. The other students were very good at it, but I wasn't."

She tried to have fun playing volleyball, and often she was able to. But the games made her nervous. "I was very short, compared to the other students," she said. "I felt I wasn't doing a very good job. To be very honest, I was a lousy player."

One afternoon, the physical education instructor told Atsuko Saeki that she was assigned to set the volleyball up for the other players on her team. "I was told that it was my job to hit the ball to them, so that they could hit it over the net."

No big deal for most people, but it terrified Atsuko Saeki. For some reason, she feared she would be humiliated if she failed—if she was unable to set the shots up for her teammates. Undoubtedly they would have forgiven her. But in this world each person's fears—each person's perceived humiliations—are private and are real.

Apparently a young man on her team sensed what she was going through. This was a coed class; he was on her side of the net.

"He walked up to me," she said. "He whispered to me: 'Oh, come on. You can do that.'

"He said it in a nice way, but he was serious. If you are the kind of person who has always been encouraged by your family or your friends or somebody else, maybe you will never understand how happy those words made me feel. Four words: 'You can do that.' "

She made it through the phys ed class. She may have thanked the young man; she is not sure.

But now five years have passed; she is out of college, and back in Japan, and living in her parents' house.

"I have never forgotten the words," she said. " 'You can do that.' When things are not going so well, I think of those words."

She is quite sure that the young man had no idea how much his words meant to her. "I'm sure that he was just a nice guy," she said. "I'm sure that he was the kind of guy who would say those words to anyone.

"But at the time it made a big difference to me. When I left the gymnasium I felt like crying with happiness. He probably doesn't even remember saying the words."

Which, perhaps, is the lesson here. You say something cruel to a person, you have no idea how long it will stick. You say something kind, you have no idea how long that will stick.

"I remember the young man's name," Atsuko Saeki said. "His name was William Sawyer. I do not know what happened to him, but he helped me just by whispering to me."

She's all the way over there in Japan. But still she hears his words: "You can do that."

# Author

I was staying as a houseguest with some people I know well, and one night I couldn't sleep.

I went out into their living room and started looking through their book collection. It was fairly extensive, and most of the books had well-known titles. I found myself attracted, though, to a thin volume with a blue cover—a book I had never seen before.

I took it back to the bedroom and opened it up. It became immediately clear to me what the book was: a "vanity press" publication.

If you don't know what vanity press books are, some explanation is probably in order. Virtually all books that you see in bookstores—the books put out by the big-name publishers—are paid for by the publishing companies themselves. The publishing companies pay the authors for writing the books, and then pay for production, distribution, promotion, advertising, etc.

However, there are many people in this country who love to write, but who cannot find a publisher to pay them to do so. For them, the so-called vanity presses exist.

With a vanity press, a person writes his or her book—and then pays the vanity press to publish the book. It's the reverse of the usual procedure. A vanity press will publish anything, as long as the author pays for it. For a certain amount of money, the vanity press will put out a certain amount of books. What the author does with those books is the author's own business.

So here I was, in an unfamiliar bedroom with this blue-bound book.

The author poked gentle fun at himself right on the first page; he had written "First [and only] Printing, June, 1971."

The book had been inscribed to the people who owned the house. That's how it had ended up in their library; the man who had written it had given it to them as a present.

In the preface, the author began with a question:

"Is there any excuse for a volume like this? To be charitable, there are possibly two. The first is the uncontrollable egomania which obsesses anyone who has had the tiniest success in stringing words side by side and interspersing them with punctuation marks. . . .

Nearer the truth is that a project like this stems from fear. You get terrified at the speed with which time is ticking you toward eternity, and you search frantically for a device to thwart the old man with a scythe. . . . So you settle for a thin book. . . .

I lay in bed and I read the man's book from beginning to end. It wasn't great; it wasn't terrible. It was the words of one human being who, for his own reasons, wanted to see those words collected between bound covers, even if he had to pay for the endeavor himself.

Even though I didn't know the author, I found myself thinking about him. I could imagine him on the day he took a deep breath and decided to do it: to write out a check and purchase a certain number of books to give to his friends and his family.

Before this I had not given much thought to vanity press authors; if anything, I suppose I felt a little sorry for them that they had to resort to getting their words published this way.

But as I read this fellow's book, I realized that there was nothing wrong with this at all. Some people spend their money on liquor, and some people spend their money on gambling, and some people spend their money on fancy trips. For his own reasons, this man had spent his money so that he could say that he had written a book. That's as noble a reason as any.

All authors, be they famous or obscure, write for one basic reason: to reach an audience on the other end. If you're Stephen King or James Clavell, you know going in that your audience is going to be huge. But even if you're not a brand name, you hope that there's someone out there to read what you have put down on paper.

That has to apply to vanity press authors, too. They must know inside that their books have no chance of being accepted by a wide marketplace. But they must hope that somewhere, somehow, someone will pick up their book and take the time to delve into it. That must be the real motivating force behind what they do.

And that is what struck me was I read this blue-bound book by the light of a lamp on the night table. Isn't life peculiar? Here I was, in someone else's house, and more than 15 years after the man had written his book, I was reading it.

He had found his audience; it had come about in a way that no one probably could have predicted. But he had found his audience, and I stuck with the book until the end. The author of the blue-bound book will probably never know it, but his book has been read. Maybe that makes the whole project worth the doing.

# Over the Fence

$T$he first one of us who ever hit a home run was in town on business, so we got together.

Now, I'm sure that in playground games back in elementary school, someone must have hit the ball far enough to make it all the way around the bases. But this boy—now a middle-aged man—was the first to do it in a real, official game. The first to knock a ball over the fence.

I didn't bring it up right away. I was happy that he had called me. He said he was attending a convention during the day, but that he was free after working hours. So we met at a restaurant, and we caught up on each other's personal histories. We have known each other since we were children, so there was a lot to talk about.

I kept wanting to say it, and finally I sort of edged it into the conversation.

"Do you remember the home run?" I said.

"I remember the home run," he said. He knew what I was talking about without me having to elaborate.

It was a junior high school baseball game, on a regulation diamond. Way off in the distance, in left field, was a tall metal fence that separated the junior high school from the high school; there were tennis courts on the high school side of the fence.

I can see it as if it were yesterday. Our team was at bat, and he came to the plate, and he swung . . . and the ball took off. It headed high and hard toward left field, and the left fielder from the other team ran back toward the fence. And then, just like that, the ball dropped over the fence, on the high school side. A home run.

298

It was the first time in our experience that someone had done something to set himself apart from the crowd. I wouldn't have been able to verbalize it for you back then, but that's what had happened. One second we were all pretty much equal, and the next second he was above us. He had hit a home run.

In adult life, of course, that goes on every day. In the business world, someone is always attaining an achievement that makes him or her special—that sets him or her apart, and makes everyone else feel somehow inadequate. But that was the first time I remember it happening. The ball dropped over the fence, and everyone was screaming and cheering, and he rounded the bases. In an instant, he had become someone different from who he was before.

Now, in the restaurant, I asked him what he was thinking about when he was running those bases.

He laughed. "Probably that I'd never be able to do it again."

"No," I said. "I'm serious."

"I'm serious, too," he said. "I don't think I ever hit another home run."

"Do you know what it was that made you hit that one?" I said.

He was still smiling. "The moon and the stars must have been aligned right," he said.

"I guess it must have been in seventh grade," I said.

"Eighth," he said quickly.

"Are you sure?" I said. "My memory says that it was seventh."

"Eighth," he said. "Gene Mechling was the coach."

"If Gene Mechling was the coach, then you're right," I said. "It must have been eighth."

We tried to talk about other things for a minute or two, and then I said, "Did it do anything for your self-esteem?"

"Self-esteem?" he said.

This time I was the one who laughed. "I guess we didn't use words like that back then," I said. "What I mean is, when you were rounding the bases, did you realize that you had risen above everybody else?"

"I don't think so," he said. "I just remember the ball going over the fence."

He started to kid me. "Do you remember your great plan to use a tape recorder on the seventh-grade geography test?" he said.

I said I sure did. Herbert Collier's class.

"You recorded all the square miles and populations of all the countries in the world on a tape recorder," he said. "You read the names of the countries and the populations and area numbers over and over, onto a whole tape. You didn't study for the test. You just went to sleep the night before and turned the tape recorder on, and you thought you'd learn the answers through osmosis."

"I remember," I said.

"Do you remember what you got on the test?" he said.

"Zero," I said.

"The worst grade you ever got," he said.

"It was worth a try," I said.

We kept talking, about one thing or another, and then he said that his business convention had a party he was supposed to attend. He asked if I'd like to go along, and I said that I was sorry, but that I was supposed to be somewhere else.

"Trying to study for a test through a tape recorder while you were asleep," he said. We shook hands and then he walked out of the restaurant, the first one of us who ever hit a home run.

# The Telephone Call That
# Freezes Time

$S$omewhere, in the back of your mind, you probably always know that someday it may come: a telephone call while you're asleep, a telephone call that might be a wrong number but isn't, a telephone call that rings at an hour when people just don't call other people. Not unless there is a message to be delivered that cannot wait—a message that you know, before you even pick up the phone, you aren't going to want to hear.

But you pick up the phone anyway.

So I listened and I got on the plane and within a few hours I was walking into a hospital. I had known that my father was going to have some tests performed; they weren't exactly routine—is there such a thing as a routine test in a hospital when you're seventy-four years old?—but I had hoped that the doctors would smile and wave and say to my dad, "Go on home."

The doctors didn't do that. What they did was get him into surgery as quickly as they could requisition an operating room.

By the time my plane landed the surgery had been completed. He made it through. Getting off that hospital elevator and hesitating outside his room on the fourth floor, though . . . I knew that whatever I saw when I walked inside the room, nothing was going to be precisely the same again.

My brother was with me, and my mother was already in the room. My dad . . . there's no reason to go into graphic details here, but when your dad is seventy-four and he is just a few hours out of major surgery, your first sight of him is not one you are likely to forget.

My family is not one that has ever been especially good at verbalizing emotions—I do it a lot better at a keyboard than I do in person—and usually we cover up this inadequacy with jokes. Walking into the room, it took maybe a thousandth of a second for me to know that this was not the time for jokes, not even the best-intentioned.

When I was a boy, my father's own father had been hospitalized suddenly, and my father had left our home and had driven for hours to be with his dad. Days later, he returned, looking exhausted. As I recall, he didn't say much when he got home. I asked him, "What did you do while you were with Grandpa last night?" I remember his weary answer: "We listened to a baseball game on the radio." I asked him, "Who won?" He wasn't very interested in talking—he hadn't even had a chance to tell my mother about what he had encountered—but he had distractedly said to me. "The Indians."

I had gone to the living room of our house and I had looked at the sports pages of the newspaper, and the baseball results reported that the Indians had lost the game the night before. So—I was very young —I had gone back to my dad, who was by then talking to my mother, and I had said, "Dad, you said the Indians won. The Indians didn't win last night. They lost."

To his credit, he did not blow up at me; if I had to guess, I would say that my mother probably shooed me out of the room. I hadn't thought about that in years, but now, out of nowhere, it came back to me. Now it was my father who was in the hospital bed, and now I was the grown son in the room. Twenty-four hours earlier, a baseball game had been very much on my mind. A team from the city where I now live had a chance to make it to the World Series; twenty-four hours earlier, I had assumed that I would be sitting in front of a television set watching intently, thinking how important the game was. You find out in a big hurry what is important and what is not.

I was at that hospital for a week, and I still am not exactly sure how this will all turn out. Religion, organized or otherwise, has never been a very big part of my life. But on a bulletin board in the hospital hallway, one of the nurses had posted a card with the heading "Footprints." I found myself returning to the board and reading the words on the card again and again:

> One night a man had a dream. He dreamed he was walking along the beach with the Lord. Across the sky flashed scenes from his life.

For each scene, he noticed two sets of footprints in the sand; one belonged to him, and the other to the Lord. When the last scene of his life flashed before him, he looked back at the footprints in the sand. He noticed that many times along the path of his life there was only one set of footprints. He also noticed that it happened at the very lowest and saddest times in his life. This really bothered him and he questioned the Lord about it. "Lord, you said that once I decided to follow you, you'd walk with me all the way. But I have noticed that during the most troublesome times in my life, there is only one set of footprints. I don't understand why when I needed you most you would leave me." The Lord replied, "My precious child, I love you and I would never leave you. During your times of trial and suffering, when you see only one set of footprints, it was then that I carried you."

When the phone call comes, waking you in the night—when the phone call is about your mother or your father—it doesn't take very long for all the other problems in your life to suddenly become very minor.

This is one of your parents. Nothing else matters. Nothing.

# Dreamgirls

$\mathbf{F}$rank Lenger is fifty-nine now, a machine setter for the Allen-Bradley electronics-manufacturing firm in Milwaukee. He has spent his entire life in Milwaukee, and that is where, at the age of fourteen, he first heard the Dinning Sisters.

"It was on the radio," he said. "My parents were divorced, and I was an only child, and my mother and I would sit in the living room and listen to the radio. I guess this would be around 1941. We would listen to Fibber McGee and Molly, and Fred Allen, and Jack Benny, and Amos and Andy. But no one on the radio affected me like the Dinning Sisters."

The Dinning Sisters—Ginger, Lou, and Jean—were not the hottest sister act in the country. The Andrews Sisters were far more popular, as were the King Sisters. There was something about the Dinnings, though, that Frank Lenger could not get off his mind.

"Basically it was the beauty of their voices," he said. "To me, they were like angels singing. The little inflections and chord changes they made —I had never heard anyone sing like that."

The Dinning Sisters were under contract to NBC, and Lenger would make a point of listening to the various shows on which they appeared. "They were regulars on Don McNeill's 'Breakfast Club,' " he said. "They sang on Garry Moore's program. They were on the Alka-Seltzer 'National Barn Dance' a lot. And they had their own fifteen-minute daily show."

He was even a fan of the commercials that the Dinning Sisters made. "They did them for Brach's candy bars and for Rit dye," he said. "I can still hear them singing that Rit dye commercial."

Lenger began to sing in a wavering voice: "All-purpose Rit, all-purpose Rit, the finest dye that money can buy, all-purpose Rit."

Even though he was constantly listening to the Dinning Sisters, he had no idea what they looked like. "But then one day I went out and bought a copy of *Song Hits* magazine," he said. "There was a photograph of the Dinnings in there, and they looked absolutely gorgeous."

At the age of eighteen, Lenger went into the Navy. "Just before I left Milwaukee for the service, I saw an ad in the newspaper that the Dinning Sisters were performing in Chicago, in the College Inn nightclub of the Hotel Sherman. On a Saturday night I had a buddy drive me down there. We walked through the lobby and found our way to the entrance of the nightclub. You had to be twenty-one to get in, but a very kind headwaiter let us stand at the back of the room.

"The Dinning Sisters were being backed up by the Vaughn Monroe Orchestra. I will never forget them singing 'Sentimental Journey.' After the show they walked past me, and I got up the nerve to ask Lou Dinning for an autographed picture. She went and got me one. We drove back to Milwaukee on a cloud that night."

In the years that followed, the Dinning Sisters all got married. They released approximately eighty songs for Capitol Records and appeared as guest performers in several movies. But times were changing; there wasn't as much call for close-harmony sister acts. By 1952 the Dinnings had retired from show business. Frank Lenger, out of the Navy and back in Milwaukee, got a job with an electrical-motor company, then another job selling ladies' shoes. Virtually every night he continued to play his Dinning Sisters records.

In 1958, after hearing nothing about the Dinning Sisters for years, Lenger read a story in *The Milwaukee Journal* that said Jean Dinning was living in Elk Grove Village, Illinois.

"I got together everything that I had of theirs," he said. "Their records, their photographs, my scrapbooks. I packed everything into a car and I headed for Elk Grove Village. I knew that Jean Dinning was married to a man named Howard Mack. I drove around Elk Grove Village all day, looking for Howard Mack's name on a mailbox. At last I found it. It was one of those country mailboxes, out by the road.

"I drove into the driveway and knocked on the front door. A man answered. He was the caretaker. He said that Mr. Mack wasn't home, and besides, Jean Dinning had divorced Mr. Mack. She wasn't living there any longer. But I got her phone number.

"I called her up. She was polite but not too outgoing. I asked if I could come and meet her. She said that would not be possible."

Lenger did get the address of Ginger Dinning, who was living in New Jersey. He wrote her a letter, and to his surprise she answered. They began to correspond regularly.

"I would try to find any piece of Dinning Sisters memorabilia that I could," Lenger said. "Anything in print—posters, magazines, what have you. Ginger wrote me and told me that none of the girls had a complete collection of their own records. But I did. So I would make tapes of the records and send them to all three of the Dinning Sisters. By this time, I had all of their addresses."

In the late 1960s, after years of corresponding, Lenger finally got the chance to meet the Dinning Sisters. They were having a family reunion, and they invited him to attend.

"It was absolutely thrilling," he said. "I went into the thing very, very nervous and tongue-tied. But they were so down-to-earth and natural, they made me feel like family. They had a little ceremony and made me an honorary Dinning Brother. They were tickled pink that someone still cared about them."

Soon after meeting the Dinning Sisters, Lenger embarked on a crusade.

"None of their records were available," he said. "I can't remember how many times I wrote to Capitol Records, asking them to reissue the Dinning Sisters records. Usually I got no response. Once I got a letter that said, 'We have listened to the masters, and we found that they were too dated.' They congratulated me on my good taste, but said, 'Not at this time.'"

So Lenger began writing to independent record companies—mostly "nostalgia labels." He got nowhere. He didn't give up, though. In 1982, leafing through a record-collector magazine, he came upon an advertisement placed by a man in France who was looking for some old records that Lenger happened to own. Lenger wrote to the man.

"His name was Gilles Petard," Lenger said. "It turned out that he worked for Pathe Marconi EMI in France, the entertainment conglomerate. And Gilles Petard, it so happened, was in charge of reissues. I sent him pictures of the Dinning Sisters and tapes of eight of their songs. He wrote back and said, 'Pick out six more songs and we'll put an album out.'

"I called the girls. They just about flipped. They couldn't believe it was happening. The album came out in 1983. It was called *The Dinning Sisters*, and in very, very tiny print on the bottom of the back of the cardboard jacket, it said 'Compilation/Documentation: Frank Lenger.' Then, two years later, the same company put out *The Dinning Sisters, Volume 2*. I wrote the liner notes for that one, and I got a by-line. And I didn't stop there. I had transcriptions of 113 songs that the Dinning Sisters had sung on the radio in the Forties. A little label in West Germany called Cattle Records took the transcriptions and put some of them out under the title *Songs We Sang at the National Barn Dance*. All three albums are available all over the world. You have to look for them, but they're available."

Lou Dinning Robertson, now sixty-six, lives in Burbank, California. "It's just amazing, what that man has done," she said. "During our career, we didn't even know that he was alive. And let's face it—the Andrews Sisters were way ahead of us. They were much bigger. We tried our darndest to be as commercial as they were, but we weren't flashy enough. We were all kind of shy. We came from a farm in Oklahoma. We never took dancing lessons or anything.

"The average person has no idea who the Dinning Sisters were. That's why we found it so hard to believe that Frank Lenger had collected so much stuff about our career. When we first heard about him, we thought there might be something kind of weird about him. But he's just a sweet, sweet man.

"The first time I met him, I gave him a hug. His whole body was shaking and trembling. It made me feel fabulously important, to have that effect on someone.

"And think about it—because of him, there are people listening to our records again. Not all that many people—but some people, and it's all due to him."

Jean Dinning Beasley, now sixty-three, lives in Bon Aqua, Tennessee. "What Frank has done means a great deal to me," she said. "He tells us that he felt we never got the credit we deserved. He says that he's always been determined to get us that credit.

"We see him at least once a year. He comes to our family gatherings. It's hard to believe that he's kept his affection for us all these years after listening to us on the radio when he was a boy."

She said that the thing she has done that has had the most impact has nothing to do with being a Dinning Sister. In 1959, long after the group retired, she wrote what turned out to be the ultimate high school tragedy song: "Teen Angel." It was recorded by her younger brother, Mark Dinning, and went to number one in the nation.

"I had read an article in a magazine about juvenile delinquency," she said. "The writer said that since there was a name for bad kids—juvenile delinquents—there should be a name for good kids. The writer suggested that good kids should be called teen angels.

"I knew right away that it was a great song title. I went to bed that night, and I woke up and wrote down the first verse: 'That fateful night the car was stalled, upon the railroad track, I pulled you out and we were safe, but you went running back. . . .' "


Ginger Dinning Lutke, now sixty-three (she and Jean are twins), lives in Vernon, New Jersey. "Frank Lenger is far and away the most dedicated fan we ever had," she said. "He very often finds things in our work that we weren't even aware of. He analyzes our songs as though they were pieces of art. We knew we had a nice blend, but Frank tells us specific things about our singing. I like the way I sound through Frank's ears better than the way I sound through my own."

During the years the Dinning Sisters were on live radio, she said, "It was hard to believe that what we sang into the microphone was going out over the air all over America. During one show Jean and I laughed during a song. The song was called 'Oooh, Lieutenant.' Jean and I looked at each other and for some reason we just broke up. The next week we got mail from all over the country asking what was so funny.

"And of course we had no idea that, sitting up in Milwaukee listening to us, was Frank Lenger."


Frank Lenger goes to work every morning at the Allen-Bradley plant. He has never married, and he has no children. The thing in his life that he is proudest of is that he is responsible for the Dinning Sisters being available on records again.

"It's like making my little mark on the world," he said. "I feel it is something I have done of some small benefit. Getting the girls heard again. Letting people hear those beautiful ladies sing.

"The Dinning Sisters had the most lovely voices I have ever heard. Now I pick up my copies of the reissued albums, and I see my own name on the back of the jackets. Maybe it's silly, but it makes me feel that after I'm gone, something will be left behind."

# "Who Went into the Men's Restroom?"

On a recent evening I was using an outdoor pay telephone on one of the Florida keys. I made a long-distance call to a friend thousands of miles away and punched in my telephone credit-card number.

As I was speaking with my friend, two girls came walking by; they had just left a nearby building. One of them said to the other, "Can you believe we did that? We went into the men's restroom instead of the ladies' restroom!"

My friend across the thousands of miles said, "Who went into the men's restroom?"

I said, "You could overhear that?"

My friend said, "Clear as day."

Only later did the thought strike me: When Alan Shepard and John Glenn and the other original astronauts were risking their lives and becoming national heroes for making the first flights into space, did they have this in mind? Did they think that their training and their courage would end up being used so some guy thirty years later could make a phone call to a friend, and the phone call would bounce off a satellite and reach the friend with such clarity that the friend would be able to overhear a conversation taking place ten feet from the pay phone?

I'm not sure what we schoolchildren thought back then, as we sat in classrooms and watched Shepard and Glenn and the others being rocketed toward space on television. I have a vague memory of assuming that going into space would give us some sort of military advantage in the event of World War III. Clearly, though, as our teachers stopped normal classroom activities so that we could watch the space shots, we knew that what was going on was vital to the future course of our nation's history.

And now . . . "Can you believe we did that? We went into the men's restroom instead of the ladies' restroom!"

I checked with AT&T to make sure that credit-card calls from pay phones did, indeed, bounce off satellites. John R. Schneider, a company spokesman, said that long-distance calls are transmitted in a number of ways, but via satellite is definitely one of them.

I couldn't stop wondering . . . is this what John Glenn had in mind?

So I asked him.

"The conversation carried that clearly, did it?" Glenn asked, laughing. He is sixty-six now and a member of the U.S. Senate.

"That's happened to me, too," he said. "I'll be making a long-distance call, and there will be a quarter-second delay and a little echo. And it will occur to me that the call is probably bouncing off two satellites instead of just one."

I asked Glenn if—as he sat in the space capsule atop that giant rocket—he thought he was putting his life on the line so that future generations could make high-quality credit card calls.

"I don't think we really knew," Glenn said. "I think all of us thought that part of the value of the program was the serendipity of it. If you know what the results of something will be, why do it?"

He admitted, though, that sometimes the irony of what the space program has resulted in gets to him. The two most recognized forms of satellite use are for phone calls and television transmissions. "We did talk about what we thought the military applications would be," Glenn said. "Whether you could put weapons on spacecrafts, weapons that could be used as you flew over other countries.

"So now we end up with Teflon on frying pans. Well, I guess we probably would have had Teflon on frying pans even if there had been no space program. You know when I think about all of this? When I'm watching the local news, and the weatherman comes on with one of those satellite pictures showing the weather moving across the country. That's routine on all newscasts now. And I find myself thinking: I was up there once and saw the weather moving across the country with my own eyes.

"It's kind of peculiar, thinking about that."

I asked Glenn if he had any message to the girls who had inadvertently stepped into the wrong restroom, and whose discussion of that fact was transmitted instantly across the country. After all, those girls were not even born when Glenn went into space.

He laughed again. "I don't know what to say," he said. "You have to remember—our main concern was not what was going to happen in the future. Our main concern was to make it a two-way trip. Get up there and get back."

# One for the Books

Ellen Berman is forty-five and her mother is seventy-five. Ellen moved away from her hometown—a lovely suburb with a population of about fifteen thousand—many years ago. Now she lives in another state.

When she returned to her hometown recently, she was talking with her mother, and the subject of her mother's eyesight came up. Like many people in their seventies, Ellen Berman's mother has eyesight that is not as sharp as it used to be. Ellen suggested that she and her mother go to the community's public library to find out if the library had any good books on audiocassette.

This was on a Saturday. On the way to the library—she had not been there in years—Ellen Berman began to think about what the place had once meant to her.

She had started to go to the library, with her mother, when she was seven. Within a year or two, she was going to the library by herself, riding her bike and leaving it in the rack near the front of the building.

"I loved that library," she recalled the other day. "Going to the library was my secret vice. It wasn't something I did with all my girlfriends. The library was about a mile away from my house. I went during all the seasons of the year, but when I think of it, I think of summer afternoons."

Her mental picture of the library remains vivid: "There were flat stone stairs leading to the front door—the stairs weren't very steep. And the door itself was heavy. You would pull hard to open the door, and immediately you would be in this cool, dark place. No matter how hot it was outside, it was so cool in the public library.

"The floor was smooth and cold, too. You would walk into the foyer, and you could hear the sound of your shoes on that smooth, hard floor. There might be traffic on the street outside—cars might be honking—but as soon as you were inside the library, you felt as if you were in a cavern. A cave.

"The whole place seemed dark. It was a nice kind of dark, though. I would go to the children's reading room and just spend hours with the books that lined the shelves there. My memory is of one librarian who seemed about a hundred years old to me, standing behind a tall, dark, formidable wooden desk.

"But my main memory . . . this is strange . . . my main memory is of the smell of the place. It was a wonderful smell. The smell was dusty and musty . . . it seemed to me to be the smell of books. Anytime I think of that library, I think of the scent."

And now Ellen Berman was back in town, if only for a brief visit, and she was taking her mother to the library.

"I had not been inside the building in twenty years," Ellen said. "The exterior looked pretty much unchanged. The leaded windows were still there, and the stone front. The first thing I noticed, though, was that there was a parking lot—and it was completely filled. The library never used to have its own parking lot. People either parked in the lot in front of the drugstore across the street or they found a place on a side street."

The front door was still heavy. When she pulled it open, though. . . .

"We were met by blinding light," she said. "The entire place had been refurbished. That dark place was now very much illuminated. I think there must be carpeting there now, too, because I didn't hear our footsteps on the floor.

"The dark wooden circulation desk, the dim entrance hall, the soft shuffling noises—they were all gone, too. And there were throngs of people. It's funny . . . when I think about what the library was like when I was a girl, it seems as if I was the only person in there. I envision myself in the children's reading room, and maybe a mother with her little child, and nobody else. I'm sure that wasn't true, but that is my memory.

"Now, though . . . the place was actually crowded. Men, women and children were busy pushing computer buttons—I suppose computers must have replaced the old card files—and they were using Xerox machines, and they were talking. Just talking in regular conversational voices, but I never remember anyone talking when I used to go to the library."

And the smell—the smell of the old library? It was gone.

"I noticed that right away," she said. "I have no idea why the smell was gone. They must have done something during the redecoration. Obviously the books were still there, but the place didn't smell the same. It smelled like . . . it smelled like nothing. It smelled like an office building. Like disinfectant and paper and Xerox fluid."

At first she was pleased that there were so many people in the library on a Saturday. Then she started to pay attention, and she figured out that most of the people were not in the library for books—they were there to check out videotapes, which the library now carried. Videotapes for Saturday night.

That was okay, though. She and her mother selected some audiocassettes. She realized that the library was now much more inviting and accessible than it had been when she was a girl. It didn't seem like a cave. She didn't feel like an adventurer in the mist. And the smell was gone.

# For You, Lou

**M**artie Relle has been married for twenty-nine years to Lou Relle, who is an electrician. Lou was about to celebrate his forty-eighth birthday, and Martie got an idea.

Martie is a voracious reader of the newspapers. Among the things she reads every day are the gossip-and-entertainment-news columns—the columns that report on the comings and goings of the world's celebrities.

She had noticed something about those columns. Often, near the end of the columns, there would be a list of the birthdays of famous people. She sometimes found herself thinking how that would really be something—to be so well-known that even your birthday is of interest to the reading public.

With her husband's birthday approaching, she got her idea. She would write a letter to one of the gossip-and-entertainment-news columns; she would explain all about her husband, and how special he was to her. She would say that she knew it was asking a lot—but perhaps the column, in its birthday section, could mention that Lou Relle was turning forty-eight.

She took great care in writing the letter. She mailed it, and before too many days had passed she received a letter back from the newspaper.

"It was a very gracious note," Martie Relle said. "It explained that, because there were so many celebrities and important people whose birthdays had to be listed, there just wouldn't be room to mention Lou's birthday."

Martie said that she really wasn't surprised. "Let's face it," she said, "Lou and I are nobodies. You have to be a known celebrity to get into the paper—you have to have a famous name in order for people to be interested in you. I can understand why Lou's name wouldn't qualify to be wished a happy birthday."

I asked her to tell me some things about her husband.

"Well, he may not be important to the world, but he's awfully important to me," she said. "We have had a long, wonderful marriage, and I have Lou to thank for that. He's an excellent husband, a good provider and a very good father. He's just a great person. He's very smart. He's my best friend.

"I think about what would have happened if Lou's birthday would have made the paper. Everyone would have seen it. All of our friends, and all of our family. I know that his name wouldn't have meant anything special to all the people who would have seen it in the paper, but it would have been special for us.

"This whole thing has made me think about what it might be like to have a well-known name, a name that everybody knows. But I never wish I was a celebrity. Celebrities are in the spotlight, and they make a lot of money, and they have their promoters to keep their names before the public. I really enjoy my life just the way it is."

She finally told her husband about the attempt she had made to get his birthday in the paper.

"He just laughed in a nice way and told me that it was a sweet thing for me to have tried," she said.

I spoke with Lou Relle and asked him what he had thought of his wife's gesture.

"She is the greatest," he said. "If you ask anyone I know, they'll tell you that I'm always saying she's the most special woman in the world. You could never find a woman who loves her husband more than my wife loves me. And I never forget that."

He said he knows that the media world seems to be increasingly dominated by celebrity journalism, whether it be in magazines, newspapers or on television. He said that he holds no illusions that he would fit into that lineup.

"Why would a Lou Relle, an electrician, be in a high-society newspaper column?" he said. "I've never had my name in the newspaper in my entire life. I told her not to worry that I didn't make the paper. To me, it's just another wonderful thing that she has tried to do for me. And that's enough."

He said that he did give fleeting thought to what it would have been like to wake up in the morning, open the paper and see his name alongside those of all the international celebrities.

"It would have been something really terrific," he said. "It would have been an awfully big thrill. But it's okay that it didn't happen. My feelings weren't hurt."

I don't know what the moral of all this is. There is a case to be made that it would, indeed, have been confusing to readers to find the name of Lou Relle next to all the instantly recognizable names. And as Lou put it, "My wife has been doing wonderful things for me for almost thirty years now. It's enough for me just to know that she tried."

That probably says it best.

Except for one more thing.

Mr. Relle?

Happy birthday.

# The New Wisdom

I have in front of me two high school yearbooks, both from Mid-western towns. One yearbook is from 1957. The other yearbook is a current one.

As you no doubt recall, the most important section in a high school yearbook is the part where the seniors' pictures are displayed. Traditionally, next to the portrait of each senior is a list of that senior's accomplishments during his or her four years in school. Also traditionally, there is a quote. The quote serves to sum up the senior's personality or philosophy. Usually the quote is printed in italics.

Now . . . what differences did I find between the 1957 yearbook and today's yearbook?

Obviously, the students looked as if they came from different worlds. But that is to be expected.

What struck me was the quotes next to the seniors' names. In the 1957 yearbook, the quotes read as if they had come from classical literature, or ancient poetry. In the 'fifty-seven yearbook, the sources for the quotes were not given. But the language spoke for itself.

For example, the quote next to the picture of a male member of the Spanish Club:

*He is wise who doth talk little.*

The quote next to the picture of a female member of Future Teachers of America, the Bowling Club and the Music Club:

*And all that's best of dark and bright, meet in her aspect and her eyes.*

The quote next to the picture of a male member of the marching band:

*In quietness and in confidence shall be your strength.*

The quote next to the picture of the male editor of the school newspaper:

*The desire of knowledge, like the thirst of riches, increases ever with the acquisition of it.*

The quote next to the picture of a female Student Council member:
*Sweetness and goodness in her person shine.*

There was one fellow in fifty-seven who had no organized activities listed beside his picture. Apparently he had not accomplished anything in high school. But even the quote next to his picture was elegant:

*Not that I love books less, but that I love pleasure the more.*

Now . . . on we move to the current yearbook. In today's yearbook, the students were allowed to list the sources of the quotations next to their senior pictures.

The tone was, you might say, a little different. A great many of the quotations came from rock singers.

The quote next to the picture of a female member of the Pep Club and the International Club came from Joe Walsh:

*I go to parties, sometimes until four, it's hard to leave when you can't find the door. . . .*

The quote next to the picture of a male member of the Drama Club and the Anthropology Club came from the Doors:

*Take it as it comes, specialize in having fun.*

The quote next to the picture of a male baseball player came from the rock group Steppenwolf:

*Like a true nature's child, we were born, born to be wild.*

The quote next to the picture of a female member of the field hockey team came from the Rolling Stones:

*You can't always get what you want, but if you try sometimes, you just might find, you get what you need.*

The quote next to the picture of a male member of the student jazz band came from the Eagles:

*Take it to the limit one more time.*

The quote next to the picture of a female who was manager of the girls' basketball team came from Sting, the lead singer of the Police:

*After today, consider me gone.*

The quote next to the picture of a female member of the Film Club and the Spanish Club came from Keith Richards of the Rolling Stones:

*Gonna find my way to heaven, 'cause I've done my time in hell.*

Of course, not all the students used rock stars for their senior quotes.

The quote next to the picture of a male member of the Spanish Club came from tennis player John McEnroe:

*My greatest strength is that I have no weakness.*

The quote next to the picture of a male soccer player came from a David Letterman monologue:

*I do and I do for you kids, and this is the thanks I get.*

The quote next to the picture of a female member of the Social Committee and the school newspaper came from football quarterback Jim McMahon:

*Outrageousness is a way to wake people up.*

And the quote next to the picture of a male member of the French Club came from Dean Vernon Wormer, the fictional dean of students in the movie *Animal House*:

*The time has come for someone to put his foot down—and that foot is me.*

# Chuck and Bob

I do my best to avoid reading celebrity autobiographies. The reason is that they're usually ghosted—written by professional writers, who are paid to have the celebrities talk into a tape recorder, and then to turn the anecdotes into books. More often than not, the book sounds more like the ghostwriter than the celebrity. The voice is all wrong.

Recently I made an exception. I read the autobiography of Chuck Berry, the rock and roll pioneer, and was delighted to find that there was no question about it: Berry wrote the book himself. The language, the cadence and the rhythm of the sentences were as fascinating and as unique as the lyrics to "Johnny B. Goode."

I had no intention of writing about the book; for one thing, Berry had just completed a nationwide promotional tour for the book and for his concert movie, and for another thing, I had done a Berry piece before the book and movie were released.

But on page 299, I read something that stunned me.

Berry wrote that he did not consider himself to be a true star. He wrote that people such as himself, Linda Ronstadt, Elvis Presley, Fats Domino, Janis Joplin and Bo Diddley were "all moons and satellites as far as I'm concerned." He said that a true star "will go down in the history books of even Russia, China, and Arabia—where we moons might circle a few years in the foreign magazines and then fade away in the next conventional war." He wrote that in December of 1981, he had "the distinct honor of playing on the same bill with someone I consider a star."

That person's name?

"Mr. Bob Hope."

At first I thought this must be a product of Berry's bizarre sense of humor. Chuck Berry looking up to Bob Hope? Bob Hope is one of America's most beloved comedians, but it would be hard to find two people as seemingly different as Bob Hope and Chuck Berry. Bob Hope is mainstream, middle-of-the-road, safe and staid. Chuck Berry has always seemed slightly nasty, on the cutting edge, artistically dangerous and just outside society's accepted boundaries.

And Berry considers "Mr. Bob Hope" to be a star, while Berry is a mere "moon"?

I had to call him to see if he was joking.

"I'm not joking," Berry said. "I definitely meant it."

I asked him what he liked about Bob Hope.

"He's quite alert and quite talented in comedy, and I like comedy," Berry said.

I said that the two men seemed almost totally opposite—but Berry interrupted and said he felt they were "very similar."

*Very similar?* I said that Berry had written all of his own songs— "Maybelline," "Roll Over Beethoven," "Sweet Little Sixteen," "School Days," "Brown-Eyed Handsome Man" and so many others. Bob Hope's jokes have always been created for him by gag writers.

"I don't know anything about his lifestyle or even where he lives," Berry said. "Where he comes from, I don't know." He said that Hope's jokes might be written by others, but "he delivers the jokes. Often there are four or five seconds before the audience can conceive [the joke] to respond. That's art.

"The way he does stand-up comedy—say a few words . . . add a few words . . . add a few more words. . . . When *TV Guide* says Bob Hope is going to be on, I make a point to watch."

I told Berry that I was sure that many people would be astonished when they learned of his reverence for Hope and his work. Berry said he didn't know why that would be, and then he stunned me again.

He said he had once gotten Bob Hope's autograph.

It was on a plane, well before the time they appeared on the same bill.

"Yes, I asked Bob Hope for his autograph," Berry said. "I would have understood if he would have turned me down. If he didn't have the time.

"I walked up to his seat and I said, 'Could I have your autograph?'

He looked up and said, 'Sure.' He was very polite to me. To my surprise, he was overpolite. He gave his entire attention to me. And he gave me his autograph."

I asked Berry if he had told Hope that he was Chuck Berry.

"I would never do that," Berry said.

And did Berry feel that Hope knew who he was, anyway?

"I still don't know if he knew I was me," Berry said. "I knew him, though, baby."

# Traveling Man

The guy spends entirely too much of his life on the road, and on this particular night he found himself waiting backstage in an ornate old theater, checking his watch every few minutes and tapping his right foot on the wooden floor, waiting to make his speech.

He does this a lot—flies into an unfamiliar town, makes a speech, then flies out in the morning—and he has gotten the routine down pretty well. If it's an evening speech, like tonight's, he rests at the hotel in the afternoon, skips dinner to avoid a jumpy stomach, has some room service afterward and gets the first flight out the next day.

Usually the speeches are in stark convention centers or soulless meeting rooms; tonight the speech is scheduled for this grand old movie palace. If he had to guess, he would say that the movie house was built in the 1920s. Its ceiling is high, and there is intricate painting and detail work up near the balcony. He can peek between the heavy curtains and see the audience arriving; the movie palace has been refurbished and repainted and reupholstered so that it is nearly as beautiful as when it was new.

"We almost lost this place," someone had told him. During the Sixties and Seventies, the person had explained, the theater had been allowed to become decrepit and dirty. At the time, no one thought there would ever again be a need for a grand old downtown movie palace. Just when things looked the worst, though, a committee had been formed, money had been raised, and the theater had been saved—resurrected not for the display of new movies like the ones in mall multiplexes, but for concerts and speeches and civic events. The theater once again was the architectural pride of the town.

"The last movie they showed here before we knew we had to save the theater. . . ." the man from the town said.

The guy who would be making the speech knew how the sentence was going to end.

"The last movie they showed here before we knew we had to save the theater was *Deep Throat*," the man from the town said. "That just seemed too sad."

Which made sense. For some reason, it seems that every grand old movie palace in every American downtown had been reduced to *Deep Throat* before the civic leaders had decided to rescue it. The guy who would be making the speech thought that the saving of all the old movie palaces in all the old downtowns was a fine thing—and this old theater was especially lovely.

The guy wandered around the backstage area. There were ropes and sandbags and metal stairs, like remnants from vaudeville. And, back near the dressing rooms, there were photographs hanging on the walls.

The photos—autographed—were from the performers who had appeared on this stage in the years since the theater had been saved. The guy looked at the glossies: Chuck Mangione, Bill Cosby, Charlie Daniels, Tammy Wynette, Itzhak Perlman, Eddie Rabbitt. The juxtaposition of some of the photos made him smile—there was a photo of the Ohio Express, and there was a photo of the Vienna Boys Choir—and some made him wonder. There was a photo of Bob Hope, for example. The guy thought: What inner drive, at this point in Bob Hope's life, keeps him on the road, brings him backstage to old movie palaces, perhaps makes him look at his watch in the moments before going on?

All of these people in the glossy photos—they spend so much of their lives on the road away from their homes and families, performing for strangers, then moving on to perform for more strangers the next night instead of sleeping in their own beds. There was once a haunting song written about this very thing, with a short but memorable refrain: "God bless the absentee."

The guy overheard some people talking. They were students in the local high school's jazz orchestra, who would be providing music to open the program. One of the students, looking at the photos, said, "Is Dizzy Gillespie still alive?" Someone said, "I think he may be dead." And someone else: "No, he's alive. Count Basie is dead."

The guy who would be making the speech stood in the wings. Out front, the audience was still arriving. A man named Fred Lewis was playing the old movie palace's "Mighty Wurlitzer" organ. Fred Lewis would play and then the jazz orchestra would play and then the guy would step in front of strangers and make his speech. God bless the absentee, he thought, looking at his watch one more time.

# Safe at Home

BEXLEY, OHIO—Port Columbus was filled with security agents and national political reporters; George Bush had just arrived in town, and it was a big story. I walked past the airport throng. I had something more important on my mind. I was thinking about Miss Barbara.

Miss Barbara—her full name is Barbara Drugan, but I do not think I have ever heard anyone call her that—was the kindergarten teacher at Cassingham Elementary School in Bexley from 1947 to 1979. She was the first teacher that thirty-two classes of Bexley children ever had. I hadn't heard from her in a long time. Then a note arrived.

Enclosed was a recent color photograph of Miss Barbara, taken in the studio at the Lazarus department store downtown. In the photo Miss Barbara was wearing a yellow crossing-guard's vest and holding a red sign that said "School—Stop."

In the note, Miss Barbara said that she had recently been named "volunteer of the year" by the Bexley schools. "I was so happy," she wrote, "because it was a surprise, and my picture would be in the school office. I truly never have left my school; my room; my friends."

A little background: In 1979—after those thirty-two years as the kindergarten teacher at Cassingham Elementary—Miss Barbara retired. She was only fifty-three at the time, and it was clear that she would have preferred to stay. There was some talk of a disagreement with a new school administration, but people didn't probe too deeply into the nature of the disagreement. In Bexley a person's privacy is usually respected.

"It took me four years to get over the hurt," Miss Barbara told me the other day. "It was a very tough thing."

We read a lot about the disappointments of public people—a Richard Nixon or a Michael Dukakis. Believe me, though, those disappointments could not cut any deeper than the disappointment Barbara Drugan must have felt when she was told that she no longer was going to teach kindergarten.

But back to the present. "There was an item in one of the community newspapers," Miss Barbara said. "The item said that the school had decided to start having crossing guards at the corner of Cassingham and Fair, and there was going to be a meeting asking for volunteers."

The corner of Cassingham and Elm—at the other end of the block —has always had patrol boys and patrol girls. Fifth graders. There is a stoplight at that corner. But at the corner of Cassingham and Fair— where there are only stop signs—there never had been crossing guards. Because of the absence of a stoplight, it was determined that adult volunteers were preferable.

Miss Barbara took a deep breath and went to the meeting. She knew that the school was expecting mothers of students to volunteer. Miss Barbara never has married.

She went to the meeting and she was the only person there. And she volunteered. And she was accepted.

Now, each school year, she stands at the corner of Cassingham and Fair in her yellow vest and her "School—Stop" sign. "It makes me so happy," she said. "The boys and girls seem so glad to see me."

As well they should. Miss Barbara claims never to have forgotten the name of any kindergartener she taught in all of those thirty-two years. No matter how old they get, she remembers.

"I was having lunch in the Grill and Skillet," she said. "Your brother and his wife and their son came in. I said to your brother, 'I know you.' He was about to tell me his name, but I asked him not to.

"It took me twenty-five minutes. But then I looked in his eyes, and I knew. I knew because of those eyes. I said, 'Those are Phyllis Greene's eyes.' " Phyllis Greene is my mother. My brother was in Miss Barbara's kindergarten class in 1958.

With the new school year about to begin, Miss Barbara said she is eagerly anticipating her crossing-guard duty. She was twenty-one years old, fresh out of Ohio State University, when she taught her first kindergarten class at Cassingham in 1947; now she is sixty-two. "Last year one little boy told me that I was the oldest crossing guard he'd ever seen in his life," Miss Barbara said. "The next day I said to him, 'Take a good look, because I'm one day older than I was yesterday.'"

The wounds are starting to heal; Miss Barbara is now warmly accepted as a substitute teacher at Cassingham, and the "volunteer of the year" award seemed to be an official welcome back. She would still love to be teaching full-time. As it is, though, she is happy to be the crossing guard at the corner of Cassingham and Fair.

"I am so proud to be there," she said. "I can hardly wait for the school year to start, so I can see all the children again."

I asked her why she was doing it. Why was she standing out there, on her own time, wearing that yellow vest and holding that red sign?

"To make sure that the boys and girls get across the street all right," she said. "To keep them safe."

God, I love this place.

# Your Next Stop . . .

WASHINGTON—There comes a point during each of these extended trips when I feel that I have crossed that invisible line into the Twilight Zone.

That moment came in the hours just after dusk. I had checked into my hotel room overlooking the Potomac River, and I had just finished harassing the telephone switchboard operator downstairs with my customary greeting, the first words I always utter after I have checked in: "What room do you have me registered in?" (At this point the operator always asks me why I would ask; obviously I know what room I am in.) "Because I want to make sure my calls go to the right room." (At this point the operator confirms that she has me listed as being in the room that I am, indeed, in.) "Good. Then all of my calls will go to this room?" (The operator says of course. She asks if any hotel has ever had me listed in a room that I was not, in fact, in.) "You'd be surprised how many times it has happened to me." (It happened to me once, in 1974.)

Anyway, I had just completed the obligatory conversation with the hotel operator, when I noticed that this particular establishment was one of the many hotels that have started to include "electronic entertainment centers" in the guest rooms. VCRs, multi-unit tape decks, cable TVs . . . you're starting to see them all the time. I also noticed—with a great deal of pleasure—that this hotel was one that had decided to provide a library in each guest room. Yes, a library, with a selection of hardbound books. I find this a very heartening development. As long as hotels are going to put in VCRs, it's a nice idea for them to provide reading material as an alternative.

**331**

I looked across the room. The hardbound books were arranged in twin bookcases. There appeared to be at least forty books.

I walked over to look at the books.

This is when the Twilight Zone kicked in.

There were more than forty books all right. But . . .

*Doo-doo-doo-doo, doo-doo-doo-doo . . .*

Twenty-eight of the books were *Snake*, the autobiography of former football player Ken Stabler. And sixteen of the books were *Betty: A Glad Awakening*, by former First Lady Betty Ford.

I stood in front of the twin bookcases, stunned. I thought I might merely be road weary.

But I counted them up again. Twenty-eight copies of *Snake*. Sixteen copies of *Betty: A Glad Awakening*.

The bindings on the twenty-eight copies of *Snake* were colored red. The bindings on the sixteen copies of *Betty: A Glad Awakening* were colored black. (The paper dustjackets had all been removed.)

Now, you might ask yourself: Who would make such a decision?

If the conscious decision had been made to provide more than forty books in the room of each guest, you might ask yourself why twenty-eight of those books would be *Snake* and sixteen of those books would be *Betty: A Glad Awakening*.

I determined not to ask myself that question. Obviously, that was just what the management wanted: for me to ask myself that question. The management was trying to drive me crazy by making me think about that.

Not me. I'm too savvy a traveler. I just removed one of the twenty-eight absolutely identical copies of *Snake* from the bookshelves—a copy of *Snake* that had other copies of *Snake* on either side of it—and I started reading:

"Some of my most vivid memories are of training camps. Although many players have compared life in a National Football League training camp to being in a Turkish prison, I loved it."

Those were Ken Stabler's words, all right (as told to ghostwriter Berry Stainback, according to the twenty-eight title pages). I was going to resist every impulse to call the hotel manager and ask why there were twenty-eight copies of *Snake* in my room, and why there were sixteen copies of *Betty: A Glad Awakening*. If the manager was trying to make me goofy by doing this, I wasn't going to fall for it. Nope. I was going to cancel all of my appointments and read each word in all of those twenty-eight copies of *Snake* and all of those sixteen copies of *Betty: A Glad Awakening.*

The trip was still young, and here I was, already in the Twilight Zone. The road is long, but my patience is longer.

BOB GREENE is a syndicated columnist for the Chicago *Tribune*; his columns appear in more than two hundred newspapers in the United States, Canada, and Japan. He is the author of ten previous books, including the national bestsellers *Be True To Your School* and *Good Morning, Merry Sunshine*.